History
TODAY

Charles Simeon
An ordinary pastor
of extraordinary
influence

Derek Prime

DayOne

© Day One Publications 2011
First printed 2011

ISBN 978–1–84625–313–3

British Library Cataloguing in Publication Data available

Published by Day One Publications
Ryelands Road, Leominster, HR6 8NZ
☎ 01568 613 740 FAX 01568 611 473
email—sales@dayone.co.uk
web site—www.dayone.co.uk
North America—email—usasales@dayone.co.uk

Cover design by Wayne McMaster
Printed by Orchard Press (Cheltenham) Ltd

Appreciations

For more than a decade now, I have been longing for someone to write fresh words and reflections on the life of Charles Simeon. With Charles Simeon: An Ordinary Pastor of Extraordinary Influence, *that desire has been wonderfully met! Writing as a pastor to pastors, Derek Prime gives us Simeon in his own words, followed by seasoned reflections that greatly encouraged my own soul. This book will soften the heart and strengthen the resolve of anyone hoping to establish a ministry known for fidelity to the gospel.*

David Helm, Pastor, Holy Trinity Church, Chicago, and Chairman, The Charles Simeon Trust, USA

For pastors facing a crisis, preachers struggling to communicate and lay leaders wanting to make an impact for the gospel, Charles Simeon is a fount of practical wisdom. Derek Prime has distilled that wisdom in this compelling story of grace, faith and perseverance. It is rich in spiritual nourishment.

Colin Smith, Senior Pastor, The Orchard Evangelical Free Church, Arlington Heights, Chicago, USA

Charles Simeon's influence on 19th-century evangelicalism in Britain was profound. Those who heard Vaughan Roberts' outstanding address on Simeon at the 2009 Evangelical Ministry Assembly will be in no doubt of his relevance for today. This is a wonderful, instructive and heart-warming book, written by a preacher and pastor with a similarly fruitful ministry in Scotland. This clearly written biography fills out the picture with care and warmth. I particularly loved the chapters about how Simeon trained preachers. Although today, in an age of widespread biblical ignorance, I think consecutive biblical exposition is generally more profitable than Simeon's method of individual texts, his training is full of practical and perceptive principles of enduring relevance. I should like to make this book compulsory reading for students at the P.T. Cornhill Training Course.

Christopher Ash, Director, Proclamation Trust Cornhill Training Course, London, UK

Appreciations

A new biography of Simeon is long overdue and Derek Prime has done us a great service in putting the spotlight on a man whose contribution to the work of the gospel is all too neglected. With this book's strong focus on Simeon's commitment and approach to expository preaching and his encouragement of others in that task, reading of his life brings to mind others like Dick Lucas and the late John Stott, not to mention Simeon's biographer himself, who embodies many of the graces and qualities identified in his subject.

John Brand, Principal, Faith Mission College, Edinburgh, UK

Charles Simeon's life straddled the 18th and 19th centuries. There were some spiritual giants in the land in these years, and Simeon was one of the most notable. It is therefore surprising that there has been no substantial biography of such an outstanding Christian leader in recent decades. I can think of no better pen than that of Derek Prime to fill this space. He has in his own ministry and example reflected so many of Simeon's qualities, and mentored innumerable aspiring preachers. He has given us a vivid and highly readable account of the fascinating life and extraordinary ministry of a great and godly servant of the gospel of Christ. You cannot afford not to read it.

Eric J. Alexander, retired minister of St George's Tron Church, Glasgow, UK

I have been keenly awaiting the publication of this book and I am not disappointed. If, like me, you have had only a scanty knowledge of Simeon, you are in for a treat. Derek Prime's interest in and knowledge of his subject is such that he is able not only to tell us about Simeon but also to convince us of the benefit (we might even say necessity) of getting to know him. I read chapter 15 first and I was hooked. He has convinced me that in Simeon's life and ministry we discover enduring principles for today. It is for this reason that the leadership team at Parkside is reading this book together.

Alistair Begg, Senior Pastor, Parkside Church, Chagrin Falls, Cleveland, Ohio, USA

Here is a rare and powerful chemistry. Ingredient one: the story of one of the most influential evangelical Anglican ministers, Charles Simeon—a pastor-preacher whose long ministry in Cambridge lastingly impacted generations of students, world missions and many other ministers, then and now. Now add ingredient two: the perspective of the author, Derek Prime, to whom many ministers today have similarly looked as an example of biblical preaching and faithful pastoral ministry. The result? A book to be recommended to all Christians, and one of those books about which we can say, 'Every minister needs to read this!' Charles Simeon: An Ordinary Pastor of Extraordinary Influence *cannot fail to instruct, challenge and enthuse.*

Sinclair B. Ferguson, Senior Pastor, The First Presbyterian Church, Columbia, South Carolina, USA

To the many encouragers God has given me over the years,
to whom I owe so much

A bust, sculpted after Simeon's death by Samuel Manning, originally located in the Cambridge University Library but now in the entrance to the History Faculty Library and said to be an almost perfect likeness, indicating why at school he gained the nickname of 'Chin Simeon'

Contents

My interest in Simeon arises from several circumstances. First, each Sunday evening for three years as a student I sat in Holy Trinity Church for the weekly Christian Union evangelistic sermon and most weekdays joined in the lunch-hour Christian Union prayer meeting in the Henry Martyn Hall, adjacent to the church. It was impossible to engage in these activities without imbibing something of the ministry of Charles Simeon and being inspired by it.

Second, on my ordination a minister approaching retirement gave me Simeon's collection of sermons—his *Horae Homileticae*—that had been given to him at his own ordination by an older minister. Over the years I found them a tremendous resource as well as an example of biblical preaching, with a clear emphasis upon Christ-centredness and the application of the Bible to daily life. On my younger son's ordination I felt I could do nothing other than pass them on to him, although I quickly missed having them at hand. This loss was more than relieved when the whole of Simeon's *Horae Homileticae* became available on one DVD. How amazed—and I think also both humbled and delighted—Simeon would have been at such a wonder of contemporary technology!

Third, on reading the two principal biographies of Simeon two questions were raised in my mind. First, coming from an aristocratic background, was he as affluent as we might imagine and seems often to be suggested? Second, how extensive and wide was his influence? My reading of primary sources has put the first question into perspective and confirmed the second.

Fourth, as a pastor and teacher I've come to recognize that in spite of the passage of 250 years and the perception we may have of what Christian ministry should be in today's society, Simeon's life and experience provide enduring principles relevant to the church at all times.

Many titles and descriptions have been given of Charles Simeon. Perhaps the most telling regarding his influence is that of Lord Macaulay in 1844, when he suggested that 'his real sway in the church was far greater than that of any Primate' (i.e. Archbishop of Canterbury).[1]

One of my main purposes in writing this book is to allow Simeon to speak for himself, as it were, by quoting as often as is possible his own words, whether from his *Memoirs*, letters or sermons. I've wanted to discover his main spiritual concerns and where he placed the emphasis in his teaching and preaching, rather than concentrate on biographical details alone. (This accounts for the longer chapter on 'Simeon and the Jews' (Chapter 12)—an area of his concern frequently overlooked.) Sometimes I have been tempted to paraphrase quotations because the style of language is so different from that of today. I've tried to avoid doing this unless clearly necessary. Quotations, unless otherwise stated, are from the *Memoirs* of his life, edited by William Carus, his successor at Holy Trinity Church.[2] I was surprised and grateful to discover that Harvard University has made the American Edition of 1847 (491 pages) available online—a remarkable resource. And other universities—such as Trinity College, University of Toronto—have done the same. Google's edition of the *Memoirs* is easily downloadable in a brief time, with the facility of typing in any quotation in the book to find its place and context within seconds.

Although I am a great admirer of Simeon's, I want to avoid any sense of wrongly eulogizing him. He had self-confessed weaknesses against which he fought a lifelong battle. Neither Simeon himself nor those who admired him regarded him as someone of outstanding intellect or oratory. But he *was* a godly pastor and teacher in whom God was perfecting his sanctifying work and who, as a consequence, served the body of Christ more than he knew as he reflected the character of his Lord.

I write with the conviction that, just as the New Testament draws attention to the lessons we may learn from the lives of God's people in the Old Testament (1 Cor. 10:6, 11), so we may gain much from the lives of godly men and women who have left their mark for good upon past generations.

Notes

1 **G. O. Trevelyan,** *The Life and Letters of Lord Macaulay*, vol. 1 (first published 1876; Oxford: Oxford University Press, 1978), p.64, n. 1.
2 *Memoirs of the Life of the Rev. Charles Simeon, M.A., with a Selection from His Writings and Correspondence. Edited by the Rev. William Carus, M.A.* (American edn., ed. Chas. P. McIlvaine; New York: Robert Carter, 1847). Hereafter referred to as *Memoirs of Charles Simeon*.

Life before Cambridge

N one of us chose the family into which we were born or the place where we were first brought up. But these circumstances are within God's providence for all of us, just as they were for Charles Simeon.

Reading in Berkshire

The family lived in Reading, where his father was a practising attorney. Both Simeon's grandfather and his great-grandfather were Anglican ministers, following each other in the same parish of St Mary's, Bucklebury, in Berkshire. His father, sadly, showed no evidence of spiritual life. If Simeon could have appeared on a contemporary TV programme such as *Who Do You Think You Are?* he could easily have traced his descent from a family of French extraction that came over with William the Conqueror. His mother, Elizabeth, also had ministers in her family's history, two of them ending their ecclesiastical careers as archbishops of York. Never, so far as I know, did Simeon refer to this part of his family background.

Charles, born 24 September 1759, was the youngest of four children, all boys. His mother seems to have died soon after Charles's birth, and this probably explains why he makes no reference to her in his writings. Richard, the eldest, died when Charles was only twenty-two. John, the second son, followed his father into the legal profession and then became a popular MP for Reading. Edward, the third son, became a wealthy merchant and a Director of the Bank of England. An impressive monument in his memory is found in Reading town centre. Significantly, books written about Reading's history draw attention to Charles rather than to his brothers as the most eminent and influential member of the Simeon family.

Eton College

Simeon's father decided to send Edward, John and Charles to Eton, less than twenty-two miles from Reading. It seems likely that this was done because of the death of his wife and the difficulties of looking after his sons while pursuing his career.

The first sight that greets visitors to the school as they enter the School Yard is the king's bronze statue, dating from 1719. Every Founder's Day, King Henry VI's prayer is used in the college chapel. Translated from the Latin it reads, 'O Lord Jesus Christ, who has created and redeemed me, and has brought me to what I now am; you know what you would do with me: do with me according to your will, for your tender mercy's sake. Amen.'

Few, if any, schools can rival Eton's reputation for its education of so many great and influential men. The Duke of Wellington, victor at the Battle of Waterloo and later Prime Minister, is one of the most famous. Eton has educated at least nineteen other British Prime Ministers, from Walpole and Pitt the Elder to Harold Macmillan and David Cameron. The memorial in the cloisters gives impressive testimony to the number of Etonians who gave their lives for their country as members of the Armed Services—129 in the Boer War, 1,157 in the First World War and 748 in the Second World War. It has also provided many bishops, including John Ryle, the first Anglican Bishop of Liverpool in 1880, and numerous ministers. The year that Charles entered Eton, an old Etonian, Frederick Cornwallis, became Archbishop of Canterbury.

Three brothers together

Charles Simeon arrived at this impressive institution in 1767, aged eight. His two brothers Edward and John were already there, having joined the school two years previously in 1765—Edward in May and John in September. The basic entrance fee was two guineas, although wealthier parents gave three, four, five and up to ten guineas. The records show that their father paid two guineas each when Edward and John entered the college, and this may be an indication that he was not excessively wealthy. Poorer parents gave either nothing or simply a single guinea.

Charles joined the school, like his brothers, as an Oppidan, a name that continues to be used. Eton remains unique in the terms it uses to describe its students. King's Scholars, or Collegers—of whom there were, and are still, seventy—lived in the school and were educated for free. From the early eighteenth century Oppidans (from the Latin meaning 'town') stayed in lodgings in the town of Eton in what were known as Dames' houses. These were sometimes run by men known as 'domines', teachers of non-classical subjects but not part of the regular school staff. In 1766, nearly two years before Charles arrived, thirteen such houses existed, three of which were run by 'domines'. Charles and his brothers boarded in the house of Mr Brian Harding, who lived at Baldwin's End. He was also a draper and maltster (a maltster treated barley with malt in his malthouse for the brewing of beer).

When Charles joined the school, numbers were something over 500, competing with Westminster School, its traditional rival. Boys represented every part of British society and some even came from abroad. Bricklayers, coal merchants, shipwrights, cooks and bakers sent their sons to Eton, along with eminent Scottish and Irish families, as well as those from the West Indies and the American colonies. Eton's reputation for educating the British aristocracy and producing eminent statesmen and politicians made it attractive to all who sought the best for their sons and had the means to fund their education.

Each boy had a tutor. Oppidans, like Charles, had one of the assistant masters. Some, whose parents were more affluent, had private tutors, either men already living in Eton or those whom the boys brought with them. The concentration of an Etonian education was primarily on the classics, and almost exclusively so.

Harsh discipline

School discipline was severe, and life was not made easier by the fag system. It was said that Eton treated every boy as a liar. Flogging, abandoned by most schools, carried on as a degrading punishment for boys of all ages.

Fags underwent hardships and privations we would associate with slavery. Besides daily cleaning, they lit fires, made beds and performed other menial tasks, frequently being kept out of bed until the early hours of a morning to do the bidding of their 'masters'. Older boys physically punished fags for the most trifling mistake or trivial delay, and floggings at the hands of both masters and older boys made life a misery. The victims were afraid of talking about the beatings they received because of possible repercussions. Charles Simeon's own comment about life at Eton—though brief—speaks volumes. Henry Venn reported that Simeon described Eton as 'so profligate a place, that he told me he should be tempted even to murder his own son (that was his word) sooner than let him see there what he had seen'.[1]

Although Eton had a magnificent chapel, instruction in the Christian faith was absent. Boys were obliged to attend chapel, not counting Sundays, at least four, five or even six times in a week, but it was a matter of mere routine and superficial duty. Prayers were read carelessly and thoughtlessly and all was done within the space of twenty-five minutes. In spite of this, one in five boys at Eton was ordained to the Christian ministry, but their schooling did nothing to point them to faith in Christ.

In 1773 Charles became a King's Scholar, two years after his brother John. Boys could become one of the seventy scholars any time up to their seventeenth birthday, although most did so between the ages of eight and twelve. The condition was that they had to be of good character, up to standard in their Latin grammar, able to read and sing plainsong (a form of repetitive chanting) and qualified scholastically to go on to King's College, Cambridge, at the age of eighteen or soon afterwards.

Chapter 1

Charles most likely benefited from having two older brothers at Eton, living initially in the same domine's house, and they probably protected him from some of the worst aspects of Eton life. Like most old boys of any school Charles could look back in later life and remember good things, especially friendships.

Memories others had of Simeon at Eton

Simeon's contemporaries at Eton remembered his somewhat eccentric character and exploits.

Dr Goodall, who became Provost of Eton, recalled in a letter to him their conversations as boys at the school on more serious subjects, as well as Charles's expertise in archery:

Above half a century has elapsed, my dear friend, since you and I occasionally conversed on sacred subjects in our walk round chamber, before we partook of certain bones of neck at the sixth-form table. I then dared to controvert some of your opinions, and you will see that the habit is not eradicated; but I should be now as much afraid to meet you in the field of argument, as Askew was to stand up against you in the shooting fields. My arrows must be shot at a distance; such as they are, they are, I hope, not poisonous, and I can say with a safe conscience they are not meant to hurt. Methinks I hear you say, 'True, Goodall, for they are blunt.' Be it so; it is at least no novelty for a fool to shoot his bolt.[2]

Dr Goodall also reminded Simeon of his feats of strength and activity in which he was surpassed by none: 'I much doubt if you could *now* snuff a candle with your feet, or jump over half a dozen chairs in succession.'[3] Others remembered his love of clothes and competitiveness in athletics. Horsemanship was his favourite physical enjoyment, and he was regarded as a good judge of horseflesh. Others recalled his meticulousness when it came to money and keeping accounts.

The whole course of Simeon's life was redirected and transformed when the time arrived for him to go to King's College, Cambridge.

Notes

1 *Memoirs of Charles Simeon*, pp. 16–17.
2 Ibid., pp. 408–409, footnote.
3 Ibid., p. 2.

Cambridge and conversion

Like every other King's Scholar at Eton, Charles Simeon waited his turn to take his place at King's College, Cambridge. It was only as one scholar from King's graduated and left that another could replace him. Vacancies occurred at random times. An election to fill a vacancy or vacancies came at the end of July 1778, and as a result Charles went up to King's on 29 January 1779 at the age of nineteen, having spent almost twelve years at Eton.

Student life at King's

Cambridge, like Eton, did not have the best of reputations. The university was much smaller than it is today. In 1781, for example, it was reckoned that only three colleges had more than fifty resident undergraduates, and only seven more than forty, with St John's and Trinity Colleges being the largest.

The life of Cambridge undergraduates was typically one of leisure. They were not well taught, no university exams had to be taken and they could be as lazy as they liked, with little to inspire personal initiative or ambition. With neither a rigorous examination system nor a carefully structured teaching programme, young men had plenty of scope for relaxation and mischief.

Leisure gave time for both dons and undergraduates to patronize the many coffee houses, popular not only for their coffee but also as places to smoke a pipe of tobacco, read daily publications such as the *Spectator* or the *Daily Post* and talk. Alongside this went a good deal of heavy drinking, extravagant living, idleness, rioting, pitched battles and indiscipline. The authorities battled constantly against the problem of prostitutes and houses of ill-fame.

King's College was nothing like it is today in size. It was a closed society of fellows and scholars, and the average number of undergraduates seldom exceeded twenty and might at times be fewer than ten. Simeon, as a King's Scholar, had benefits which scholars of other colleges did not enjoy. Providing he behaved himself, and after being in residence for three years, he would automatically be elected into a fellowship, which could be held for life providing he did not marry. In addition, he could proceed to the degrees of Bachelor and Master of Arts without undergoing any examination or performing any of the prescribed exercises. It is not known how this privilege originated. Scholars and fellows had their room and board paid for life, and once they became fellows they received dividends from the college's rental and farming income. From this they probably had to pay for their own servants and horses but they had use of the college's stables and pastures. What men in other colleges would have had to compete for, Simeon was to receive as a benefit as a King's Scholar. But this did not, as we might be inclined to think, lead to the idleness that was the norm in the university. The evidence is that King's gained a creditable number of university scholars and prizes.

As with all new students, Simeon's early days focused upon understanding how student life worked and what was expected of him. One of the first things he had to do was to furnish his rooms and buy a cap and gown, both essential for going out of college into town. A usual day began with chapel at eight o'clock and then a lecture in Greek or English at eleven. This might be followed by a visit to Deighton's, the Cambridge bookshop, or reading the morning's newspapers. In most undergraduates' cupboards there would be some Stilton cheese for lunch, plus ale and bread from the college buttery, where provisions within the college were kept. Some might have gone for something more substantial but attendance at Hall, the main feature of the day, was at four o'clock sharp, when an ample dinner was served. This meal was invested with a certain amount of dignity and most would dress carefully for it. At the beginning of winter the floor was covered with sawdust which was turned over regularly with a rake and removed when the weather became warmer. The waiters were the bed-makers and gyps,[1] and the undergraduates carved for themselves, pushing the joints along the tables to one another.

A complete surprise

The most significant piece of information Simeon gleaned on the third day after his arrival was that in about three weeks' time he was expected to attend and take part in the celebration of the Lord's Supper in the college chapel. A genuine sense of alarm seized him. Little did he appreciate it at the time, but God's Spirit was graciously working in him and preparing him for the understanding he was to gain of his own sinfulness and of God's mercy to sinners. 'On being informed that I must,' he later wrote, 'the thought rushed into my mind that Satan himself was as fit to attend as I, and that if I must attend, I must prepare for my attendance there.'[2]

Not having anyone with whom he could share his concern, he immediately sought help from religious books. The only one of which he had heard was *The Whole Duty of Man*, not to be confused with Henry Venn's *The Complete Duty of Man*. It was written anonymously, but was reliably attributed to Richard Allestree (1619–1681). Published originally in 1657 and then repeatedly reprinted, its latest edition of 1773 was available to Simeon. The book was divided into seventeen chapters, so that one chapter could be read every Sunday and the whole book read three times a year. It also contained private devotions for special occasions. Simeon records that he read the book 'with great diligence, calling my ways to remembrance, and crying to God for mercy'.[3]

The section on the Lord's Supper proved especially relevant. It underlined the priority of understanding God's new covenant and of how inappropriate and wrong it is to come to the Lord's Table without understanding what we do. It called for self-examination and dependence on the Lord Jesus Christ for salvation. It was both spiritual and practical in its advice. George Whitefield was critical of the book, particularly because he could find in it no mention of regeneration. Whatever its limitations, it reminds us that God may use less than what we regard as ideal means to meet the need of an individual genuinely seeking salvation.

Increasing apprehension

As Simeon contemplated the arrival of the day of the Communion service he made himself quite ill with his 'reading, fasting and prayer'.4 Clearly God's Spirit was making him realize that the most important issue was the well-being and salvation of his soul through a right relationship with God. His spiritual distress continued until Easter 1779.

He read without any benefit a book by John Kettlewell (1653–1695) with the long title *An Help and Exhortation to Worthy Communicating; Or, A Treatise Describing the Meaning, Worthy Reception, Duty, and Benefits of the Holy Sacrament*. He also read in the week preceding Easter yet another book on the Lord's Supper. It was by Thomas Wilson, Bishop of Sodor and Man between 1697 and 1755, and had an equally long title, part of which was *A Short and Plain Instruction for the Better Understanding of the Lord's Supper*. This was a popular book, and its twenty-second edition had been published just ten years before Simeon's acquisition of it. God used it as a potent instrument to give him understanding of how his growing sense of sin and guilt could be relieved.

One part in particular was used by the Holy Spirit to enlighten him. He wrote,

But in Easter week, as I was reading Bishop Wilson on the Lord's Supper, I met with an expression to this effect: 'That the Jews knew what they did when they transferred their sin to the head of their offering.' The thought rushed into my mind, What, may I transfer all my guilt to another? Has God provided an offering for me, that I may lay my sins on his head? then, God willing, I will not bear them on my own soul one moment longer. Accordingly I sought to lay my sins upon the sacred head of Jesus; and on the Wednesday began to have a hope of mercy; on the Thursday that hope increased; on the Friday and Saturday it became more strong; and on the Sunday morning (Easter-day, April 4), I awoke early with those words upon my heart and lips, 'Jesus Christ is risen to-day! Hallelujah! Hallelujah!'[5]

Christian assurance

Assurance of salvation was immediate and memorably transformed his approach to the Lord's Table on Easter Sunday.

From that hour peace flowed in rich abundance into my soul; and at the Lord's Table in our chapel I had the sweetest access to God through my blessed Saviour. I remember on that occasion there being more bread consecrated than was sufficient for the communicants, the clergyman gave some of us a piece more of it after the service; and on my putting it into my mouth I covered my face with my hand and prayed. The clergyman seeing it smiled at me; but I thought, if he had felt such a load taken off from his soul as I did, and had been as sensible of his obligations to the Lord Jesus Christ as I was, he would not deem my prayers and praises at all superfluous.[6]

While in no way regarding it a good thing that students should be compelled to attend the Lord's Supper, and aware of how damaging such a rule could be to their spiritual understanding, Simeon realized that God in his sovereign mercy had used it to bring about his repentance and faith in Christ.

Notes

1 The name 'gyp' is still used in Cambridge colleges for those who look after the rooms of

undergraduates. In Simeon's day, they looked after the needs of two or more students, rather like a gentleman's valet. They were different from bed-makers in that they ran errands, waited at table, woke students for morning chapel, and did other practical things like brushing their clothes. The derivation of the word 'gyp' is uncertain. A short jacket worn by valets of Oxford colleges was called a 'gippo' in the seventeenth century, and this may then have been abbreviated to describe the valets themselves. The other explanation nineteenth-century dictionaries give is that it comes from the Greek word for vulture, implying that they preyed upon their employers.

2 *Memoirs of Charles Simeon*, p. 4.
3 Ibid.
4 Ibid.
5 Ibid., pp. 5–6.
6 Ibid., p. 6.

Chapter 3

Evidences of spiritual new birth

More than perhaps most Christians Simeon remembered the circumstances and dramatic effect of his conversion upon his life, calling forth unceasing thankfulness and gratitude. Writing in 1807 he declared,

The Passion-week I look forward to with more peculiar delight. It has always been with me a season much to be remembered, not only on account of the stupendous mysteries which we then commemorate, but because of the wormwood and the gall which my soul then tasted, twenty-eight years ago, and the gradual manifestations of God's unbounded mercy to me, till on Easter-day I was enabled to see that all my sins were buried in my Redeemer's grave.[1]

He pondered God's providence in the provost of King's requirement that he should attend Communion.

Writing in 1832 in answer to a friend's question about new birth, he replied,

I can only answer by saying, that, under God, I owe everything to Provost Cooke. I see you full of utter amazement: 'Pray explain yourself,' I hear you say. I will in few words. On the 29th of January, '79, I came to college. On February 2nd I understood that, at division of term, I MUST attend the Lord's Supper. The provost absolutely required it. Conscience told me that Satan was as fit to go there, as I; and that if I MUST go, I MUST repent, and turn to God, unless I chose to eat and drink my own damnation. From that day I never ceased to mourn and pray, till I obtained progressive manifestations of God's mercy in Christ in the Easter week, and perfect peace on Easter day, April 4th.[2]

While rejoicing in the joy of God's salvation, Simeon went on to express the desire that he might never lose his awareness of his sins and his dependence upon his Saviour. Three years before his death, in one of his tea parties for students, he was asked what he considered to be the principal mark of regeneration. He first responded by saying, 'The very first and indispensable sign is self-loathing and abhorrence. Nothing short of this can be admitted as an evidence of a real change.' At the conclusion of their time together he movingly added,

And that you may be able the better to pursue it, and properly to enter into it, allow me to state to you what have sometimes been my feelings while seated in this chair by myself, shut in with God from the world around me. I have thought thus within myself in my retirement: I now look around me, and behold this apartment. I see all is comfort and peace about me. I find myself with my God, instead of being shut up in an apartment in hell, although a hell-deserving sinner. Had I suffered my deserts, I should have been in those dark abodes of despair and anguish. There I should have thought of eternity,—eternity! without hope of escape or release. From all this I am delivered by the grace of God, though I might have been cut off in my sins, fifty-four years ago. While engaged in these thoughts they sometimes overpower me. Were I now addressing to you my dying words, I should say nothing else but what I have just said. Try to live in this spirit of self-abhorrence, and let it habitually mark your life and conduct.[3]

Simeon often referred to the experience of new birth in his preaching.

We have heard of men, even of good men, as Job and Jeremiah, cursing the day of their birth: but who ever cursed the day of his new birth? At every period of life this is a subject that will bear reflection and impart delight.[4]

To be children of God, we must be 'begotten of God': and that being admitted, I am indifferent as to the name by which it shall be called: call it a new birth, a new creation, a renewal in the spirit of the mind, or a conversion of soul to God; only let an entire change of heart and life be included in it, and (though one word may more strictly and appositely express it than another) we are satisfied. Suffice it to say, that 'a new heart must be given us, and a new spirit be put within us'; and that this change is essential to us, as children of God.5

Distinguishable marks of Simeon's experience of regeneration and conversion were evident.

1. Conviction of sin

The first was personal conviction of sin. He found himself reviewing his past with deep shame and sorrow, especially his personal vanity, foolishness and wickedness. He felt that his sins were more in number than the hairs of his head or the sand upon the seashore. When speaking of this, he chose not to enter into precise details except to affirm that a prodigal had returned to the Father's house. As he put it, 'God will be in no ordinary measure glorified in me, the abundance of my sinfulness will display in most affecting colours the superabundance of his grace.'6 Some might think that as a nineteen-year-old student he exaggerated the sins of his youth, but it was all part of that necessary and developing understanding of his utter dependence upon the Lord Jesus Christ for salvation.

2. God's prior work

The second mark was Simeon's realization, on reflection, that God had been at work in him long before this time, without any awareness of it on his part. He recalled how a few years before he left Eton, a day of fasting was observed at the college and elsewhere on 13 December 1776 because of the British reverses in the American War of Independence. The boys gathered in the chapel twice that day for services, at one of which the provost, Dr Barnard, preached a sermon. The day made a deep impression on Simeon. He wrote,

I was particularly struck with the idea of the whole nation uniting in fasting and prayer on account of the sins which had brought down the Divine judgments upon us: and I thought that, if there was one who had more displeased God than others, it was I. To humble myself therefore before God appeared to me a duty of immediate and indispensable necessity. Accordingly I spent the day in fasting and prayer.7

Sadly, he then fell into the snare of publicly and ostentatiously displaying his fasting rather than keeping it secret. His companions ridiculed him for shutting himself within his study, instead of joining them for meals, and contenting himself with a hard-boiled egg. His contemporaries called him a hypocrite and his good desires were quickly dissipated so that he returned to his thoughtlessness and sin.

Nevertheless, his dress and manners from that time became plainer and unfashionable. A boy who slept within a few feet of his bed tells how many a direct and indirect jest was directed at Simeon as the senior boys met together of an evening. They particularly mocked him when they discovered that he now 'kept a small box with several divisions, into which, on having been tempted to say or do what he afterwards considered as immoral or unlawful, it was his custom to put money for the poor'.8 The boy who slept next to him recorded, 'His habits from that period became peculiarly strict ... We used to have a song about him, ridiculing his strictness and devotion: and the chorus of that song, referring to his box, I am ashamed to say I once joined in: and it haunts me to this day.'9

When conviction of sin begins in us, not uncommonly we may foolishly imagine that our own salvation may be achieved by religious observance; and that was Simeon's experience. He wrote, 'I do not remember that these good desires ever returned during my stay at school; but I think that they were from God, and that God would at that time have communicated richer blessings to me, if I had not resisted the operations of his grace, and done despite to his blessed Spirit.'10

3. A changing attitude to money

The third mark was a changing attitude to money. By nature and habit Simeon was extravagant, especially in his delight in clothes and horses. He considered it legitimate to spend his money upon himself without a second thought and he would have been quite hard upon any who dealt with him at all unfairly. This changed significantly. He began to practise the most rigid economy. As a result he was able to complete his three years' scholarship at King's without any student debt, the opposite of most of his contemporaries, who ended up owing several hundred pounds. Rather than indulging himself in spending, he spent less than half what might have been expected and began to set apart some of his income for God. He maintained meticulous accounts with this objective, and the records he kept show that he regularly gave a third of his income to charity. Henry Venn's comment confirms this change: 'This is the young man so vain of dress that he constantly allowed more than £50 a year for his own person. Now he scruples keeping a horse, that the money may help the saints of Christ.'[11]

4. An appetite for Christian books

The fourth mark was an appetite for Christian books to aid his spiritual understanding of the Bible. *The Whole Duty of Man* and Thomas Wilson's book on the Lord's Supper continued to be important to him. He refers to reading the latter on a Sunday after receiving Communion and praying 'fervently for several graces out of the Whole Duty'.[12] He became a member of the Society for Promoting Christian Knowledge, thinking that its books would be the most useful of any that he might obtain and then profitable for passing on to others. He read printed sermons, of which there were many, and particularly Bishop Beveridge's on Common Prayer.

His occasional journal shows that he was quick to act upon practical suggestions for spiritual growth. The first entry in his diary on 18

February 1780 records, 'I took the hint of keeping a diary of my thoughts and actions from Stonhouse's *Spiritual Instruction to the Uninstructed*, and shall think my religion cooled very much when I remit it.'[13] This was one of the tracts (although fifty-six pages long) distributed by the Society for Promoting Christian Knowledge and was written by Sir James Stonhouse (1716–1795), a physician and Anglican clergyman. It was another popular piece of contemporary Christian literature that went into at least twelve editions. Explaining the relationship between faith and works, it emphasized that sanctification was the consequence of salvation. Direction was provided in the practice of prayer, together with prayers to be used both morning and evening and encouragement to discover the benefits of family prayers.

What particularly struck home with Simeon was Stonhouse's footnote comment about keeping a diary:

That you may make the better progress in religion, I would above all things (if you have leisure and capacity) recommend to you the keeping a Diary, or daily account how you employ your time. This would be of great use, both with regard to your spiritual and temporal concerns. But if you cannot keep a Diary in so full a manner you could wish; yet you may occasionally commit to writing a few observations on the state of your mind, and your progress or decline in religion; which the oftener they are repeated, the greater advantage you will receive.[14]

While never regularly keeping a journal or diary, Simeon adopted the practice on an occasional basis when he felt it beneficial.

5. Growing understanding

The fifth mark was an increased spiritual understanding. Initially, for about a year, Simeon had difficulty in appreciating the nature of saving faith and assurance. He came to the conclusion that assurance is not necessary to saving faith: what God's Word requires is a simple reliance on the Lord Jesus Christ for salvation. Assurance is a privilege, but not a duty or condition of salvation. He was convinced that Christians may be assured of the Lord Jesus Christ's power and willingness to save them, and yet not be assured that he has actually imparted salvation to them.

Preaching on Romans 8:16, he said,

The Spirit, as a 'Spirit of adoption', testifies to the believer's soul, that he belongs to God. Not that this testimony is given without any reference to the Scripture; yet it is imparted in a more instantaneous manner, and in a far higher degree, at some times than at others. God by his Spirit sometimes 'sheds abroad his love in the heart' in such a measure, and shines so clearly on the work he has already wrought there, as to convey immediately a full persuasion and assurance of an interest in his favour. As by 'the sealing of the Spirit' he stamps his own image on his children for the conviction of others, so by 'the witness of the Spirit' he testifies of their adoption for the more immediate comfort of their own souls. These manifestations are vouchsafed, for the most part, to prepare the soul for trials, to support it under them, or to comfort it after them: but they cannot be explained for the satisfaction of others; yet may they be sufficiently proved from Scripture to be the privilege and portion of true believers.[15]

As he read books arguing for different positions on such subjects, he was helped to understand that where differing views divide Christians or become their hobby-horses, safety is found in understanding the Scriptures themselves. He wrote, 'I love the simplicity of the Scriptures, and wish to receive and inculcate every truth precisely in the way and to the extent that it is set forth in the inspired volume. Were this the habit of all divines, there would soon be an end of most of the controversies that have agitated and divided the Church of Christ.'[16]

6. God-honouring conduct

The sixth mark was a growing awareness of the kind of behaviour that befits a Christian. The August after his conversion, Simeon went to the

Reading races, as was his usual practice, and attended the race balls that followed. But the pleasure he had known in them before had disappeared. He wrote, 'I felt them to be empty vanities; but I did not see them to be sinful; I did not then understand those words, "be not conformed to this world".'[17]

Events surrounding the races taught him a hard lesson that he never forgot. Invited to join a cricket match at Windsor and to spend a few days with a military friend, something happened that he determined 'ever to remember with the deepest shame, and the most lively gratitude to God'.[18] On the Sunday his friend suggested visiting a friend about fifteen miles away, and Simeon agreed. But here he wrote, 'I sinned against God and my own conscience; for though I knew not the evil of races and balls, I knew full well that I ought to keep holy the Sabbath day.'[19] They travelled for about ten miles in his friend's four-wheeled open carriage and the rest of the way on horseback. The day was hot, and upon arrival at the friend's house Simeon drank a good deal of what was known as 'a cool tankard'—a drink made of wine and water, with lemon and sugar. After eating dinner, he drank wine, forgetting how much of the earlier drink he had drunk and its potency. When he set off to return on horseback, he was 'in a state of utter intoxication'.[20] The motion of the horse increased the effect of the liquor and deprived him entirely of his senses. His friend rode on ahead and Simeon's horse chose to turn in to an inn. Seeing the state he was in, the people took him off his horse. When his friend discovered what had happened, he put him into a fast carriage and transported him to the inn where they had picked up their horses, in order to stay the night.

Simeon's embarrassment increased when the next day, on returning from a public breakfast and dance at Egham, he went through Salthill, now part of Slough, and saw the inn-keeper there, whom he knew. She asked him if he had heard of the accident that had happened to a gentleman from Reading the previous Sunday evening: how he had fallen from his horse in a state of intoxication and had been killed on the spot. Her words spoke to Simeon's conscience.

What were my feelings now! I had eighteen miles to ride, and all alone: how was I filled with wonder at the mercy of God towards me! Why was it not myself instead of the other gentleman? Why was he taken, and I left? And what must have been my state to all eternity if I had then been taken away! In violating the Sabbath, I had sinned deliberately; and for so doing, God had left me to all the other sins that followed! How shall I adore his name to all eternity that he did not cut me off in these sins, and make me a monument of his heaviest displeasure![21]

In the years to come, sanctification became a frequent theme in Simeon's sermons. Preaching on Leviticus 14:4–9 he declared,

We need still to be renewed, both in our outward and inward man, day by day. Sin cleaves to us … it spontaneously rises up in us: so that though we be washed ever so clean, we shall need to be washed again … we shall not be many days without manifesting that the work of sanctification is not yet perfect. Besides, there are higher degrees of holiness to which the regenerate are to be constantly aspiring. They are 'not to account themselves to have yet attained; but, forgetting the things which are behind, they are to press forward for that which is before'.[22]

In spite of many a fall, God's good work in Simeon had undoubtedly begun.

7. A spiritual appetite

The seventh mark of his new birth was an appreciation of anything and everything that nurtured and strengthened his faith. We have already noted his reading of some of the best-known Christian books of his time. He attended the services in King's College Chapel with a different attitude and spirit. He wrote,

The service in our chapel has almost at all times been very irreverently performed but such was the state of my soul for many months from that time that the prayers were as marrow and fatness to me. Of course, there was a great difference in my frames at different times; but for the most part they were very devout, and often, throughout a great part of the service, I prayed unto the Lord 'with strong crying and tears'.[23]

Rather than being fed by the teaching and preaching of God's Word—benefits that were absent from the services—his soul found spiritual food and nourishment in the liturgy of the Anglican prayer book. For the rest of his life he retained a profound respect and thankfulness for it. It was a proof to him, he testified,

that the deadness and formality experienced in the worship of the Church, arise far more from the low state of our graces, than from any defect in our Liturgy; if only we had our hearts deeply penitent and contrite, I know from my experience at this hour, that no prayers in the world could be better to our wants, or more delightful to our souls.[24]

He found the same spiritual nourishment when he was on vacation at home in Reading, as he testified: 'I used to attend the parish church at Reading every afternoon, and frequently in a morning; and I used to find many sweet seasons of refreshment and comfort in the use of the stated prayers.'[25]

At the same time he began to discern that he gained more spiritual feeding in some places than in others. He discovered more profit for his soul when attending St Giles's Church in Reading than in the parish church where he had been baptized. The minister of St Giles's, the Hon. William Bromley Cadogan, someone with whom Simeon later became friendly, was associated with many evangelical leaders, including the Countess of Huntingdon. So effective was his preaching that a huge gallery was built in the church in 1784 to accommodate the congregation, and yet still many people had to stand. He founded Sunday schools for the children of the parish and at his own expense fed the poor on meat and broth during the winter months. Simeon's father and brothers were not happy at Charles's association with Cadogan because he was regarded as a troubler of the religious establishment in Reading.

On Cadogan's death in 1797 Simeon described him as 'a burning and a shining light'[26] and the sermon that he preached on that occasion still exists. The vicar who followed Cadogan, the Revd Joseph Eyre, did not share his evangelical faith and the flock was sadly scattered. The year after Cadogan's death, part of the congregation left the church to form an independent evangelical chapel called St Mary's Butts in Castle Street, a large building belonging to the Countess of Huntingdon's Connexion. Others joined Nonconformist chapels.

8. A spiritual concern for others

The final mark of his new birth was his immediate spiritual concern for others. It began with anxiety for his college servant—his gyp or bed-maker—and others who performed the same functions. Their duties precluded them from attending church on a Sunday. Simeon determined to do something to help them. He wrote,

From the time that I found peace with God myself, I wished to impart to others the benefits I had received. I therefore adopted a measure which must have appeared most singular to others, and which perhaps a more matured judgment might have disapproved; but I acted in the simplicity of my heart, and I am persuaded that God accepted it at my hands. I told my servant, that as she and the other servants were prevented almost entirely from going to church, I would do my best to instruct them on a Sunday evening, if they chose to come to me for that purpose. Several of them thankfully availed themselves of the offer, and came to me; and I read some good book to them, and used some of the prayers of the Liturgy for prayer; and though I do not know that any of them ever received substantial benefits to their souls, I think that the opportunities were not lost upon myself; for I thereby cultivated a spirit of benevolence, and fulfilled in some measure that divine precept, 'Freely ye have received, freely give'.[27]

This concern was no flash in the pan since Simeon showed the same anxiety when he returned home to Reading at vacations. He described his endeavours the first summer vacation after his conversion:

In the long vacation I went home; and carried with me the same blessed desires. I had then a brother, eight years older than myself, living with my father, and managing, as it were, his house. I wished to instruct the servants, and to unite with them in family prayer; but I had no hope that a proposal to that effect would be acceded to either by my father or my brother: I therefore proposed it to the servants, and established it myself, leaving to my brother to join with us or not, as he saw good. To my great joy, after it was established, my brother cordially united with me, and we … worshipped God, morning and evening, in the family. I take for granted that my father knew of it; but I do not remember that one word ever passed between him and me on the subject.[28]

On reflection, he recognized that his early enthusiasm inclined him to trust his own resources rather than to depend upon God. He had to learn that God's work needs to be done in God's energy. He wrote, 'During my Scholarship at King's College, I made many attempts to benefit my friends, and sometimes thought I had succeeded in conveying to them some spiritual good; but I now see that I expected too much from my own exertions, and from their resolutions. If good be done to any, the work must be God's alone; "the help that is done upon earth, he doeth it himself"'[29]—a quotation from the 1662 *Book of Common Prayer*'s choral rendering of Psalm 74:13, an indication of how the liturgy nurtured Simeon's spiritual growth.

One of the most remarkable circumstances surrounding his conversion is that for the three years afterwards he failed to identify in

Chapter 3

Cambridge anyone who had had the same experience of conversion as himself. Thankfully, this was all suddenly to change.

Notes

1 *Memoirs of Charles Simeon*, p. 131.
2 Ibid., p. 414.
3 Ibid., p. 381.
4 Sermon on Ecclesiastes 12:2, *Horae Homileticae*, vol. 7 (London: Samuel Holdsworth, 1836 / Logos Bible Software, 2007). Hereafter referred to as *Horae Homileticae*.
5 Sermon on 1 Peter 1:3–5, *Horae Homileticae*, vol. 20.
6 *Memoirs of Charles Simeon*, p. 3.
7 Ibid.
8 Ibid., p. 4.
9 Ibid.
10 Ibid., p. 3.
11 Ibid., p. 17.
12 Ibid., p. 11.
13 Ibid.
14 Ibid.
15 Sermon on Romans 8:15, *Horae Homileticae*, vol. 15.
16 *Memoirs of Charles Simeon*, p. 7.
17 Ibid.
18 Ibid.
19 Ibid.
20 Ibid.
21 Ibid., p. 8.
22 Sermon on Leviticus 14:4–9, *Horae Homileticae*, vol. 1.
23 *Memoirs of Charles Simeon*, p. 6.
24 Ibid.
25 Ibid., p. 9.
26 Ibid., p. 88.
27 Ibid, pp. 6–7.
28 Ibid., p. 7.
29 Ibid., p. 10.

Ordination and Holy Trinity Church

S imeon's conviction about his call to ordained ministry came soon after his conversion. This was understandable. First, such a step was common for old Etonians and King's Scholars; second, as we have seen, his family had a history of providing ministers for the Church of England; and third, and most important of all, the reality of his spiritual understanding of the necessity of new birth and the urgent need for faithful ministers of the gospel to proclaim its truth must have stimulated his thoughts and prayers in that direction.

He was ordained on Trinity Sunday, 26 May 1782, at the age of twenty-two, by the Bishop of Ely. We may wonder what training he had for this important step. The answer is: little. Theological training for ordination scarcely existed within Britain. In Cambridge the ordination examination—taken on the day of the ordination—consisted only of translating aloud a passage from the Greek New Testament.

St Edward's Church

During the Long Vacation after his ordination he was given the opportunity to serve in St Edward's Church, where the minister, Christopher Atkinson, was someone for whom he had high regard. From 1781 to 1785 Atkinson was what was called the Vicar-Chaplain of the Church of St Edward King and Martyr. Previously a fellow of Trinity College, he became a fellow of Trinity Hall for the period he was at St Edward's. The church, one of Cambridge's oldest and smallest, had been given to Trinity Hall, one of the university's smaller colleges, in the fifteenth century.

As a young minister, Simeon must have been thrilled at St Edward's history. It had been at the centre of the English Reformation, a place in which some of the influential Reformers had preached—men such as Thomas Bilney, Robert Barnes and Hugh Latimer, all of whom gave their lives for their faith. It was Latimer who, put to death beside Nicholas Ridley, declared, 'Be of good comfort Master Ridley, and play the man: we shall this day light such a candle by God's grace in England, as (I trust) shall never be put out.'[1]

Simeon already had some knowledge of the congregation. After his conversion on Easter Day 1779 he looked without success to find others who shared his experience and he naturally explored the Cambridge churches. Perhaps because it was the university church and close to King's College, he went first to St Mary's, known now as Great St Mary's. But he found little there to help and encourage him in his Christian life. Then later, at the time he became a fellow of King's, he visited St Edward's, which was nearer still, down a lane opposite King's College. To his joy and delight he found that its minister preached the truths through which he had been converted and in which he now delighted.

He was astonished that Mr Atkinson never spoke to him after a service. This was surprising since no other university students attended, and they were easily identified by their wearing of a gown. It puzzled Simeon, as well it might. 'I thought,' he wrote, 'that if I were a minister, and saw a young gownsman attending as regularly and devoutly as I did, I should invite him to come and see me; and I determined, if he should do so, I would avail myself of the opportunity to get acquainted with him.'[2] Already Simeon showed indications of pastoral sensitivity that were to develop and blossom to the profit of many in the years to come.

His longing for spiritual fellowship with like-minded Christians was so great that, on his ordination, he thought seriously of putting an advertisement in the newspapers, in the following words:

That a young Clergyman who felt himself an undone sinner, and looked to the Lord Jesus Christ alone for salvation, and desired to live only to make known that Saviour unto others, was persuaded that there must be some persons in the world whose views and feelings on this subject accorded with his own, though he had now lived three years without finding so much as one; and that if there were any minister of that description he would gladly become his curate, and serve him gratis![3]

Eventually, Atkinson invited Simeon to visit him. He also asked an artist to join them. The latter was neither Christian nor religious and the conversation proved unprofitable. Simeon responded by inviting them both to eat with him one evening, but the artist could not join them, so Simeon had Atkinson to himself. Simeon explains,

I soon dropped some expressions which conveyed the idea of my feeling myself a poor, guilty, helpless sinner: and Mr A was quite surprised, for he had set it down, as a matter of course, that I must be a staunch Pharisee; he had, even for the whole space of time that I had been at college, noticed my solemn and reverent behaviour at St Mary's, so different from that which is generally observed in that place, and concluded, as three of his pious friends had also done, that I was actuated by a proud pharisaical spirit; when therefore he found that I was of a very different complexion, he manifested a union of heart with me.[4]

The first taste of ministry

Immediately after his ordination Simeon was delighted to begin his Christian ministry in Christopher Atkinson's parish. He had around seventeen Sundays in all at St Edward's. They began with four to six weeks during the minister's absence when he had complete care of the congregation as well as the responsibility of preaching, and he gave a series on the Ten Commandments. It was a unique and stretching experience for Simeon, one he never forgot. His preaching began to fill the church, something unknown for the best part of a century. He wrote,

'In the space of a month or six weeks the church became quite crowded; the Lord's table was attended by three times the usual number of communicants, and a considerable stir was made among the dry bones.'[5]

This evidence of God's hand upon him was an unexpected and wonderful confirmation of his call to pastoral ministry. Significant from the point of view of his understanding of that task, he at once began to visit from house to house in the entire parish, making no distinction between Anglicans and Dissenters. Later he recalled having a friendly dispute with a Dissenting minister about the doctrine of election in the course of his visitation.

His pastoral heart came to light after the first service he conducted at St Edward's. As he walked back to King's College through the narrow St Edward's Passage, he heard the loud voices of a husband and wife in an argument. As their door was open, he entered the house and rebuked them for neglecting to be in church and for disturbing the peace of those who had been. He then knelt down to pray for them. Passers-by, intrigued by such unusual behaviour, crowded into the room. News of what was happening through this new minister of the gospel soon spread.

The Venn family

One of Atkinson's most influential actions was introducing Simeon to John Venn, who took him to meet his father, Henry, parish minister of Yelling, a village about twelve miles from Cambridge. John had told his father of the reports he had heard of Simeon and his father had encouraged him to make contact with him, but he had not done so. It was Atkinson who, in God's providence, brought it about.

Simeon's appreciation of this introduction was immediate. 'O what an acquisition was this! In this aged minister I found a father, an instructor, and a most bright example: and I shall have reason to adore my God to all eternity for the benefit of this acquaintance.'[6] Every young minister may profit from an older minister's friendship and godly counsel and this benefit was now Simeon's. Time and time again he visited Yelling to obtain the older man's advice and through him he gained knowledge of other evangelical ministers throughout England. Venn found Simeon quick off the mark to exercise pastoral responsibility. On Venn's suggesting that Simeon should visit a man he knew to be in prison awaiting execution, Simeon responded, 'Oh, I have been with him several times, and have good hopes he will go from the gallows to glory.'[7]

In addition Charles had the friendship of John Venn, the friendship with someone of the same mind he had looked for those three years since his conversion. He wrote to John, 'I used formerly to think that I had some idea of real friendship, but my acquaintance with you has convinced me it was a very faint conception rather of what it should be, than of what it is. The Lord Jesus Christ, I trust, has given me to know something more of it now.'[8] It was during this period that the telling story is told of John Venn's sisters laughter at his new friend's look and manner when he visited them at Yelling. They described his distorted facial expressions when he spoke as 'beyond anything you can imagine'. Observing the girls' hilarity, their father asked them to go outside and pick him a peach. Not guessing what he had in mind, they obeyed. Being early summer, the peach was green, unripe and inedible. 'Well, my dears,' commented their father, 'it is green now, and we must wait; but a little more sun and a few more showers, and the peach will be ripe and sweet. So it is with Mr Simeon.'[9]

Family relations

Charles told Henry Venn of his father's disapproval of and antagonism towards his evangelical zeal. Venn wrote,

Mr Simeon's father, who used to delight in him, is all gall and bitterness. I should not wonder if he were to disinherit him. The Lord will be his portion if it be so; and he would be rich nevertheless. Such storms we have weathered—for what remains may we be ready, and at last be guided into the haven where we would be.[10]

Charles's father's reaction may have been not so much on account of what he heard of his son's ministry in Cambridge but because of the spiritual concern Charles demonstrated for both his father and brothers, and his identifying no longer with the family's parish church when on vacation in Reading.

The relationship may well have been made easier between father and son through the sad death of Charles's oldest brother, Richard, in October 1782. Charles showed concern and respect for his father by agreeing to the suggestion that, because his father was now left to live on his own, he should leave King's and return home. Charles was to have part of the house to himself so as to be able to entertain his friends without disturbing his father. The move was just a fortnight away, with his books packed ready, when an event occurred that determined the course of the rest of his life.

Holy Trinity Church

Regularly when walking through the centre of Cambridge, Simeon passed Holy Trinity Church, one of the largest churches in the town. It is even more central to town and university life than Great St Mary's, the university church. (Godly Richard Sibbes had served Holy Trinity Church as a lecturer in the seventeenth century.) Often Simeon had said to himself, 'How should I rejoice if God were to give me that church, that I might preach the Gospel there, and be a herald for him in the midst of the University.'[11] But he could not see how this could possibly happen. Yet such an ambition had clearly been implanted in him by God's Spirit.

At this time, when he was packed and prepared to leave for Reading, he heard that the minister of Holy Trinity had died. He immediately wondered if this was God's opportunity for him. He remembered that, providentially, the only bishop with whom his father had any acquaintance was the Bishop of Ely, whose responsibility the appointment was. He wrote to his father, asking him to apply to the bishop for the living on his behalf. His father acted upon his request and the move to Reading was put on hold.

But obstacles existed to frustrate Charles's hopes. A curate, John Hammond, had served Holy Trinity Church for some time and the congregation, not surprisingly, wanted him to be the new minister. To achieve this they engineered a political manoeuvre. The main source of income for a minister of the parish was a lectureship and the power of appointment to it lay not with the bishop but with the congregation. They assumed that no one would want to become vicar without the financial benefit of the lectureship. Somewhat militantly, they therefore signed a petition on behalf of the curate in which they informed the bishop of their action in giving him the lectureship.

Aware of their violent reaction to the possibility of the appointment of anyone other than the curate, Simeon told them that he was 'a minister of peace'[12] and that he had no wish to be their minister other than for their good. On reflection, having originally thought of writing to the bishop, he decided not to do so. He determined that if the bishop chose to appoint him rather than the curate, he could appoint Hammond as his substitute, and give him the income that came from the living for as long as he chose to hold it. Then, if Simeon was still alive when Hammond wished to leave it, he could take possession without anyone else obtaining it. This shows the quite remarkable calling and commitment Simeon felt to the parish. Having made this decision, he resigned himself to the possibility of waiting many years to see his vision fulfilled.

But the parishioners did not know their bishop! He liked neither their spirit nor their indiscreet language. On 9 November 1782 he wrote to Simeon offering him the parish, telling him that if he did not accept it, he would certainly not offer it to the curate. Charles's response was, 'Truly "the judgments of God are unsearchable, and his ways past finding out".'[13]

An unhappy reception

Scarcely a worse start to a ministry could be imagined. The sense of hostility was tangible. His pastoral wish to visit people was impossible because of their bitterness at his appointment: none would admit him to their homes. They went so far as putting locks on the pews, determined that not only would they not go to church themselves but that they would also hinder others who wanted to do so. At his own expense, he brought benches and seats into the church, but the churchwardens threw them out.

John Hammond, the previous vicar's curate, exercised his lectureship once a week and gained the income from it. Simeon decided to set up his own lectureship on another evening, but the churchwardens shut the church doors against him. On another occasion, as the congregation gathered, they discovered that one of the churchwardens had locked the door and gone away with the key in his pocket. Simeon employed a locksmith to open the door and pondered what he should do.

A criticized initiative

A number of Nonconformist or Dissenting churches met in the town and Simeon was worried lest the potential congregation he was building up would be lost to such meetings. He decided to hire a private room in the parish where he could expound the Scriptures and the people meet to pray. It quickly became too small for the numbers wanting to attend. He then obtained a larger room in a neighbouring parish, aware that many would criticize him for doing this and even persecute him. Committing his cause to God, he wrote,

He knew the real desire of my heart; he knew that I only wished to fulfil his will. I told him a thousand times over that I did not deprecate persecution; for I considered that as the necessary lot of all who would 'live godly in Christ Jesus'; and more especially, of all who would preach Christ with fidelity; but I deprecated it as arising from that room.[14]

Simeon's friends, alarmed at his action, decided to get Henry Venn to speak to him, knowing Simeon's respect for his mentor. The explanation Simeon gave Venn convinced him of the sensitivity he had to the issues involved and the necessity of his actions. Venn's response was, 'Go on, and God be with you'; he was even prepared to preach for him.[15] He wrote to a friend, 'He preaches twice a week in a large room … and his people are indeed of an excellent spirit—merciful, loving, and righteous.'[16] His encouragement of Simeon was vindicated even though convening a meeting in another church's parish was highly irregular. Simeon's later testimony was that, while his convening a meeting in another church's parish was abnormal, 'The persecutions in my parish continued and increased; but during the space of many years no persecution whatever arose from that room, though confessedly it was the side on which my enemies might have attacked me with most effect.'[17]

2 Timothy 2:24

Simeon was learning an invaluable lesson that in the years to come he passed on many times to men in the ministry. He would have sunk beneath the burden and anxiety of it all had not God shown him that the key response and remedy to all opposition is faith and patience.

The passage of Scripture which subdued and controlled my mind was, 'The servant of the Lord must not strive' [2 Tim. 2:24]. It was painful indeed to see the church, with the exception of the aisles, almost forsaken; but I thought that if God would only give a double blessing to the congregation that did attend, there would on the whole be as much good done as if the congregation were doubled, and the blessing limited to half the amount. This has comforted me many, many times, when, without such a reflection, I should have sunk ...[18]

It was not for just a brief period that this situation continued, but for ten years. When after about five years John Hammond vacated the lectureship, instead of Simeon being able to assume it, the son of a parishioner competed for it. Although by this time Simeon's standing in the parish had improved, 'a bitter and persecuting spirit'[19] continued and the leaders of the parish declared that he had lost the vote. They also kept most of the pews shut. Acting upon 2 Timothy 2:24, Simeon looked to God to bring about the change. He recognized that trials are part of God's necessary instruments for character transformation, and not least the character of his ministers. He wrote to a friend,

Certain it is, that the saints whom God has most approved, have been most abundantly exercised in different manners for the trial of their faith: and they who are most earnest in prayer for grace, are often most afflicted, because the graces which they pray for, *e.g.* faith, hope, patience, humility, &c., are only to be wrought in us by means of those trials which call forth the several graces into act and exercise; and in the very exercise of them they are all strengthened and confirmed.[20]

His trials increased his conviction that more important than status or remuneration, 'the most valuable, most honourable, most important, and most glorious office in the world' is that of being 'an ambassador of the Lord Jesus Christ'.[21] God was working not only in his convictions, but also in his character. He was learning invaluable lessons that could be learned only in the hard school of experience. Significantly, he spoke of the worship of God as 'the adoration of humility',[22] and humility and love as 'the chief ornaments of a Christian'.[23] So great was the battle he experienced throughout his life against pride that 'he sometimes spoke of his own salvation, as of that which would be the very masterpiece of Divine grace, and of the probability of his being the last and least in the kingdom of heaven'.[24]

Notes

1 **John Foxe,** *Acts and Monuments* (1583); quoted in *Oxford Dictionary of National Biography*, vol. 23 (Oxford: Oxford University Press, 2004), p. 638.

2 *Memoirs of Charles Simeon*, p. 13.

3 Ibid., p. 14.

4 Ibid.

5 Ibid., p. 15.

6 Ibid., p. 14.

7 Ibid., p. 28.

8 Ibid., p. 17.

9 **H. C. G. Moule,** *Charles Simeon* (London: Hodder & Stoughton, 1977), p. 45.

10 *Memoirs of Charles Simeon*, p. 28.

11 Ibid., p. 24.

12 Ibid., p. 25.

13 Ibid., p. 26.

14 Ibid., p. 27.

15 Ibid., p. 27.

16 Ibid., p. 50.

17 Ibid., p. 27.

18 Ibid., p. 26.

19 Ibid., p. 39.

20 Ibid., pp. 42–43.

21 Ibid., p. 17.

22 Ibid., p. 304.

23 Ibid., pp. 369–370.

24 Ibid., p. 397.

The early years at Holy Trinity: a tough beginning

A lthough duly appointed to Holy Trinity Church, twelve years passed before Simeon was able to exercise fully his calling as its pastor and teacher. A lesser man—or perhaps better expressed, anyone lacking the conviction of God's call and help—would have soon removed himself from the scene.

As early as January 1783, just months after his appointment, Henry Venn wrote, 'Cambridge is going to be in a ferment—Mr Simeon's ministry is likely to be blessed. We may indeed say, "a great door is opened!" for several gownsmen hear him. What follows is as true[:] "and there are many adversaries" … But "the Wonderful Counsellor" is with him.'[1]

Venn's quoting of Paul's words in 1 Corinthians 16:9 was relevant. As well as locking the pews and even the church itself to hinder Simeon's pursuit of his calling, the leaders of the parish made a formal complaint to the Bishop of Ely. They accused Simeon of preaching 'so as to alarm and terrify them, and that the people came and crowded the church, and stole their books'.[2] The bishop wrote to Simeon regarding their complaint, and he in turn replied at considerable length to vindicate his preaching and deny the charges.

Lessons to be learned

Simeon later regretted the length of his answer and understood why the bishop was displeased with it. He confessed that his letter was more like a syllabus with a number of distinct headings than a letter with a clear argument. 'I was not then skilled in writing to bishops: were I to answer the same accusations now (1813), I should frame my reply in a different way.'[3]

He was also sorry that, while the parishioners' complaint was unjust and an indication of hostility to the gospel, it also drew attention to his own over-enthusiasm.

I thought that to declare the truth with boldness was the one object which I ought to keep in view; and this is a very general mistake among young ministers. I did not sufficiently attend to the example of our Lord and his apostles in speaking as men were able to hear it, and in administering milk to babes, and meat to strong men. My mind being but ill-informed, my topics were necessarily few; and the great subjects of death, judgment, heaven and hell, were prominent in every discourse, particularly as motives to enforce the points on which I had occasion to insist. Were I now to enter on a new sphere, especially if it were in a town and not in a village, I would, in the Morning Services especially, unfold the parables, and endeavour rather to take the citadel by sap and mine, than by assault and battery. I would endeavour to 'win souls', and 'speak to them the truth in love'; not considering so much what I was able to say, as what they were able to receive. But this requires more extensive knowledge, and a more chastised mind than falls in general to the lot of young ministers, especially of such as have never had one letter of instruction given them on the subject.[4]

A discernible turning point

Patience bore its fruit and there were encouragements along the way. In December 1786 Simeon was invited to preach for the first time before the university, and this had considerable impact. The Saturday beforehand Dr Glynn, a leading Cambridge physician and friend from King's, called on Simeon and had him read the sermon to him so that he might help him correct and improve upon it.

When the time came for the service to begin, St Mary's, the university church, was packed and it looked as if undergraduates had come to disturb and annoy the preacher. The record of what happened reveals the opposite to what was expected:

But scarcely had he proceeded more than a few sentences, when the lucid arrangement of his exordium, and his serious and commanding manner, impressed the whole assembly with feelings of deep solemnity, and he was heard to the end with the most respectful and riveted attention. The vast congregation departed in a mood very different from that in which it had assembled; and it was evident, from the remarks which were overheard at going out, and the subdued tone in which they were made, that many were seriously affected, as well as surprised, at what they had heard. Of two young men, who had come among the scoffers, one was heard to say to the other, 'Well, Simeon is no fool!' 'Fool!' replied his companion, 'did you ever hear such a sermon before?'5

In 1790, with the consent of his churchwardens, Simeon established a Sunday evening lecture at Holy Trinity. Legally he could have insisted earlier on his right to do so, but increasingly he was learning to wait God's time for the fulfilment of his wishes. His natural temperament was to respond too quickly to challenges, as already illustrated when complaints were made about his preaching to his bishop; but greater self-knowledge helped him to submit to his Lord's example.

The purpose of the evening lectures was instruction of poorer members of the community who could not easily attend a church service in the earlier part of the day. An evening service was something of a novelty in Cambridge, although not in college chapels. It was a deliberate evangelistic outreach and some would have regarded it as being more what was expected of Methodism than of Anglicanism. The religious community in Cambridge viewed it with either jealousy or contempt. Undergraduates initially attended with the motive of disturbing and disrupting the worship, some in a state of intoxication. They walked about the aisles, ignoring the stewards directing them to seats and often insulting members of the congregation during and after the service. Knowing that he would get little support from their college authorities to discipline them, Simeon positioned stewards in the aisles to look out for troublemakers and went to the door at the end of the service to make sure he could apprehend any undergraduate whose intention was to insult those who had attended the service. Once more, his growing gentleness, coupled with firmness, showed itself. He requested those who withstood his authority not to compel him to demand their names, because if they put him under pressure to do so, he would have to take further disciplinary measures.

Initially inclined to abandon the lectures, he recognized that the opportunity they afforded of instruction and evangelism was too good to forfeit. After consultation with the university's vice-chancellor, he made an example of a young man who had the nerve to break a window and then come into the service. Adopting what he called a kill or cure approach, he required the young man to read, in the presence of the congregation, a public acknowledgement of his crime, written for him by Simeon. This he did the next Sunday evening. It read,

I — ..., sensible of the great offence I have committed in disturbing this congregation, do, by the express order of the vice-chancellor, thus publicly beg pardon of the minister and congregation; and I owe it only to the lenity of Mr Simeon, that the vice-chancellor has not proceeded against me in a very different manner; for which lenity I am also ordered by the vice-chancellor thus publicly to acknowledge my obligation to Mr Simeon: and I do now promise never to offend in like manner again.[6]

As the young man's voice was not very loud, Simeon himself then read the statement again to a church packed with undergraduates, many of them standing upon the benches and seats to see and hear what was happening.

It was then a dramatic moment when Simeon went up into the pulpit and preached on Galatians 6:7–8: 'Do not be deceived: God cannot be mocked. A man reaps what he sows.' A sense of awe fell upon the congregation and Simeon recorded,

My sermon was heard with the deepest attention; and for a long time my enemies were all subdued before me. I have sometimes doubted whether I was not guilty of undue severity in reading the paper a second time myself; but when I consider the extremity to which I was reduced and the dreadful alternative to which I must resort, in case the misconduct of the young men was not effectually checked, I am disposed to think that I did right. It was God's cause alone that I vindicated, and for him alone I acted: and when I reflect that the interests of immortal souls, during the whole remainder of my life, were at stake, I think the importance of the object to be attained justified the measure to which I resorted for the attainment of it.[7]

This was not a unique experience and Simeon discovered that gentleness with firmness was the right way to proceed, as on the occasion when two young men entered the church in a disorderly way. He tried to catch their eyes and indicated his displeasure by his look. While one of them was clearly ashamed, the other deliberately sought to stare Simeon out in defiance. Simeon sent for him the next morning and challenged him about his behaviour, reminding him that it was not mere man that he was despising but God and his Word. He instructed him not to come to church again unless he changed his attitude and spirit. To his surprise, the man was there the next Sunday and the Sundays following, and he came to a full knowledge of the gospel of Christ and a year or two afterwards became a minister of the gospel.

Teaching made attractive by good works

Throughout all these years of opposition Simeon maintained his high view of what it means to be a minister of the gospel, considering it, as we saw in the previous chapter, 'the most valuable, most honourable, most important and most glorious office in the world'.[8] While many chose to despise his evangelical preaching, they could not ignore how attractive that teaching was in the good works that it produced.

Relief of the poor

When bread became scarce at the end of 1788 and continuing into 1789, a fund was set up for the poor of Cambridge to enable them to obtain it at half-price. Simeon contributed a large amount of money to the fund and his acquaintance with the surrounding villages made him as concerned for them as for the people of Cambridge. 'What is to become of them?' he asked. 'That is more than we can undertake to answer for,' was the reply. Simeon's response was, 'That shall be my business.'[9] Accordingly, he set on foot a plan by which they too might be included in the benefit.

Assuming personally a large share of the cost and trouble he inspired others with the same desire to bring relief in twenty-four villages near Cambridge. Every Monday he rode to the villages within his reach to see that the bakers performed their duty in selling to the poor at half-price. He displayed exceptional organizational ability in the way in which a fair distribution was arranged.

The growth of the flock and the appointment of an assistant

The next insight we gain into the size of Simeon's flock is in February 1794, nearly twelve years after his settlement at Holy Trinity, when a friend wrote, 'He has above one hundred whom he considers as his flock, whom he has reason to believe the Lord hath called and blessed.'[10] These were Christians who gave evidence of a living and lively faith. Careful in his pastoral care, he visited them in their homes and met with them every week in a room in the town hired for the purpose. He did all he could to encourage their spiritual growth. His exhortations to them were described as 'close and heart-searching'.[11] None could have accused him of doing what he did for financial reward, for the church gave him scarcely forty pounds a year. When this was commented on, his response was, 'If they would not let me preach, I would give them forty pounds to make them do it.'[12]

The year 1794 provided another important turning point when twelve years of patience were rewarded and Simeon became the chosen Lecturer of Holy Trinity Church without opposition. This, however, brought the responsibility of three services on a Sunday, and he soon recognized the wisdom and necessity of having help. In October 1796 he invited his young friend Thomas Thomason to be his assistant and at the same time obtained for him the curacy of Stapleford, a village four miles south of Cambridge, where he could minister in the morning and Simeon in the afternoon.

Notes

1 *Memoirs of Charles Simeon*, p. 28.
2 Ibid., p. 38.
3 Ibid.
4 Ibid., pp. 38–39.
5 Ibid., p. 54.
6 Ibid.
7 Ibid., pp. 54–55.
8 Ibid., p. 48.
9 Ibid., p. 59.
10 Ibid.
11 Ibid.
12 Ibid.

Patience rewarded

Pastoral care was a priority on Simeon's agenda. He saw the tremendous spiritual benefit of meeting with his people regularly—a shepherd can only shepherd his flock if he knows his sheep. He observed how effectively Nonconformists, and especially Methodists, exercised spiritual care through gathering believers together in small groups or societies.

With a growing congregation at Holy Trinity he concluded that if he and others did not do something similar the members of any church would be 'only as a rope of sand and may easily be scattered with every wind of doctrine, or drawn aside'[1] by some unhelpful enthusiast.

His solution was to divide those who came to Holy Trinity from Cambridge itself and whom he knew to be 'spiritually enlightened'[2] into six societies, each with a membership of about twenty. He formed the societies according to sex and to how he thought the individual members would relate to one another. One such society was made up of those whom he considered the most spiritually mature and experienced. They were also responsible for the funds collected from all six societies for the relief of the poor, and it was their task to dispense these resources.

Now that he was meeting with the individual members of his flock only once a month rather than weekly, he appointed someone within each group, called a 'steward', in whose judgement he trusted. It was the responsibility of these stewards to report any spiritual concern they had for those within their groups, particularly if they were turning away from God or perhaps finding themselves drawn away to Dissenting groups. He gave these leaders guidance in dealing with minor problems and reserved to himself the right to interpose where he thought it necessary.

Sensitive to the danger of creating societies or groups within a church, he saw the importance of their spiritual oversight; we can never have spiritual benefits without spiritual dangers. Writing of his use of societies, he declared,

That it is open to abuse is certain; and what is there that may not be abused? Even the Apostolic Churches were more or less distracted by the conceit of some, or the violence of others; and whilst human nature is what it is, we cannot hope to find any society of men on earth free from some kinds of evils.3

The need for supervision

A particular experience around 1811 taught Simeon the dangers of meetings without supervision. During the Napoleonic Wars (1803 to 1815) many weekly prayer meetings met throughout the nation, and that was so at Holy Trinity. But when the wars ceased, the prayer meeting at Holy Trinity continued without Simeon, with around fifty people meeting together. As often happens when supervision and leadership are absent, the wrong people came to the fore and saw it as an area of power and influence, making it more than simply a prayer meeting. They had no desire to be led but rather were determined to be in control. Instead of simply reading the Scriptures and praying, they became self-appointed expounders of Scripture and preachers. In addition, rather than making it a meeting for those who belonged to the six societies of Holy Trinity, they extended an invitation to others, making it, in effect, another church.

If this had come to the ears of Simeon's bishop, it could have brought an end to his ministry at Holy Trinity. Aware that he had to deal with the problem, lest he be considered a patron and encourager of the meeting's irregularities, he tried to bring a change, but to no avail. He summoned his stewards to share his concern and expelled one of their number. He recommended that, rather than meeting together in such a large group, they should meet for prayer in smaller groups of ten or twelve and limit themselves to members of Holy Trinity. They refused. Simeon had no option but to tell their leader that if they were determined to go their own way, he wished them to separate themselves from Holy Trinity. 'If they chose to let off fire-works, they were at liberty to do so, only I desired they would not put them under my thatch, to burn down my house.'[4]

But they declined to leave and determined to go their own way. When Simeon suggested that, although he could not stop them coming, he could—as an act of discipline—keep them from attending the Lord's Table, their response was that since it was not Simeon's Table but the Lord's, it was open to all. He told them that he would not refuse any of them the first time but afterwards he would warn individuals not to come again, so that they might consider their ways.

With many tears, Simeon urged them to repent, and some did. After exercising patience for a whole year on the issue, he expelled some from his societies, deliberately beginning with those who were not the leaders, recognizing that if he began with the latter they would carry others with them. His judgement proved right and terms of peace were forthcoming, bringing to an end one of his most difficult pastoral experiences, one that took its toll on him physically as well as spiritually.

An undiminished conviction

His view of the importance of pastoral groups within a church was not weakened by this sad experience. He wrote in 1815,

My judgment most decidedly is, that without them, where they can be had, a people will never be kept together; nor will they ever feel related to their minister, as children to a parent; nor will the minister himself take that lively interest in their welfare, which it is both his duty and his happiness to feel. A minister is to be 'instant in season and out of season': and if his public labours are comprehended under the former period, these private exercises seem especially intended by the latter; and one who would approve himself to God, as St Paul did, should be able to say, 'I have taught you publicly, and from house to house, and have warned you night and day with tears.' But then great care should be taken about the manner of conducting them. The people should never, if it can be avoided, be left to themselves: the moment they are, there is danger of unhallowed kind of emulation rising up among them; and those, who by reason of their natural forwardness are most unfit to lead, will always obtrude themselves as leaders among them; whilst the modest and timid will be discouraged, because they cannot exercise those gifts which they behold in others. On such occasions, too, the vain and conceited will be peculiarly gratified; and mistaking the gratifications of vanity for truly spiritual emotions, they will attach a pre-eminent importance to those opportunities which tend to display their talents; and they will begin to entertain low thoughts of their own minister, whose labours do not afford them the same pleasure. This spirit, too, they will encourage among the people at large, and this will spread among them a disposition to criticize and sit in judgment on the labours of their ministers. It is probable, that this will not fall on their stated minister, to whose exertions they owe, under God, the salvation of their souls: they, in general, will idolize him and make him a standard whereby to judge of others: but other ministers, who shall occasionally address them, will be applauded or censured by them with as much confidence, as if their taste were perfect and their judgment infallible. This, therefore, a minister must guard against with all his might: and if he make it a rule to conduct the service in the private societies himself, he will, for the most part, keep down these evils.[5]

Reflecting later still upon what had happened, he wrote,

The true state of the case is, that the corruption of human nature will sooner or later show itself in every church. There were those who said to Moses, 'You take too much upon you'; whilst the charge was in truth applicable only to themselves. There ever was, and ever will be, some Diotrephes, 'who loves to have the pre-eminence', and who will find some occasion or other to manifest and diffuse his own evil dispositions. If even St Paul found this to be the case, yea, and the loving John too,—who am I, that I should minister for thirty-three years, and not find it? This is only a fresh proof that human nature is the same in every country and in every age.[6]

The opening of the church galleries

A year later a change was apparent. The respect and kindness shown to him in the whole university far exceeded anything he had known previously and the numbers attending Holy Trinity greatly increased. He could write at the end of 1816, 'My people, who remained steadfast, are in a blessed state: my church better attended than ever: my delight in my work greater: my health is good: my strength is renewed, so that I preach with ease. I do hope that God has yet something for me to do before I die.'[7]

During the summer of 1817 his preaching through 1 Thessalonians caused some who were proud and not submissive to God's Word to leave the congregation. His humble spirit and weeping over them seemed to enrage them more than anything, whereas it drew those of a humbler spirit closer to him.

At the end of the year the church was more crowded with undergraduates than ever. For the first time Simeon had to open the galleries for them, but still many had to stand in the aisles. His regular congregation was in better spiritual health than for many years. 'The bad spirits are withdrawn, and peace and love are abounding in the midst of us.'[8] He sensed that since the withdrawal of the proud and conceited there had been 'a peculiar unction' upon his ministry and 'a rich blessing' on the word.[9] When he preached a series of five sermons upon the Law (Gal. 3:19) at St Mary's, the university church, the numbers were so great that many had to be turned away. The number of societies—or pastoral groups—within his own congregation had increased to thirty and achieved great good.

When the fiftieth anniversary of his appointment to Holy Trinity arrived in 1832 the testimony of love given to him by his people overwhelmed him and filled him with thanksgiving. He wrote to a friend, 'Who would have ever thought that I should have to behold such a day as this? My parish sweetly harmonious!'[10] And so it continued, with the church being enlarged to hold 1,100 people.

Chapter 6

This change prompted him to recall how once in his early years in Cambridge he had attended Holy Trinity Church to hear a popular preacher and had remained afterwards for the Lord's Supper. Besides those who administered it, he was one of but three communicants.

Important lessons

More than half a century's ministry taught Simeon many lessons about pastoral ministry and God's service. Besides those that we may deduce ourselves as we read his story, he himself commented on many of them and it is helpful to identify them.

1. THE PRIORITY OF FAITH AND PATIENCE

The primary lesson he had learned was the importance of waiting God's time by exercising patience. The challenges he faced drove him to the Scriptures and served to confirm the priority of living with difficulties confident of God's sovereignty. When the members of Holy Trinity locked the pews, although they had no right to do so, Simeon could write,

I was restrained from attempting to open them by that Divine declaration, 'the servant of the Lord must not strive'. Many hundreds of times has that one word tied my hands, when a concern for immortal souls, and a sense of the injury done to my ministry, would have prompted me to take off the locks. I hoped that God would at last effect a change; and I found, after about ten years, that I was not disappointed.[11]

2. DIFFICULTIES AS THE PATH TO GOD'S BLESSING

He discovered that difficulties are not to be equated with unfruitfulness, and that even the opposite may be true: they may be the outworking of God's eternal purposes of salvation. Earlier we recorded the distress and hassle of the interruption of services by disorderly students at Holy Trinity and the two young men who came together with that deliberate purpose, one of whom Simeon had to discipline as an example to others.

Both were subsequently brought to faith in our Lord Jesus Christ and became eminently godly men and his friends. They were Richard Godley and the later biographer of Henry Martyn—John Sargent.

While the obvious doors for ministry at Holy Trinity were closed for Simeon for a number of years, others opened up for him—part of the programme of good works that God prepares in advance for his people to do. A particular door of opportunity was the influence he was able to exercise in his own college; and those close to him recognized this. One, also a member of King's, urged him in 1789,

You have already, my dear friend, gone through much evil report; the scene now changes; and your good report is commencing. This you are to consider as a new talent, of no small importance, put into your hands: O! use it faithfully; and remember you are as much accountable for the improvement of it, as for the discharge of your parochial duty. Lay yourself out for usefulness no less in the University than in the town. The Lord indeed seems to be calling you to it; for the fresh sphere you expected in Trinity church seems to be shut up, at least for the present; and your influence in your own college is evidently increasing ... Give the present state of our college and of the University at large its proper proportion of your attention and your prayers. You have zeal; use it then in the way which God by his providence points out to you; and not in that way only to which your inclination may lead.[12]

The year before he received this letter, at the age of twenty-eight, Simeon had been elected Junior Dean of Arts and then the next year Dean of Divinity. This gave him great moral influence in the college, especially over undergraduates. When his year of service as Dean of Arts expired, he was elected Vice-Provost in November 1790, the highest office he could hold as a fellow. His ability and leadership found an almost immediate test when during the absence of the provost, a senior member of the college had to be disciplined for gross misconduct. He handled it with integrity and prudence.

The provost's appreciation of how he had acted drew unqualified approval: 'It is a high satisfaction to me, under my absence, that I have so faithful a representative';[13] and Simeon was re-elected Vice-Provost for the following year. The exercise of these duties in no way diminished his commitment to Holy Trinity but, in God's providence, enhanced his reputation and ministry. Some have suggested that he played little part in the life of King's College during his years there. That is plainly erroneous, especially as his influence was not simply in the offices he held for a brief period but undoubtedly also in his character.

3. THE MIND OF CHRIST AND CHRISTIAN CHARACTER

Simeon's testimony was that a pastor's trials are good for his character. More important than insisting upon his rights was the privilege and duty of exhibiting the mind of Christ. Early on he wrote, 'I did not, however, choose to exercise my right … but desired rather to wait till God himself should accomplish my wishes in his own time and way. To this I was led by various considerations.'[14] One such was his Saviour's words,

'Blessed are ye when men shall revile you, and persecute, and say all manner of evil against you falsely for my sake: rejoice, and be exceeding glad, for great is your reward in heaven.' So far from being diverted from what is right by the censures or even the persecutions of mankind, they become stimulatives and encouragements to our perseverance; they are, you see, to excite joy, exceeding great joy, not grief, disappointment, and melancholy.[15]

His conviction grew that our enemies may benefit us. 'If I suffered with a becoming spirit, my enemies, though unwittingly, must of necessity do me good; whereas, if in acting I should have my own spirit unduly exercised, I must of necessity be injured in my own soul, however righteous my cause might be.'[16] This was no mean testimony because Simeon's natural disposition—as he frequently admitted—was to react strongly. His achievement of gentleness was an evidence of God's grace to him and in him. He observed,

That which is characteristic of a man's disposition, and is his besetting sin in a state of nature, will most generally remain so when he is in a state of grace; with this difference only, that in the former case it has the entire ascendant over him—in the latter it meets with continual checks, and is not suffered to have dominion. It is promised that if 'we walk in the Spirit, we shall not fulfil the lusts of the flesh'; but not that we shall find no temptations to fulfil them.[17]

4. INFLUENCE NOT A MATTER OF NUMBERS

An outstanding lesson of Simeon's long ministry is that the influence of a church or a pastor is not necessarily related to a church's numerical strength. A subtle form of worldliness may lead us to judge both ministers and churches by their apparent success and size. For many years Simeon laboured with a congregation that did not number much more than a hundred. Attendances of large numbers at Holy Trinity Church occurred only in Simeon's final years, but his influence was as great in the years when the numbers were few, and not least through his influence upon young men at his tea parties and sermon classes—the subjects of our next chapters.

Notes

1 *Memoirs of Charles Simeon*, p. 81.
2 Ibid.
3 Ibid., p. 82.
4 Ibid., p. 191.
5 Ibid., p. 194.
6 Ibid., p. 245.
7 Ibid., p. 254.
8 Ibid., p. 274.
9 Ibid., p. 289.

10 Ibid., p. 413.

11 Ibid., p. 39.

12 Ibid., pp. 49–50.

13 Ibid., p. 57.

14 Ibid., p. 51.

15 *Horae Homileticae*, p. 21.

16 *Memoirs of Charles Simeon*, p. 52.

17 Ibid., p. 43.

A teapot and skeletons

Holy Trinity Church, Cambridge, possesses a number of interesting artefacts relating to Simeon—for example, his Bible, his umbrella, his armchair and his portrait of Henry Martyn. But perhaps the most unexpected and unusual artefact is his teapot!

Both his tea parties and sermon classes for young men began in a small and insignificant way, illustrating the truth of Ecclesiastes 11:6: 'Sow your seed in the morning, and at evening let your hands not be idle, for you do not know which will succeed, whether this or that, or whether both will do equally well.' The value of individual parts of any pastor and teacher's ministry are impossible for us to determine and are known only to God, but these two distinctive features of Simeon's work appear to have been among the most influential.

The sermon class

Which began first? We cannot say with certainty, but the sermon class gains the first mention in his *Memoirs*. His memory of his own difficulties when he began to preach prompted this initiative. Like other young ordained men of his day he had received no instruction in preaching and was dependent upon whatever role models he might have—and good ones were few. All too many entered the ministry with little or no sense of vocation and sadly failed to rightly divide the Word of truth. In the hard school of experience, therefore, he hammered out rules and principles for himself. For the benefit of his sermon classes he then condensed his method into brief statements and read them out to the young men. Afterwards he got them to write down what he had said at his dictation.

Jean Claude on preaching

A few years after his ordination he came across an *Essay on the Composition of a Sermon* by Jean Claude, a minister of the French Reformed Church in the seventeenth century. To his surprise and delight Claude's rules coincided much with his own. This reassured him that he was on the right track. It provided the encouragement he needed to impart to others what he had learned, using Claude's rules as his initial foundation. As early as 1792 he provided an abridgement of Claude for his class, and at the end of the manuscript he appended 'additional observations' of his own. He made preparations to publish a new edition of Claude's work, adopting the translation from the French already made by Robert Robinson.[1]

Having revised and considerably improved Claude's *Essay*, Simeon published it in 1796 with an appendix containing one hundred skeletons of sermons, several being the substance of discourses he had preached before the university. This was the beginnings of his *Horae Homileticae* that ultimately extended to twenty-one large volumes and that he regarded as his life's most important work.

The recommended procedure

Simeon's method was simple and straightforward. He chose a text for the young men to consider and for which they had to produce a sermon in skeleton form. As they shared these with him, he commented on them, pointing out where he felt they could improve them and particularly express their understanding of God's truth more effectively. To use Simeon's own words, 'I give the text for the elucidation of each distinct topic. They treat the text; and I make my remarks on their compositions, pointing out what I conceive to be the more perfect way.'[2]

The basic and essential truth of every biblical text, whether long or short, had to be reduced to a simple statement within one sentence so that the truth to be conveyed was not in doubt. Then a simple and straightforward skeleton outline had to be produced that unfolded or unpacked the identified truth and topic. This might mean that not every part of the text had to be expounded if other parts did not throw light on the main subject. His emphasis was upon simplicity. The person who understands truth most clearly gains the ability to express it most simply.

He stressed that everything had to be subject to a clear statement of the essential truth. The students had to ensure that their presentation of biblical truth could be easily comprehended so that a child could understand it. With that purpose in view, he stressed the importance of writing out what they intended to say, for this then gave them the ability to be self-critical and to see if they were following the rules they knew to be best. On some occasions, rather than giving a specific Bible verse or passage, Simeon suggested a topic such as the nature of the Christian's separation from the world. His comment about simplicity is worth pondering: 'The distinguishing mark of the religion of Christ is its simplicity, and its suitableness to the condition of all men, whether rich or poor, wise or unlearned.'[3] It is not to our credit when people listen to us and remark how clever we are; whereas it is greatly so when they say, 'Now I understand.'

Personal testimony

For the students' encouragement, Simeon frequently referred in a playful manner to the awkwardness of his own first efforts, both in the composing and in the delivering of his discourses. Occasions like this, when he opened his heart to his hearers and shared his own battles, must have been an invaluable help and encouragement to them. They knew the benefit of being taught by a pastor whom they could hear Sunday by Sunday and of witnessing the principles he taught being put into practice.

No doubt Simeon found it stimulating for his own preaching skill to address a text of Scripture with a group of eager students keen to learn, aware of the added challenge that having instructed these young men they would examine all the more closely his public utterances on a Sunday.

The best teachers of homiletics

'Homiletics' comes from a Greek word meaning to put or assemble together. It is learning to communicate the teachings of the Bible in a way listeners can understand. Simeon was unconsciously demonstrating that the best teachers are those who are themselves engaged in what they teach. While there are happy exceptions, unfortunately those who teach homiletics in theological colleges may not always be pastors and teachers. When asked how his theological institution trained preachers, a distinguished contemporary theological professor replied, 'We recognize that the best provision is not what we provide in homiletics but the role models that able ministers provide where our students may worship Sunday by Sunday.'

Simeon had a high regard for Thomas Chalmers, with whom he corresponded and who was conspicuous as a theology teacher because of his practical experience as a pastor and teacher. Simeon recognized Chalmers as a man raised up by God 'for a great and peculiar work'.[4] He admired 'his depth of thought, originality in illustrating, and strength in stating',[5] and considered him to be unrivalled in those areas. The generous way in which Chalmers gave of himself to training young men for the ministry meant that, in effect, he reproduced himself in some measure in them. William Carus, Simeon's biographer and his desired successor at Holy Trinity Church, declared, 'This was one of the most important services which Mr Simeon rendered to the younger members of the University; and it was a labour of love peculiarly his own.'[6] It is not surprising that he has been called the father of homiletics.

Simeon's concern for young men in Cambridge was matched by his like concern for young men everywhere who felt God's call to the ministry. He was instrumental with others in forming in 1816 the Society for Educating Pious Men for the Ministry, longing that it might become a powerful instrument in God's hands. William Wilberforce was one of the trustees.

An invitation to tea

The tea meetings met an altogether different need, although no doubt some who first came to the tea meetings went on to join the sermon classes. They became a spiritual oasis. Simeon's own experience as a gownsman or undergraduate revealed how little spiritual life, generally speaking, was to be found in college chapels. The tea meetings provided the spiritual nourishment and encouragement that Christian Unions in coming years were to provide.

Whereas the sermon classes were by invitation, the tea meetings were not. All who desired to come were free to do so. 'I have an open day,' Simeon explained, 'when all who choose it come to take their tea with me. Every one is at liberty to ask what questions he will and I give to them the best answer I can.'[7]

If undergraduates came across difficulties in their studies or in their discussions with others, they could share them freely and openly and look for answers. This meant that a great variety of subjects, not easily discussable from the pulpit, were considered. There was no prayer or deliberate exposition of Scripture, but it was easy for Simeon always to use the Scriptures in providing the answers. His purpose was to display not his superior knowledge but rather the adequacy of God's Word. He then encouraged his hearers to pray for God's help as they turned the application of the Scriptures over in their minds.

A typical Friday evening

We are able to imagine ourselves at a tea meeting from a first-hand account compiled around 1829. On a Friday evening upwards of forty students made their way up the stairs to his rooms. The sitting room was set out ready with benches to make maximum use of the space. If they were insufficient, the window recesses were filled with seats.

As each young man entered, Simeon greeted him personally. If it was an undergraduate's first attendance, he produced his notebook and carefully wrote down his name and college. (No doubt that notebook was turned into a prayer diary in the weeks that followed.) Sometimes he would make a witty comment about the name he was writing down that amused the students.

When the time for starting arrived, he sat upon his chair at the right-hand side of the fireplace. With his hands folded upon his knees, and his head turned a little to one side, he would address his audience: 'Now—if you have any question to ask—I shall be happy to hear it—and to give what assistance I can.'[8]

Most questions were a genuine enquiry after truth. Some—asked by typically mischievous students—were intended to fox him. As one in later life admitted,

I fear that, in some instances, those who were present abused the privilege afforded us, and asked 'foolish and vain questions', for the purpose of displaying their own wit and cleverness … and, perhaps, with the mean hope of being able to say, 'I have puzzled Mr Simeon'; yet much do I err in judgment, if many will not have occasion to praise God with eternal praises for benefits received at those important and instructive meetings.[9]

At a suitable juncture Simeon asked two attendants to provide tea for the young men. Most of them were happy to forgo this provision as it tended to eat into the time they had for questions, but they accepted it as part of his courtesy.

Let's sit in on a tea meeting

We can give more or less word-for-word examples of the questions that were asked and the answers given. One undergraduate wrote down his observations on leaving the room as correctly as his memory would allow.

One student asked, 'Pray, sir, how do you understand Romans xi. 32 ['For God has bound everyone over to disobedience so that he may have mercy on them all']?'

Simeon turned to the passage and after a moment's consideration replied,

All men have sinned; and there is but one way of salvation for all. Both Jews and Gentiles must look for mercy only in the free grace of God by Jesus Christ. Deep humiliation is what most becomes guilty rebels. Having no hope but in the mercy of God, we should approach him as Benhadad approached king Ahab, with sackcloth on our loins, and ropes upon our heads: and our language should be that of his servants, 'Behold now, we have heard that the kings of the house of Israel are merciful kings.'[10]

Then someone else asked, 'What does the apostle mean, sir, when he says, in 1 Tim. iv. 10, "that God is the Saviour of all men, specially of those that believe"?'

Simeon immediately discerned that the questioner hoped to spark a controversial discussion and he gave a short and pithy reply that frustrated that intention: 'Of all, potentially; of them that believe, effectually. Does that make it clear to you?' Then he added,

Faith is a simple apprehension of Christ. It is not merely believing that he is the Saviour of the world; but it is believing in him as peculiarly suited to our own individual cases. It is not the saying, Oh, now I see I am to be saved in this way, or in that way; this, so far as it goes, is very well; but the Gospel simply declares, 'Believe in the Lord Jesus Christ, and thou shalt be saved.'[11]

At once another question was posed. 'What, sir, do you consider the principal mark of regeneration?'

'The very first and indispensable sign is self-loathing and abhorrence,' Simeon replied. He continued,

Nothing short of this can be admitted as an evidence of a real change. Some persons inquire, 'Do you hate what you once loved, and love what you once hated?' But even this mark cannot be so surely relied upon as the other. I have constantly pressed this subject upon my congregation, and it has been the characteristic of my ministry. I want to see more of this humble, contrite, broken spirit amongst us. It is the very spirit that belongs to self-condemned sinners.

Then, wanting his hearers to ponder this, he directed them to Ezekiel 36:31: 'Then you will remember your evil ways and wicked deeds, and you will loathe yourselves for your sins and detestable practices.' He urged them,

Take home with you this passage … and to-night on your beds, or in the morning, meditate thus within yourselves: Loathe?—why if I loathe and abhor anything, I cannot look upon it without disgust. The very sight of it gives me great pain and uneasiness. I turn away from it as from something abominable and hateful. Have I ever thus loathed and abhorred myself, at the remembrance of my iniquities and abominations? … I have been in the company of religious professors, and have heard many words about religion: but give me to be with a broken-hearted Christian, and I prefer his society to that of all the rest. In these days there is too much of talking about religion, and too little of religion itself.[12]

The next question concerned the Lord Jesus's words in Matthew 11:25: 'I praise you, Father, Lord of heaven and earth, because you have hidden these things from the wise and learned, and revealed them to little children.' Simeon's explanation was,

The revelation which God has given to man is precisely such as he required; it is not intended to be a subject of speculation; nor does it admit any scope for the exercise of an ungoverned imagination. Faith apprehends what reason cannot comprehend. The distinguishing mark of the religion of Christ is its simplicity, and its suitableness to the condition of all men, whether rich or poor, wise or unlearned. At the same time, its humbling truths are offensive to the wise in their own conceits. These may be able to talk about it, and write about it, and lay down an exact system of religion; but still their conceptions of it are confused and indistinct. It is just like giving a person a fine and laboured description of some beautiful scenery, or of some magnificent building—King's College, for instance—and filling his imagination with crude ideas. Such a person, be he ever so learned and clever, cannot comprehend the object so clearly as the poor ignorant man who has it placed immediately before his eyes. Were an angel from heaven to describe the properties of honey to an individual who had never seen or tasted anything like it, this individual would not conceive of it so justly as the little child who has tasted it; although the child might be quite unable to communicate to others what it tasted like. Bring a wise man and an ignorant man into this room, and tell them both that the house is on fire; I know the ignorant man would know how to make his escape quite as well as the wise man. It is just the same in matters of religion. We must all forsake our own wisdom and conceit, and stoop to enter in at the strait gate; we must become as little babes, if we would be saved. Many are the ways in which men endeavour to avoid this humility of heart, by substituting in its place some outward act of voluntary humility … Others, with the same notion of gaining the favour of the Deity, have undertaken long and dangerous pilgrimages. But there is nothing in all this to gain for guilty sinners acceptance and reconciliation with God. The plain and simple way is unfolded in the Gospel. Our salvation is procured with the blood of Christ; and by coming to God through him, with lowliness of mind and deep self-abasement, we receive the benefit of his death and resurrection.[13]

The next topic was of a practical and personal nature. 'What is the way to maintain a close walk with God?'

Simeon's reply was immediate:

By constantly meditating on the goodness of God and on our great deliverance from that punishment which our sins have deserved, we are brought to feel our vileness and utter unworthiness; and while we continue in this spirit of self-degradation, everything else will go on easily. We shall find ourselves advancing in one course; we shall feel the presence of God; we shall experience his love; we shall live in the enjoyment of his favour, and in the hope of his glory. Meditation is the grand means of our growth in grace; without it, prayer itself is an empty service. You often feel that your prayers scarcely reach the ceiling; but oh, get into this humble spirit by considering how good the Lord is, and how evil you all are, and then prayer will mount on wings of faith to heaven. The sigh, the groan of a broken heart, will soon go through the ceiling up to heaven, aye, into the very bosom of God. Without this habitual experience of our sinfulness and natural depravity, even an active religion is a vain thing. I insist upon this point so earnestly, because I feel it to be so exactly in accordance with the will of God. I have found it to be a good state for my own soul, when I have known what it is to loathe and abhor myself. I was once brought very low before God, when mine eyes were first opened to see my real state.[14]

Simeon then did what he often did—he reflected on God's gracious dealing with him at the time of his conversion:

A passage which I found in a book was the means of giving me deliverance from my bondage; I read that the Israelites believed that their iniquities were forgiven and taken away, by being placed upon the head of the victim that was sacrificed according to the ceremonial law. I thought of this, compared their state with my own, saw that Christ was sacrificed for me, took him as my Saviour, and was determined that the burden should not remain upon my conscience another hour; and I am confident it did not remain another hour.[15]

He concluded by expressing his hopes for the future and his confidence in God's providence.

This almost verbatim record of one tea party illustrates the variety of subjects that Simeon dealt with and the deep impressions that were made on the minds and hearts of young men over a number of decades. Many were the acknowledgements made by them over the years of the benefit they received.

The difference, as we have indicated, between the sermon classes and the tea parties was that the latter were open to all whereas the former were by invitation only. In both these spheres Simeon was innovative and acted contrary to the norm. In both he showed and made himself accessible to people, a mark of a good pastor and teacher.

Notes

1 Robert Robinson was the author of the hymn 'Come, Thou Fount of Every Blessing' (1758) and the minister of the Baptist church in Cambridge later associated with Robert Hall.
2 *Memoirs of Charles Simeon*, p. 377.
3 Ibid., p. 345.
4 Ibid., p. 323.
5 Ibid.
6 Ibid., p. 37.
7 Ibid., p. 376.
8 Ibid., p. 380.
9 Ibid.
10 Ibid., p. 381.
11 Ibid.
12 Ibid.
13 Ibid., p. 382.
14 Ibid.
15 Ibid.

Simeon and sermon preparation

Preaching was at the heart of Simeon's ministry and his consequent influence was immense. While exercising that ministry for fifty-four years in Cambridge he developed firm convictions about how to go about the task and shared them on numerous occasions.

As we observed earlier, like most of his contemporaries, he never received formal instruction in preaching. That was true not only of ministers in England. In Scotland, for example, Alexander Stewart, whom Simeon greatly influenced and helped, testified, 'At the Divinity Hall where I studied, or rather attended, we never got one direction how to make a sermon.'[1]

Simeon began his preaching ministry with no clear agenda of priorities. In the early days of his Christian life he was aware of how little he and others profited from the preaching they heard. Immediately upon his conversion, he had a desperate and urgent desire to share the gospel of our Lord Jesus Christ and then to see Christians built up in their faith. These aspirations motivated him to aim at the highest standards.

Although when Simeon took up his position at Holy Trinity he was restricted in his opportunities to preach there because of the opposition he faced, he was active in preaching elsewhere:

Having but one sermon in the week at my own church, I used on the week-days to go round to the churches of pious ministers, very frequently, to preach to their people; taking one church on Mondays, another on Tuesdays, another on Wednesdays ... and these seasons I found very refreshing to my own soul, and they were peculiarly helpful to me in my composition of sermons; for as I preached extempore, as it is called, I had opportunities of re-considering the subjects I had preached upon at Cambridge, and of rendering them more clear in the statement, and more rich in the illustration.[2]

Preaching's true focus

Simeon's experience of conversion—when compelled to attend the Lord's Supper—early underlined to him the centrality of the cross of our Lord Jesus Christ and it became the foundation of his teaching and preaching. He saw that Paul's words to the Corinthians, 'I resolved to know nothing while I was with you except Jesus Christ and him crucified' (1 Cor. 2:2), were 'the exclusive subject' of Paul's ministry, for nowhere else do we see displayed the wisdom and power of God, which 'will to all eternity form, as it does already form, the great subject of praise and adoration in heaven'.[3] Ever more keenly aware of his personal sinfulness, he declared, 'My only comfort is, that there is a fountain opened for sin and uncleanness, and that I am yet at liberty to wash in it.'[4]

The preacher's proper focus

Writing to a minister preoccupied with prophetic views of Christ's second coming, Simeon directed him to Paul's example, emphasizing that 'Not Jesus Christ, and him *reigning* on earth, but Jesus Christ, and him *crucified*' was his focus. 'This is the subject in which as sinners we are most deeply interested.'[5]

He saw that concentration upon any other aspect of Christian truth to the detriment of this primary focus only feeds pride, alienates Christians from one another and does the devil's work. In contrast, the preaching of the cross unites believers, keeps them right in their relationship to God and achieves God's work of translating men and women from the kingdom of darkness into the kingdom of his dear Son. His advice was, 'Only get your soul deeply and abidingly impressed with the doctrine of *the Cross*, and labour from day to day "to comprehend the height, and depth, and length, and breadth, of the love of Christ" displayed in it, and everything else will soon find its proper place …'[6]

An essential consequence

At the same time Simeon understood that the preaching of the cross and entering into the benefits of salvation must always lead to cross-bearing. In 1831, years after the event, he shared an experience that stamped this truth upon his heart.

Many years ago, when I was an object of much contempt and derision in this University, I strolled forth one day buffeted and afflicted with my little Testament in my hand. I prayed earnestly to my God, that he would comfort me with some cordial from his Word, and that on opening the book I might find some text which should sustain me … I thought I would turn to the Epistles, where I should most easily find some precious promise; but my book was upside down, so without intending it I opened on the Gospels. The first text which caught my eye was this, 'They found a man of Cyrene, Simon by name; him they compelled to bear his cross.' You know Simon is the same name as Simeon. What a word of instruction was here— what a blessed hint for my encouragement! To have the Cross laid upon me, that I might bear it after Jesus—what a privilege! It was enough. Now I could leap and sing for joy as one whom Jesus was honouring with a participation in his sufferings.[7]

Relating this incident on another occasion, he added, 'And when I read that, I said, Lord, lay it on me, lay it on me; I will gladly bear the Cross for thy sake. And I henceforth bound persecution as a wreath of glory round my brow!'[8]

Simeon would have agreed with one of the important questions the Puritans asked of every biblical passage: 'What relationship do these words have to the saving work of our Lord Jesus Christ, and what light does the gospel as a whole throw upon them?' (See Appendix 3.) But he warned against a slavish and unintelligent application of this principle. Its application must be honest and without distortion of the truth.

A snare of which we are always in danger is that of turning a good thing into something bad. He wrote, 'There is another point also, in respect to which it has been his [referring to himself] aim not to offend; and that is, in not so perverting the Scripture as to make it refer to Christ and his salvation, when no such object appears to have been in the contemplation of the inspired writer.'9 He had in mind the practical lessons many passages are intended to convey, recognizing 'that lessons of morality are, in their place, as useful and important as the doctrines of grace. In a word, it has been his endeavour faithfully to deliver, in every instance, what he verily believed to be the mind of God in the passage immediately under consideration.'10

Unconscious role model
Within ten years of his settlement at Holy Trinity many young men who felt God's call to the ministry were influenced by the role model Simeon provided. One student, who was later to become his assistant, wrote of the helpfulness of Simeon's sermons and example: 'This should be a great spur to us, that we may ... live in continual dependence upon, and communion with God; that thus, by every effort in our power, aided by the grace and assistance of God, we may at length realize his wishes concerning us.'11

Fundamental principles and essential preliminaries
Simeon expressed his convictions about preaching in a variety of ways over the years in his many recorded conversations and letters. It is worthwhile collating them.

1. GOD'S WORD MUST FIRST SPEAK TO US
A sermon commences before ever we begin our preparation. We cannot

overestimate, wrote Simeon, 'the importance of a devout personal reading of the Scriptures for ourselves, in order to qualify us to speak to others. There is, I am persuaded, more in this than even pious ministers are in general aware of. God does draw nigh to the soul that seeks him in his word, and does communicate an unction, that is in vain sought for in the books of men.'[12]

2. COMMENTARIES ARE NOT TO BE OUR FIRST RESORT BUT RATHER OUR OWN IMMEDIATE CONVICTIONS AS WE READ AND STUDY A VERSE OR PASSAGE

Our starting point must be what God's Word says to *us*. We should write down, therefore, our own thoughts before we consult the thoughts and understanding of others. First thoughts about a text or a passage may well prove to be our best, much as they may need to be checked and improved upon.

3. IMPORTANT QUESTIONS NEED TO BE ASKED OF EVERY VERSE AND PASSAGE

• What is the main subject this verse or passage presents? What must I explain and illustrate?

Such questions will often bring to mind other passages of Scripture that throw light upon the passage in hand and show where the emphasis should be. Scripture is always the best interpreter of Scripture. If different interpretations seem possible, the true one will agree with what the Bible teaches elsewhere on the same subject. Our first determination must be to discover the mind of God in the verse or passage before us. Simeon's concern was to let the text itself speak to his hearers. He spoke of so preparing that he 'might have nothing to do, but to let God himself speak'.[13]

Be not afraid of speaking all that God has spoken in his word, or of giving to every word of his the measure of weight and emphasis and preponderance, that it has in the inspired writings. The instant that you are afraid or averse to do this, you stand self-condemned, as sitting in judgment upon him, from whom every word has been inspired for the good of the Church ... preach the word freely and fully, without any fear of man, or partiality for human systems.[14]

He emphasized the identifying of one main subject in each sermon, using the illustration of a telescope that focuses upon just one object. We should be so clear about the precise subject of the text or passage that what we say about it will suit no other text in the Bible. His conviction was that every text has its proper subject, which should be brought forth without mutilation or addition of any kind. Just as each of us has an identity that distinguishes us from other people, so should every sermon.

- What is the character of the passage? Is it a declaration, a precept, a promise, a threatening, an invitation, an appeal? Or is it a cause, and effect; a principle, and a consequence; an action, and a motive to that action?

Whatever we discern to be the character of the text must then direct us in our preparation and presentation of its truth. We may feel that this takes time, but it is time well spent, and will be to the profit of our hearers.

- What is the spirit of the passage? Is it, for example, tender and compassionate, or indignant, or menacing? Is its purpose to console, alarm, warn or instruct?

The answer to this must determine the spirit of our address. 'To be tender on an indignant passage, or indignant on one that is tender, would destroy half the force and beauty of the discourse. The soul should be filled with the subject, and breathe out the very spirit of it before the people.'[15]

He used the illustration of a government's ambassador conveying a message on behalf of his sovereign. The ambassador's delivery of the message needs to express not only the message but also the spirit in which his sovereign sends it. 'As God's ambassadors, we should speak all that he speaks, and as he speaks it. God himself should be heard in us and through us.'[16] He wrote to John Venn, 'You are an ambassador of the Most High God, sent to entreat sinners, with floods of tears, to be reconciled to him.'[17] Simeon stressed that in dealing with any verse or passage of the Bible, 'The spirit of the words should pervade the discourse upon them. Whatever peculiarity there be either in the matter or manner of the text, that should be transfused into the discourse, and bear the same measure of prominence in the sermon, as it bears in the text itself.'[18]

4. DETERMINE WHAT THE CATEGORICAL PROPOSITION IS

By this he meant determining its principal subject and then stating what it either does say or does not say about the particular subject that is important in the light of God's revelation elsewhere in his Word.

'If the passage contain a great diversity of matter, the simple proposition should declare its main scope only; and the other points which are contained in the text, should be no further noticed, than as they elucidate the one great point which is intended to be considered.'[19] His concern was for 'efficiency as well as fidelity' in preparation.[20]

He amplified this in a conversation with a friend by giving an example from weaving:

When I compose a sermon, I take a single text, and consider the main subject to which it relates as the warp. The peculiar language in which it is couched supplies me with the woof. The series of cross-threads with which I weave the subject may be handled in various ways. You may take it up by the right-hand corner, or by the left-hand corner, or by a projection in the middle. [While he was saying this he was handling a little parcel on the table, by way of illustration.] But you must never wander beyond its true limits, you must not patch up your text by borrowing any extraneous ideas from other passages of Scripture.[21]

5. FORM A TENTATIVE SKELETON OR PLAN OF THE SERMON

This means establishing the main points that are to be made, together with the texts of Scripture that come to mind that will drive home the main message. This encourages clarity of thought and aids directness of presentation so that we stick closely to our subject and do not ramble away from it. A rambling address helps neither the preacher nor the hearer. Simeon used the picture of a house on fire: you do not show much concern for the person in danger if you do not go directly to the point. 'Keep in mind the motto,' he urged, quoting Richard Baxter, 'I'd preach as though I ne'er should preach again, I'd preach, as dying, unto dying men.'[22]

The skeleton should display a logical sequence of ideas. Although it is helpful to number the divisions in a sermon, the sequence of thought should be obvious without them. Clear divisions and sequence, however, frequently make it easier for people to remember what they hear.

Having established the principal parts of the skeleton, we should list under each part how we will explain and illustrate each part, ensuring that we do not get sidetracked from what we believe the main message of the passage to be.

6. BE CLEAR AND DELIBERATE IN YOUR APPLICATION

The nature of the application must depend in some measure on the subject that has been discussed, and on the state of the congregation to whom it is addressed. Where there are many who make a profession of godliness, it will be necessary to pay some attention to them, and to accommodate the subject in part to their state, in a way of conviction, consolation, encouragement, &c. But where the congregation is almost entirely composed of persons who are walking in 'the broad way' of worldliness and indifference, it may be proper to suit the application to them alone. In either case it may be done by inferences, or by address to distinct characters, or by a general address: but, for the most part, either of the former methods is preferable to the last.[23]

Daniel Wilson, Bishop of Calcutta, underlined Simeon's carefulness in never pushing his conclusions from Scripture too far. 'Unless the conclusions themselves, as well as the premises, were expressly revealed, he was fearful and cautious in the extreme.'[24]

7. CONCLUDE YOUR PREPARATION BY DETERMINING THE SERMON'S INTRODUCTION

Simeon felt he had little to add to what Claude says in his *Essay*. Claude saw the purpose of the introduction as the means of gently leading the minds of the hearers to the subject or subjects of the sermon. We must not assume that they already understand them or have ever thought before about them. 'The principal design' of the introduction is 'to attract or excite the affections of the audience—to stir up their attention—and to prepare them for the particular matters'[25] of which we are going to speak, and with as few words as possible. In our natural desire to be interesting we should not try to be clever but rather simple.

The introduction must *introduce*—it must 'be naturally connected with all the matter of the text'.[26] Nothing in it must be foreign to our subject. It must 'prepare the mind of the hearer for the matter to be discussed'.[27] At the same time it should so relate to the text or passage in hand that it could not be used easily to introduce any other.

Should the preacher write out in full what he intends to say?

In the early days of his ministry Simeon wrote out what he was going to say. But later he felt it better to preach from a skeleton outline and then to write it out in a fuller form afterwards in the light of the improvements he felt he could make.

For those beginning to preach his advice was not to start that way. He urged young ministers to write their sermons out in full for some years to help them to express their thoughts properly and to ensure that they were clear, comprehensive, wise and careful in their dealing with their subject. But he did not believe that they should always do this. 'The perfection of writing is, to communicate our ideas clearly, forcibly, impressively ... without loading our statements with ten members of a sentence, when four will suffice to convey all that a hearer or reader can receive.'[28]

After listening one Sunday to an unnamed preacher, Simeon wrote,

The sermon, though a good sermon (on 1 Thess. iv. 1) and well delivered (according to the general notion of delivery), had no effect, and made not the least impression on me. Doubtless this was my own fault; but yet I cannot help ascribing it much to the mode of delivering written sermons, for I was lively in my own soul in a more than ordinary degree, and well disposed to hear an exhortation to abound in holy duties; but the solemn sameness of the delivery (unrelieved by any occasional relaxation of more familiar address, or any animated, energetic address to arrest the mind and inflame the soul) deadened my attention, and left me not only unimpressed, but almost uninstructed. For want of more rapidity in connecting the beginning and end of the sentences, I lose the sense of them; or, if I comprehend them ever so clearly, I remain unaffected by them. I cannot but think it a great pity that a minister, well qualified to preach extempore, should still adhere to written sermons. He possesses all the qualifications that are necessary to make a most distinguished and useful preacher; and that in a very eminent degree; extensive knowledge, deep acquaintance with the heart, a clear, strong voice, a commanding manner, a tender and affectionate spirit, an ardent love to souls, and a most unfeigned desire to approve himself to God.[29]

Experience proves that once we are accustomed to writing everything out in order to express truth clearly the habit becomes one from which it is difficult to depart. Simeon understood this danger and lamented it. He would have said that, having followed this discipline, we should not be bound by what we have written, and certainly not fall into the snare of simply reading it.

Simeon's own testimony to his practice was,

When I began to write at first, I knew no more than a brute how to make a sermon—

and after a year or so, I gave up writing, and began to preach from notes. But I so stammered and stumbled, that I felt this was worse than before and so I was obliged to take to a written sermon again. At last however the reading a sermon appeared to be so heavy and dull, that I once more made an attempt with notes; and determined, if I did not now succeed, to give up preaching altogether.[30]

This method of preaching from notes, carefully arranged and prepared, he pursued till within a few years of his death. From an early period, it was his practice to write out on his return from church the principal remarks he had made while preaching from his notes; and in this manner he composed (with the exception of his complete discourses) almost the whole of his sermons, which now occupy the twenty-one volumes of his entire works.

Someone who changed his method in the light of Simeon's recommendation gave this testimony: 'I have for four months past preached … from short skeletons, without reading or committing to memory; a thing I had never attempted before. My discourse is less correct, and must offend a critic; but it is more energetic, and may profit a soul that is hungry for the bread of life.'[31]

Notes

1 *Memoirs of Charles Simeon*, p. 77.
2 Ibid., p. 36.
3 Ibid., p. 384.
4 Ibid., pp. 373–374.
5 Ibid., p. 370.
6 Ibid., p. 385.
7 Ibid., p. 395.
8 Ibid.
9 Ibid., p. 311.
10 Ibid.
11 Ibid., p. 58.

12 Ibid., p. 174.

13 Ibid., p. 216.

14 Ibid., p. 423.

15 Ibid., p. 379.

16 Ibid.

17 Ibid., p. 416.

18 Ibid., p. 379.

19 Ibid.

20 Ibid., p. 84.

21 Ibid., p. 396.

22 Ibid., p. 296.

23 Preface, *Horae Homileticae*, p. vii.

24 *Memoirs of Charles Simeon*, p. 488.

25 *Horae Homileticae*, vol. 21, *The Book of Revelation and Claude's* Essay (1832), p. 399.

26 Simeon quotes here from chapter 9 of Claude's *Essay on the Composition of the Sermon* at the end of his *Horae Homileticae*, p. 404.

27 Ibid.

28 *Memoirs of Charles Simeon*, p. 391.

29 Ibid., p. 123.

30 Ibid., p. 37.

31 Ibid., p. 77.

Simeon and preaching imperatives

Exercising such a long ministry, Simeon made many observations on preaching to those who looked to him for guidance, sharing with them significant lessons he had learned. Our primary focus now will be upon imperatives he identified, followed by some lessons and principles he felt to be important.

Be varied in your handling of the text or passage

With a complicated or unusual text or passage, the emphasis may need to be upon straightforward explanation and simple application of its relevance to the hearer.

If the text or passage states a truth that is immediately clear, the approach may be to apply it then to situations relevant to the hearers as they try to live God-pleasing lives.

Sometimes the right approach may be to identify and spotlight a particular truth or truths that are in view in the text or passage and suggest its logical consequences to Christian faith and living.

Yet another approach may be continuous explanation and application of a passage. Simeon would urge us to vary our approach and not to be predictable.

As you begin to set out your thoughts, have before you your hearers and their needs

We need to understand where our hearers are in their spiritual understanding and then gently and lovingly lead them into greater understanding. Writing to someone who had been urged to 'preach very strongly', Simeon asked,

My dear Sir, What is your object? Is it to win souls? If it be, how are you to set about it? by exciting all manner of prejudices, and driving people from the church? How did our Lord act? He spake the word in parables, 'as men were able to hear it'. How did St Paul act? He fed the babes with milk, and not with strong meat ... True, you are not to keep back the fundamental doctrines of the Gospel; but there are different ways of stating them; and you should adopt that which expresses kindness and love, and not that which indicates an unfeeling harshness. Only speak from love to man and not from the fear of man, and God will both accept and prosper you.[1]

Simeon argued that passages such as 1 Corinthians 3:2, Hebrews 5:12, 14 and Hebrews 6:1–3 teach this principle of teaching and preaching according to the capacity of our hearers. He wrote to a minister,

I would not have you withhold the strongest meat from those who are able to digest it, but I would select proper seasons for administering it, and if administered at a time when there were persons present who were likely to be choked by it, I would administer it with that measure of tenderness towards the weak, that should at least convince them that I was anxious for their welfare. In relation to all these matters, take counsel not of fear but of love. Whatever be the number or quality of your counsellors, always put love in the chair and give him a casting vote.[2]

Watch your style of preaching and be open to criticism, so that you may not be blind to your faults

We all have failings, whether in communication skills, mannerisms or style of preaching. All preachers will benefit, therefore, from honest and constructive criticism, and not least from those who offer it out of love and the best intentions.

Having heard of a minister who had sacked his curate for voicing his concern about the minister's style, Simeon felt it his duty to write to the minister, and his introduction to his long and careful letter shows his sensitive approach:

My very dear Friend … I have heard with deep concern, that, whilst all unite in loving and honouring your general character, a great number of persons are grievously offended with the style of your preaching (not with the doctrine, but with the style), which I am told is unnecessarily harsh and offensive; and that on this being suggested to you by Mr — you gave him notice to quit the curacy. Will you forgive me, my dear friend, if I say, that in both these respects you have erred. It is not by coarseness of expression, or severity of manner, that we are to win souls, but by 'speaking the truth in love', and if we are offended at such a suggestion being offered to us in a kind and affectionate way, it shows that humility and love have not a due ascendant over us… 3

The minister's reply does not exist.

After every sermon ask, 'How could I have improved it?'

The sermon—whether in full or in skeleton form—should be examined afterwards and note made of anywhere, on reflection, where it could have more effectively proclaimed the truth or been better illustrated. Unconsciously this will promote lasting effectiveness. Simeon was convinced that 'Nothing is to be done without pains'.4 Most, if not all, preachers will know the experience of having preached a sermon and then feeling so discouraged at not having handled it well that they just want to tear up their notes in despair. But it is better the next day to examine the notes carefully and recognize where lessons can be learned.

Learn to listen to other preachers with profit

Probably many pastors and teachers find difficulty in this area. We may tend to listen critically, or to imagine how we might better deal with the text or passage in hand. But we ought to give the same attention to the preaching we hear that we would expect our hearers to give us. Visiting Edinburgh Simeon went to 'the high church', almost certainly St Giles' Cathedral.

I expected to have heard Dr Davidson, one of the most popular preachers in Edinburgh; but was grievously disappointed. The preacher was Mr —, one of the most drawling and uninteresting teachers I ever heard. I am happy, however, to hear that he is a good man; and I desire to take shame to myself, that I cannot more divest myself of all regard to good sense or propriety in a sermon, and hear it, however weak it be, as the word of God to my soul.[5]

Writing one morning before going to a church other than his own, Simeon said, 'I hope I shall meet my God there. I feel as if it were my earnest desire to enjoy him more, and serve him better.'[6]

Take care of your voice

In giving this advice Simeon spoke from bitter experience, not having the benefit of our contemporary microphones and sophisticated sound systems. From about 1807 onwards Simeon's voice caused him acute problems because of over-exertion in speaking. Its weakness prevented him preaching as often as he wished. He experienced almost a total loss of his voice, so that for the space of two years he could say little in public or in private. At one stage he found that 'even to engage in family prayer twice in the day is, notwithstanding the utmost care in speaking low, a greater exertion than my voice will bear'.[7] 'I greatly regret indeed that I am able to do very little in the way of reading or conversation. If I attempt it a second time in the day, though I only whisper, it overcomes me. But, though from a prudent regard to my public duties I abstain, I think that I would most gladly spend, and be spent for him.'[8]

Rules without dogmatism

Simeon did not lay down his rules dogmatically. He regarded them as 'hints': 'If these few hints be thoroughly understood and duly attended to, the composition of a sermon, which is supposed to be so difficult, will become extremely easy.'[9] While he advocated not having a fully written manuscript before us as we preach, having heard someone preach extemporarily he commented, 'It was a very poor attempt at extempore speaking.'[10] 'It is not possible to say', he wrote, 'what is the best mode of preaching for every individual, because the talents of men are so various, and the extent of their knowledge so different.'[11]

Simeon's style of delivery

Many remarked upon Simeon's effective presentation of truth. To the end of his life it was remarkably lively and impressive. 'In his earlier days' he 'was earnest and impassioned in no ordinary degree. The intense fervour of his feelings he cared not to conceal or restrain: his whole soul was in his subject, and he spoke and acted exactly as he felt.'[12]

'Occasionally indeed his gestures and looks were almost grotesque, from the earnestness and fearlessness of his attempts to illustrate or enforce his thoughts in detail; but his action was altogether unstudied—sometimes remarkably striking and commanding—and always sincere and serious.'[13] He himself testified, 'I preach to the people with my tongue, my eyes and my hands; and the people receive what I say with their ears, their eyes and their mouths.'[14] Such manifestations of feeling were 'unusual in the pulpit; and it is therefore highly probable, that the opposition and ridicule he encountered, in the earlier part of his ministry, may be attributed as much to the manner as to the matter of his preaching'.[15]

But what seems to have stood out were his 'unusual earnestness and fervour … whether in public or in private, liable as it was to be misapprehended by strangers'.[16] 'His evident sincerity, his unwearied and disinterested exertions, and entire consistency of character … won for him the devoted attachment of those who had the opportunity of most intimately observing him.'[17] While he was clearly bold in his speech, he was respectful of his hearers. The careful preparation of what he said was obvious and he was direct in his appeal to every part of his audience.

Simeon's final preparation before preaching

Careful and disciplined preparation for preaching was not without cost and attention to detail. At the time of Simeon's death the Bishop of Calcutta drew attention to 'the labour he bestowed on the preparation of his sermons ... Few cost him less than twelve hours of study—many twice that time, and some several days. He once told the writer that he had recomposed the plan of one discourse nearly thirty times.'[18]

Visiting Edinburgh, Simeon was interviewed by a biographical sketch-writer who asked him about the time his preparation took and, interestingly, what he did once he had completed it. His interviewer wrote, 'So careful was he in his preparation for preaching, that he sometimes read his sermon five times over in private, and twice as nearly as possible with the tone, attitude and manner he purposed employing in the pulpit.'[19]

This reference to 'tone, attitude and manner' brings to mind an occasion when, preaching in Edinburgh on ministerial duties and faithfulness, he used the word 'Asleep' dramatically in an illustration. He spoke of

the keeper of the light-house on Inchkeith, the island situated in the middle of the Firth of Forth, between Mid-Lothian and Fife. He supposed the keeper to have let the light go out, and that as a consequence, the coast was strewn with wrecks, and with dead and mangled bodies; and ... the wailings of widows and orphans were everywhere heard. He supposed the delinquent brought out for examination before a full court and an assembled people; and at last the answer to be given by him, that he was 'asleep!'—'Asleep!' ... he made this 'asleep!' burst on the ears of his audience, who were hanging in perfect stillness on his lips, contrasting the cause with the effects.[20]

That sermon was long remembered.

An interesting moment of reflection

Simeon helpfully reflected upon how he would begin again on being introduced to a congregation. His conclusions confirm what we have noted earlier about the need to appreciate the capacity and understanding of our hearers.

When we begin, we may have big ideas and strong convictions about the best way to teach God's people. Looking back, Simeon saw that he had neglected simplicity and the well-known parts of the Bible, and that his preaching had not been with gentleness and love. His suggestion of dealing with the parables (that we noted in Chapter 5) is interesting. We can overlook the simple truth that the parables were an important part of the teaching method of our Lord Jesus. They have the great benefit now as they certainly did then of providing narrative that is interesting to listen to and easy to remember. All hearers—from the youngest to the oldest, from the newest Christian to the most mature Christian—will find something relevant and beneficial in them.

A necessary reminder

Faithful preaching will never be popular and acceptable to all. While the faithful teaching and preaching of God's Word—living seed—remains the only way to see our Saviour's kingdom and church established and built up, not all will appreciate it. Inevitably it sorts out the genuine from the counterfeit, the true believer from the unbeliever.

None of Simeon's curates was closer to him than Thomas Thomason, and to none did he open his heart more. In a letter to him in India he confessed,

I am concerned, though not surprised, to hear that some of your richer hearers have left you. They would rather hear smooth things prophesied unto them, that they may sleep on, and take their rest. They 'went out from you, because they were not of you': but they who value the Gospel will abide with you, and be your 'joy and crown of rejoicing'.[21]

Simeon wrote from the hard school of experience. Asked to preach before the university in December 1805, he took his sermon, entitled 'The Churchman's Confession', from 2 Corinthians 1:13, where Paul writes, 'For we do not write to you anything you cannot read or understand.' Subsequently, on reflection, Simeon felt that this 'sermon seems to have made more stir and impression than any of my sermons (some have said, more than altogether)'.[22]

We know what Simeon said because the sermon is to be found in Volume 16 of *Horae Homileticae*. In it he declared, 'There are three things, which, as it is our duty, so also it is our continual labour, to make known; namely, *Our lost estate—The means of our recovery*—and *The path of duty*.'[23] Having begun with our alienation from God and deserving of his judgement, he showed the need for repentance and faith in our Lord Jesus Christ, concluding with God's call to holiness and devotion to him. After unpacking these biblical truths he demonstrated how 'The General Confession' in the 1662 *Book of Common Prayer* exemplifies these three gospel priorities.

The then Master of Sidney College, Cambridge, wrote a letter to the *Orthodox Churchman's Magazine* attacking Simeon's sermon. The ground of complaint was what he described as Simeon's 'evident design of supporting the unfounded notions, entertained by *Evangelical* or *Calvinistic* divines, of the total corruption of human nature, and of justification or salvation by *faith only* as opposed to *obedience*'.[24]

The offence of the cross

The teaching of the total corruption of human nature and justification or salvation by faith alone rather than by human obedience offends human pride, as does even more the essential nature of what our Lord Jesus Christ did upon the cross as the propitiation for our sins. Simeon's reaction was to affirm that the arguments he drew from both Scripture and the General Confession were tenable 'against the whole world; and therefore I have spoken the more boldly. O that God may be pleased to bless it to the conviction and conversion of many!'[25]

A coveted blessing in preaching: divine unction

The preacher is never able to judge how effective his preaching is, this being a judgement that God alone can make. It cannot be judged by the appreciation he gains from his hearers, or simply by how he feels at the time or afterwards. Our subjective and personal feelings are so easily influenced by pride or temperament.

Nevertheless, there are tokens of God's approval that sometimes we may discern but which we cannot demand or even expect. Scattered throughout Simeon's various writings there are a number of expressions of this sort. He could write, for example, 'God was peculiarly present with us.'[26] At the end of his first tour in Scotland he wrote in his journal,

Respecting all the sermons I preached, since my first departure from Cambridge to this hour, I must acknowledge, to the glory of my God, and with most unfeigned thanks to his name, I have experienced the Divine presence in a manner that I never have in my whole life during so long a period together. O that I may be constrained by this mercy to devote myself more entirely to the service of my blessed Lord and Master! My labours had rather a good effect on my bodily health; and I rested well through the night. Adored be my God! Amen.[27]

He does not define the nature of this experience of God's presence, for it is certainly more 'felt than telt'. He wrote on another occasion of how he 'preached to a good congregation—found my soul tolerably happy'.[28]

Sometimes he found so much profit to his own soul on a Sunday that 'he generally appeared at the close of the day to be invigorated, rather than exhausted, by them [his duties on the Lord's Day]. "I am an eight-day clock," said he; "now I am wound up for another week."'[29]

He knew the difference between preaching 'with a sweet unction upon my soul'[30] and preaching without it. He encouraged a correspondent to 'set apart a day for fasting and prayer', with the comment,

You need not be told that, by putting oil to the wheels of a carriage, the labour to the horses is diminished, and the progress of the traveller accelerated in a degree that an ignorant and inexperienced person could never conceive. I trust you have often found the blessed effect of a Divine unction: how sweetly and rapidly have you proceeded when in a heavenly frame![31]

Nevertheless, having used these kinds of expressions, Simeon realized how subjective they were and how often unreliable. Nowhere did he prove that more than when he visited Moulin, near Pitlochry, in Scotland. On the Sunday evening he wrote,

On the whole, this Sabbath was not like the last. Then I was very much affected: now I was barren and dull: God however is the same, and his word is unchangeable: and in that is all my hope. Woe be to me if I were to be saved by my frames: nevertheless, I would never willingly be in a bad one.[32]

But it was a result of that visit to Moulin, when Simeon felt so barren, that Mr Stewart, the minister, came to experience new birth, followed not long after by a period of spiritual revival in Moulin. The lesson is plain: we should thank God for every spiritual encouragement and token of his presence as we preach, but we should let neither their presence nor their absence determine the estimate we place on the value of what we do.

Simeon also learnt the danger of preaching the same sermon several times and falling into the snare of relying upon past blessing rather than looking to God afresh. After repeating a sermon during his travels in Scotland he wrote,

In the evening I preached at Mr D.'s chapel: there was a very crowded congregation;

but I found myself a good deal straitened. I thought, that as I had preached twice on this subject with great liberty, I need not to bestow any time in reflecting upon it. I thank my God for rebuking me, and hope to look more to him in future.[33]

A difficult decision

The final lesson the preacher must learn is when to stop exercising his calling. Even when retirement from responsibility for a church or congregation comes, he may still be invited to preach. But there comes a time to stop, lest he be finally remembered for his weakness rather than for his strength.

Aware of that danger, not least perhaps because he did not have a wife to be honest with him, Simeon experienced that moment of decision when the vice-chancellor of the university called upon him, wanting to allow him to nominate Simeon as one of the university preachers for the next year. Previously he had preached sermons on the Gospels, but Simeon recognized that he was now seven years older. He knew it was right to decline. He wrote, 'But the offer itself is a token of God's merciful acceptance of my efforts to serve him, and a strong incentive to me to devote myself to him, as long as any power shall be vouchsafed to me, even to my dying hour. I do not however … forget the lesson I inculcate, "Prudence".'[34]

Notes
1 *Memoirs of Charles Simeon*, pp. 272–273.
2 Ibid., p. 423.
3 Ibid., p. 268.
4 Ibid., p. 489.
5 Ibid., p. 69.
6 Ibid., p. 126.
7 Ibid., p. 122.
8 Ibid., p. 139.
9 Ibid., p. 380.
10 Ibid., p. 124.
11 Ibid., p. 85.

12 Ibid., p. 38.

13 Ibid.

14 Ibid., p. 394.

15 Ibid., p. 38.

16 Ibid., p. 94.

17 Ibid.

18 Ibid., p. 488.

19 John Kay, *Kay's Original Portraits and Biographical Sketches*, vol. 2 (Edinburgh: [publisher not known], 1836), p. 298.

20 *Memoirs of Charles Simeon*, pp. 93–94.

21 Ibid., p. 216.

22 Ibid., pp. 120–121.

23 Discourse 407, *Horae Homileticae*, vol. 16.

24 *Memoirs of Charles Simeon*, pp. 120–121, note.

25 Ibid., p. 121.

26 Ibid., p. 90.

27 Ibid., pp. 73–74.

28 Ibid., p. 88, note.

29 Ibid., p. 138.

30 Ibid., p. 90.

31 Ibid., p. 82.

32 Ibid., p. 71.

33 Ibid., p. 69.

34 Ibid., 420.

Chapter 10

The Scottish connection

S imeon made many visits to Scotland. Those of 1796, 1798, 1815, 1817 and 1819 are recorded or mentioned in his *Memoirs*. They proved to be much more significant than he realized, especially the first. While he greatly appreciated and enjoyed the unique Scottish scenery, especially of Ben Lomond, Glencoe and Tayside, it was the friends that he made there that came immediately to his mind when he thought of Scotland. We may best consider his relationship to it through three friends in particular: Walter Buchanan, James Haldane and Alexander Stewart.

Walter Buchanan (1755–1832)

Buchanan and Simeon were close in age, with Simeon being but four years younger and dying four years after him. Simeon considered it 'one of the greatest blessings'[1] of his life ever to have known him. First meeting in London in 1796, they enjoyed a friendship of thirty-six years.

Educated at the University of Glasgow and ordained to his first charge in Stirling in 1780, Buchanan was called to the prestigious congregation of Canongate Kirk in Edinburgh's Royal Mile in 1789, where he served for forty-three years until his death. He had much in common with Simeon in that he came from an affluent background and used his resources generously for the benefit of his parish. The Canongate area then had a reputation for its noise and dirtiness. He and others transformed it into one of the quietest and cleanest parts of the city.

Buchanan, like Simeon, was concerned for the spiritual well-being and equipping of those training for the ministry. On Monday mornings he kept open house for breakfast in the manse, when he encouraged young men in their studies and generally looked after their welfare. Again, like

Simeon, he was committed to missionary enterprise and was a Director and Secretary of the Edinburgh Missionary Society, which preceded by a few years the forming of the Church Missionary Society, with which Simeon was vitally involved (see Chapter 11).

Like Simeon, Buchanan also exercised great influence in the national church, one of the avenues of which was his editorship of *The Religious Monitor*, also known as the *Scots Presbyterian Magazine*, first published monthly in Edinburgh in 1803. It tackled contemporary issues and contained thought-provoking articles on basic Christian doctrine, as well as missionary reports, including Baptist missionaries' work in India and what was described as 'Religious Intelligence': news from bodies like the General Assembly of the Presbyterian Church in the United States of America.

No evidence seems to exist as to how the friendship of Buchanan and Simeon began. It seems probable that the initiative was with friends of Buchanan, because Simeon wrote that it was in 1796 that Dr Buchanan 'was introduced' to him.[2] As a result Simeon 'went with him to Edinburgh'[3] for his annual holiday before proceeding to the Highlands, a visit he was to repeat two years later.

The trip from London to Edinburgh gave opportunity for the two men to get to know each other. From the first day of their two weeks' journey they prayed and read the Scriptures together, 'not without tears of joy'.[4] Simeon took great pleasure in first showing Buchanan Windsor Castle and St George's Chapel, followed by a visit to Eton.

A MEMORABLE VISIT

The memory of the time spent with Buchanan in Edinburgh long remained in Simeon's memory. First, he enjoyed the generous hospitality of Buchanan's home, making it his base on his arrival in Scotland and then immediately prior to his departure back home. He observed the care with which Buchanan catechized both a niece and his servants on Sunday and was astonished 'at their readiness in answering his questions, and in giving an account of what they had heard in the day'.[5]

Second, he had the opportunity of hearing Buchanan pray and preach in the Canongate church. 'How wonderfully well he prays!' he wrote; 'and how admirably does he expound! Blessed be God for enduing him with so much grace and wisdom.'[6]

Third, Buchanan gave Simeon the opportunity of leading worship as well as preaching in the Canongate church and introduced him to other like-minded ministers in the city, who then chose to invite him to their pulpits.

Although the preaching of a minister of the Church of England to a Scottish Presbyterian congregation had happened before, it was unusual. Simeon was careful to conform in every way possible to Presbyterian practice. He wrote, 'I officiated precisely as they do in the Kirk of Scotland: and I did so upon this principle; Presbyterianism is as much the established religion in North Britain, as Episcopacy is in the South: there being no difference between them, except in church-government.'[7] He describes an afternoon service:

I preached at the Canongate, and conducted the service in the usual manner—a psalm—a general prayer—a sermon—a particular prayer for the spread of the Gospel, for the king and royal family, the magistrates and ministers, those presiding in that church, the sick &c.—a psalm and the benediction. According to my instructions, I remembered to close the whole with bowing to the magistrates who sat before me. They also politely bowed to me.[8]

Fourth, Buchanan was 'unwearied in his endeavours to introduce' Simeon 'to the most godly people'[9] in Edinburgh as well as showing him as much of the city as he could. He introduced him to Dr Kemp, the Secretary of the Society for Promoting Christian Knowledge, whom Simeon described as someone in whom 'are united the gentleman and the minister of Christ'.[10]

He records how he joined one afternoon with Buchanan at 'the monthly meeting of a few friends, to which they did me the favour to admit me. After tea we retired to a room, and having prayed, read the Greek Testament (Rom. vi) with useful criticisms and observations. We then prayed again, and walked afterwards till the time for family prayer.'[11]

Through Buchanan he also met James Haldane.

James Haldane (1768–1851)

James Haldane was the younger brother of Robert Haldane; they were two men whose spiritual influence was to prove significant to the church in Scotland. They have been described as shining lights in the darkness in a period called 'the midnight of the Church of Scotland'.

James was born in Dundee and educated first at Dundee Grammar School, then at the Royal High School in Edinburgh (where Robert McCheyne was also later educated) and finally at Edinburgh University. When he was seventeen, as a midshipman he joined a ship called the *Duke of Montrose*, an East Indiaman: a ship operating under charter or licence to the East India Company, running principally to India. After four eventful voyages to Bengal, Bombay and China, in which he displayed courage and inspiring leadership, Haldane was nominated to the command of the *Melville Castle* in the summer of 1793.

During his voyages he began to study the Bible and also came under the teaching of David Bogue of Gosport. The more he read the Bible, the more convinced he became of its divine inspiration, and after serious examination of the evidence he became persuaded of the truth of Christianity and the relevance of the gospel for all. His spiritual growth after his conversion was marked by total commitment to the Lord Jesus Christ and a passionate desire to see him honoured by the preaching of the gospel. He terminated his naval career in 1794, aiming to retire into private life with a view to buying a private estate.

In God's providence, while staying in Edinburgh Haldane met Dr Buchanan and others, who introduced him to those who were busy in a variety of schemes to instruct the poor and neglected people of Edinburgh and its surrounding villages. He warmed to such enterprises. It was also at this time that Dr Buchanan introduced him to Charles Simeon on his visit to Edinburgh, a meeting that proved significant to them both in terms of fellowship and the sharing of convictions about preaching and evangelistic strategy. Haldane offered to accompany Simeon on part of his journey to the Highlands and he introduced him to Sir John Stirling, another friend of Buchanan's, who suggested that Simeon might like to use his mare for his northern tour. Simeon's response was praise to God: 'How wonderful is the goodness of God to me! Everything that I could wish, and much more than I could have expected, has taken place ... Surely goodness and mercy are following me all my way. Bless the Lord, O my soul, and all that is within me bless his holy name.'[12] Stirling then took Simeon north to Stirlingshire in his carriage on his way to join Haldane at his family home in Airthrey, the location today of the University of Stirling.

Beginning their journey on 20 June, Haldane and Simeon travelled on horseback through the Highlands. Rather than taking up the offer of Sir John Stirling's mare, Simeon chose to buy a horse of his own for his stay and then to sell it before he returned south. On account of its colour and country, he playfully named it Dun Scotus, after a thirteenth-century Scottish theologian. In spite of his earlier reputation of being a good judge of horseflesh, however, it proved to be a bad buy!

They visited Killiecrankie near Moulin, the scene of the Battle of Killiecrankie in 1689, when the Jacobite rebels fought King William's government army. A soldier famously jumped across the river at what is now known as the Soldier's Leap. As they approached the pass, Simeon's horse was seized with a fit and fell to the ground, throwing him to the edge of the precipice. Simeon and Haldane had just been talking together about heaven, and having recovered from the fall, Simeon reflected with Haldane on how wonderful it would have been for him to have been transported so immediately to glory.

One of Robert Haldane's servants accompanied the two men, carrying their saddlebags. They rode down the Forth Valley, along the southern base of the Ochil Hills, through Alloa and Dollar to Balgonie in Fife, where they enjoyed the hospitality of Lord and Lady Balgonie. After visiting Melville House, the home of Lord Balgonie's father, the Earl of Leven and Melville, they went to St Andrews and St Madoes, and then on to Perth, Dunkeld, Moulin and Blair Athol. They arrived in Blair Athol on the Saturday hoping to find lodging, but none was available.

They returned to Moulin, where Alexander Stewart ministered, and he gave them hospitality. After what proved to be a significant time there, they completed their journey back to Edinburgh. Although the purpose of Simeon's visit was to respond to Walter Buchanan's invitation to visit Scotland for a holiday and enjoy its unique scenery, his journal records that he preached in almost every place that he visited, more than twenty times altogether.

James Haldane's friendship was a refreshment and blessing to Simeon, not least in the times of prayer they enjoyed together. When they arrived at the top of Ben Lomond Simeon records how they 'then went to prayer, and dedicated ourselves afresh to God'.[13] Haldane prayed a parting prayer the night before they separated, and Simeon wrote, 'We were mutually affected with fervent love to each other, and with thankfulness that we had been permitted so to meet together.'[14] Their leisurely journey gave them good opportunities to share their mutual spiritual concerns, not least in how best to further the proclamation of the gospel.

James Haldane and his brother were both members of the Church of Scotland. By the end of the eighteenth century, James Haldane had preached the gospel as an itinerant evangelist in every part of Scotland, making great use of religious tracts.

The opposition that the brothers' gospel preaching prompted, together with prohibitions against any missionary enterprise in cooperation with Christians who were not members of the Church of Scotland, made them unhappy and uncomfortable within the Church. When in 1799 the General Assembly issued a 'Pastoral Admonition', warning people against strange preachers and prohibiting Episcopalians, like Simeon, from occupying the pulpits within the denomination, they had little alternative but to leave it and to pursue their gospel ministry independently of it.

Alexander Stewart (1764–1821)

During his first journey to Scotland Simeon became aware of God's gracious providences. None was more significant than his meeting with Alexander Stewart. Both Stewart's grandfather and his father were ministers and, having entered St Andrews University at the age of thirteen, he began to study divinity with a view to the ministry at the age of eighteen. Obviously religious, though, he sadly lacked a personal knowledge of God.

In 1786, at the age of twenty-two, he became the minister of Moulin, about a mile from Pitlochry in Perthshire, where he preached in both English and Gaelic. Stewart described his people in these terms:

The opinion of their own works recommending them to the favour of God, and procuring a reward from his bounty, was almost universal. It discovered itself in their ordinary speech, in their common remarks on more solemn occasions, and in almost every religious sentiment that was uttered. Their apprehension of the demerit and consequences of sin, were exceedingly defective. I have heard many on a sick-bed, after acknowledging in common form that they were sinners, deny that they ever did any ill. And in view of death, they have derived their hopes of future happiness from the reflection, that they never had wronged any person.[15]

The Moulin congregation was not well taught and did not have high spiritual expectations of its new minister. At the time of his appointment to Moulin, Stewart confessed,

Although I was not a 'despiser' of what was sacred, yet I felt nothing of the power of religion on my soul. I had no relish for its exercises, nor any enjoyment in the duties of my office, public or private. A regard to character, and the desire of being acceptable to people, if not the only motives, were certainly the principal motives that prompted me to any measure of diligence or exertion. I was quite well pleased when a diet of catechizing was ill attended, because my work was sooner over; and I was always satisfied with the reflection, that if people were not able, or did not choose to attend on these occasions, that was no fault of mine. I well remember, that I often hurried over that exercise with a good deal of impatience that I might get home to join a dancing party, or read a sentimental novel.

My public addresses and prayers were, for the most part, cold and formal. They were little regarded by the hearers at the time, and as little recollected afterwards. I preached against particular vices, and inculcated particular virtues. But I had no notion of the necessity of a radical change of principle; for I had not learned to know the import of those assertions of Scripture, that 'the carnal mind is enmity against God'; that if any man be in Christ, he is a new creature; and that 'except a man be born of water and of the Spirit, he cannot enter into the kingdom of God'.

I spoke of making the fruit good, but I was not aware that the tree was corrupt, and must first be itself made good, before it could bear good fruit. The people were satisfied with what they heard, and neither they nor I looked further. Almost the only remark made by any on the discourse, after leaving church, was 'What a good sermon we got today!' to which another would coldly assent, adding, 'Many good advices do we get, if we did but follow them' … I was in a great measure ignorant of the peculiar doctrines of Christianity, the corruption of the human will, the fullness and freeness of the redemption which is in Christ, justification by faith, and the necessity of the Holy Spirit's agency on the human soul; and what I knew not myself I could not declare to others.[16]

Simeon and Haldane knew nothing of this when they met him.

They had intended to arrive in Moulin on a Friday to stay just one night with Mr Stewart, to whom they had been given a letter of introduction by David Black, an Edinburgh minister and friend of Walter Buchanan, before continuing their journey. Because Simeon was too tired to travel they postponed it for a day and arrived on the Saturday. This particular Saturday turned out to be 'a high day', the day before the annual celebration of the Lord's Supper, with two services, the first in English and the second in Gaelic. They therefore decided to extend their visit to share in the Sunday's services. As mentioned above, they had planned to stay at Blair Athol, but they found all the accommodation there taken. Having introduced themselves earlier that day to Mr Stewart, they returned to Moulin, and he offered them the warm hospitality of the manse.

GOD'S PROVIDENCE

Later Simeon often reflected on these circumstances, which, contrary to his own intention, brought about his stay in the manse for the weekend rather than just for the Friday night.

It has often brought to my mind that expression of the Evangelist, 'he must needs go through Samaria'. Why so? It lay in his way, you will say, from Judea to Galilee; true, but how often had he taken a circuit, going through the towns and villages round about. But the Samaritan woman was there, and for her God designed an especial blessing. What thanks can we ever render to God for those turns in his Providence, which at the time appear insignificant, but afterwards are found to have been big with the most important consequences! It is our privilege to expect those invisible interpositions, if we commit our way to him, and every instance that comes to our notice, should encourage us to acknowledge him in all our ways.[17]

Mr Stewart invited Simeon to share in the English, rather than the

Gaelic, celebration of the Lord's Supper and to preach again in the evening to those who understood English. At the first service the congregation was large, with almost 1,000 communicants. Simeon preached a short sermon, and while people were partaking of Communion, he spoke a few words of encouragement and bade them depart in peace. He expressed his 'fears respecting the formality which obtains among all the people, and urged them to devote themselves truly to Jesus Christ'.[18]

In himself Simeon felt barren, sluggish and dull throughout the day. When he preached in the evening the numbers were few and he did not feel that the people understood him. It did not appear to have been a profitable day. He rebuked himself at the time for judging usefulness by his feelings: 'God however is the same, and his word is unchangeable: and in that is all my hope.'[19]

But when he retired to his room in the manse afterwards, his host accompanied him and they 'had much and useful conversation about the ministry'.[20] Alexander Stewart spoke of his feelings of unprofitableness, and 'was obviously much affected during the conversation'.[21] They prayed together, and Simeon prayed that Stewart might be fitted for the important and responsible charge which he held as a minister of Christ. That prayer spoke to Stewart's heart and he promised to write to Simeon.

Little did Simeon know at the time but their meeting was the means God used to bring about Stewart's new birth. As Stewart put it, Simeon spoke to him 'the words of life'.[22] When it was suggested that it was simply the reviving of his spiritual life, Stewart replied,

It was no revival: I never was alive till then. I think, however, I was in a state of preparation. I was gradually acquiring a knowledge of divine truth. It was given me to see that such truths are contained in the Scriptures; but I did not feel them. Indeed, I yet feel them but very imperfectly. I know nothing to which I can so fitly compare myself as to Ezekiel's dry bones, when they were covered with flesh and skin, but were without life or sensation. It was reserved for Mr Simeon to be the man, who should be appointed to prophesy to the wind and say, 'Come from the four winds, O, breath, and breathe upon this dead body that it may live.'[23]

Reflecting on this meeting fifteen years later, Simeon wrote,

Mr Stewart, the minister, was a man in high repute, both for amiableness of manners and for learning; but he was defective in his views of the Gospel, and in his experience of its power. When we were all retiring to go to bed, I had him with me alone in my chamber, and spoke such things as occurred to my mind with a view to his spiritual good; and it pleased God so to apply them to his heart, that they were made effectual for the opening of his eyes, and bringing him into the marvellous light of the Gospel of Christ.[24]

The consequences for Alexander Stewart were immediate and dramatic. 'From that moment he changed the strain of his preaching, determining to know nothing among his people but Jesus Christ, and him crucified.'[25] He immediately put his early sermons on the fire, and his comment written in Latin on those remaining was translated as, 'Youthful Trifles, produced in the season of ignorance and darkness, possessing nothing of the savour of the gospel, abounding in errors, fit only to be pitied, fit only to be destroyed; to be pardoned solely by the clemency of a merciful God, through the grace of his only-begotten Son.'[26] His faith grew and he became conscious of newness of life. Whereas before he spoke of Christ doubtingly, he now spoke with assurance.

His preaching was transformed, as a course of sermons on the fundamental doctrines of Christianity demonstrated.

I was now enabled to shew, from scripture, that all men are by nature enemies to God, disobedient to his law, and on that account exposed to his just indignation and curse. I therefore addressed them, not as persons who were already, from education, birth-right or local situation, possessed of saving faith and other Christian graces, but as sinners, under sentence of death ... The novelty of the matter, and some change in my manner of preaching, excited attention. People began to think more, and sometimes to talk together, of religious subjects, and of the sermons they heard.[27]

The following month he began a course of practical sermons on regeneration. The signs of revival were present. These sermons 'were attended with a more general awakening than had yet appeared amongst us. Seldom a week passed in which we did not see or hear of one, two or three persons, brought under deep concern about their souls, accompanied with strong convictions of sin, and earnest inquiry after a Saviour.'[28]

He wrote,

Having lately made an enumeration of those of our congregation, whom, to the best of my judgment, I trust I can reckon truly enlightened with the saving knowledge of Christ, I find their number about seventy. The greater part of these are under thirty years of age. Several are above forty; six or seven above fifty; one fifty-six; and one above seventy. Of children under twelve or fourteen, there are a good many ... but we find it difficult to form a decisive opinion of their case. Of persons who have died within these twelve months, three we are persuaded, and we hope two or three others, have slept in Jesus.[29]

This gracious visitation continued for about two years, with many showing by their 'heavenly walk and conversation'[30] that their hearts were renewed.

Among the earliest of the converts were a Highland farmer and his wife, James and Jean Duff. Years later they remembered how, at the age of seventeen, they sat one Sunday in church listening to a strange and fervent preacher from England, whose accent they found difficult to understand. James Duff contributed much to the well-being and improvement of his neighbourhood. He superintended Sunday schools and held weekly meetings in his own home or elsewhere for prayer and Bible exposition. He delighted in prayer and in declaring the dying love of his Saviour, both in Gaelic and in English. It was into this home that their son Alexander Duff was born on 25 April 1806; he later became the first Scottish missionary to India. Alexander Duff once visited Cambridge in the interests of missionary work in India and there met the elderly Simeon.

Another person converted through the preaching of their converted minister was a man who shared his name, Alexander Stewart. He trained under the Haldane brothers and in 1818 emigrated to Canada to be a pioneer missionary, there establishing the first Baptist church in York (now Toronto). Little did Simeon know how significant in God's purposes and plan his visit to Moulin would prove and the fruit that would follow in thousands of lives.

Simeon was delighted to call on Stewart when he returned on his next visit to Scotland and to be able to note that he was 'much grown in grace'.[31] Stewart showed Simeon some of the sermon skeletons he had made after Simeon's plan.

Sadly, Stewart's first wife died and he later married again. He accepted a charge in around 1805. Then both he and his wife were unwell in 1814 and 1815. In 1819 he decided to go to Edinburgh for the winter, with his family, as the symptoms of his illness had become so alarming in the spring of that year and better medical advice was available there. The medical opinion was not encouraging and he did not gain permanent relief. In the summer of 1820 a vacancy occurred at the Canongate and he had the joy of working with Dr Buchanan, with whom we began this chapter. But the privilege lasted less than a year on account of his death.

Simeon was invigorated by his Scottish visits, although they were physically and spiritually demanding. His itinerary for his second visit, for example, was Berwick, Dunbar, Haddington, Edinburgh, Carnock, Dunfermline, Forgan Denny, Perth, Dundee, Montrose, Stonehaven, Aberdeen, Aden, Banff, Forglin, Elgin, Nairn, Fort George, Tain, Dingwall, Ferntosh, Inverness, Croy, Fort Augustus, Fort William, Glencoe, Oban, Arosh, Loch Nagaul, Lagganulva, Staffa, Oban, Inverary by Loch Etive and Loch Awe, Arrochar, Glen Croe, Dumbarton, Glasgow, and then back to Edinburgh.

On this second visit he learned in detail what had been reported to him about those who opposed his evangelicalism in his previous visit. They had complained that all who had given him the opportunity to share in their services had acted contrary to the laws of the Church of Scotland. Although they were well answered by those who rejoiced in Simeon's ministry, it seemed clear that they would most likely bring in an 'overture' the following May to prevent anyone like him from officiating in their churches, something that would cut off, in effect, all intercourse between English ministers and Presbyterian congregations. (An 'overture' remains the term still used in the Church of Scotland for a motion or proposal to be placed before the General Assembly.) And this they did. Simeon rested in the assurance that God is sovereign and would support his own cause. So rich was his fellowship with like-minded men like Walter Buchanan, James Haldane and Alexander Stewart that, in spite of all that might have discouraged him, he returned home not tired but encouraged, and prepared for even more exertions in Cambridge.

A letter from Walter Buchanan to Simeon illustrates how his Scottish friends felt about him:

Many, I trust, have cause to thank God for your visit to Scotland; as for myself, I consider it as one of the greatest mercies I have received for a long time; and had nothing else been the result of my journey to England, I would have thought myself amply repaid. The friendship that has taken place betwixt us is founded not on the fluctuating principles of the world; and shall continue, I hope, to exist when this world and all its fleeting vanities shall be for ever at an end.[32]

Simeon's feelings were the same: 'I desire to give glory to my God for all the love which I meet with, and ardently wish that it may be the means of humbling me in the dust, and not puffing me up with pride, as though I merited such regard.'[33]

Many benefits and spiritual fruit

Simeon benefited from the Scottish practice of exhortation at the Lord's Table and he described how one exhortation 'was exceedingly precious to my soul: I was quite dissolved in tears; I made a free, full, and unreserved surrender of myself to God. O, that I may ever bear in mind his kindness to me, and my obligations to him!'[34] So precious was this experience that he was afraid, lest he should lose 'the blessed frame in which his soul then was'.[35]

His visits to Scotland also made him appreciate more the Church of England's prayer book and liturgy. His attendance at Presbyterian churches prompted him to write, 'I have on my return to the use of our Liturgy been perfectly astonished at the vast superiority of our mode of worship, and felt it an inestimable privilege that we possess a form of sound words, so adapted in every respect to the wants and desires of all who would worship God in spirit and in truth.'[36] He had in mind particularly the comparative helpfulness of extempore prayer and written forms of prayer. He frequently observed, 'If *all* men could pray at *all* times, as some men can sometimes, then indeed we might prefer extempore to pre-composed prayers.'[37]

Some of the fruit that followed his visits was obvious, and some hidden. It has been suggested that the first public distribution of Christian tracts in Scotland was made by Simeon, who throughout his tour handed out a tract entitled *The Friendly Advice* at every opportunity. It seems almost certain that Simeon had written it. In a letter of 1783 he mentions that he had some tracts printed.

The copy of *The Friendly Advice* in the National Library of Scotland (full title: *Friendly Advice to All Whom It May Concern*) was printed in both Scotland and England. A small leaflet of four pages, it is marked by directness and urgency. It begins,

You have a soul, an immortal soul, a soul which must shortly either live with God in heaven, or with the devils in hell. Do you ever think of this? Do you seriously reflect upon it? For which state is your soul prepared? To which is it hastening? The enquiry is important; for what will it profit you to gain the whole world and lose your soul? O delay not to think of eternity, till it be too late! If you should be lost can you endure everlasting burnings? But you hope to be saved; take care then, that your hope is well founded ...[38]

Halfway through, the writer bids the reader to put down the tract for two or three minutes and consider whether or not he or she knows how the soul is to be saved. He then writes of the Philippian jailor, who was directed to believe in Jesus Christ. 'He [Jesus] took our nature upon him, in order to obey that law which we had broken, and bear that vengeance which our sins deserved.'[39] It then warns of the danger of trusting in good works or the reader's repentance or amendment of life; new birth is necessary. 'You are not necessarily born again by baptism; baptism is an outward work upon the body; the new birth is an inward work upon the soul.'[40] At the end of the tract are the words 'Do not destroy this Paper, but read it again, and then lend it to your Neighbour'.[41] There is little doubt that James Haldane's extensive distribution of tracts and the fruit from them was the result of his witnessing Simeon's use of them.

In Edinburgh—on what seems to have been his second visit—Simeon established a lecture, probably annually, as well as a Female Society for Visiting and Relieving the Sick. On his way to Scotland he had discovered a similar society in England, and when he was in Leith near Edinburgh he thought that God might give him the opportunity to initiate the same there. Having suggested the idea to the minister, and invited to preach that evening, he shared with the congregation his hopes and promised on his return a few weeks later to preach a sermon to set up the society. But, he was able to write,

On my return I had the happiness to find a society established upon my plan, and a large sum of money raised to carry it on; so that instead of having occasion to beg for subscriptions, as I intended, I had only to return thanks for the activity shown, and the sums already subscribed; and I believe the society flourishes to this very day. O! that every journey I may in future take may abound with such instances of God's kindness towards me, and be so sanctified to the good of my fellow-creatures![42]

In 1817 Simeon travelled to Scotland again, only this time in the interests of work among the Jews (see Chapter 12). He was accompanied by a colleague, Mr Marsh, who shared his concern for the Jews. Simeon relished the opportunity of renewed fellowship with Dr Buchanan at the Canongate church and they intentionally arrived at the time of the General Assembly of the Church of Scotland. He wrote,

Our success at Edinburgh exceeded our most sanguine hopes, even if I estimated it by the money obtained: but on a review of our whole journey, I consider that as nothing in comparison of the interest excited and the good done. In five weeks Mr Marsh and I brought home 800 guineas clear gain; the journey having cost the society nothing.[43]

Something of what Simeon saw and heard of work in the Scottish Highlands influenced his view of how missionary work should be attempted. In September 1796, when he had returned from his time in Scotland, he took part in a discussion about the right way to advance world mission. Money had been left in a will for such work but uncertainty existed about how to use it: whether to support existing work or to initiate new. The question before the meeting was, 'Is it practicable and expedient to form an Institution for educating young men professedly with a view to their becoming missionaries under the sanction of the Established Church?'[44] Among Simeon's careful notes he refers to how missionary enterprise was engaged in throughout the Highlands of Scotland and the success experienced there. The convictions he had formed through his discussions with James Haldane clearly had a bearing upon his ongoing discussions about missionary work.

He was warm in his appreciation of his Scottish brothers. The love they showed him overwhelmed and humbled him. He discovered helpful initiatives, as in the case of a godly minister in Tain, who convened a meeting of ministers in his neighbourhood 'eight times in the year for conversation and prayer',[45] something that Simeon so much appreciated in the Eclectic Society in England (for more on this society see Chapters 13 and 18). The same minister had many praying societies among his people, and many who were truly alive to God.

Simeon was grateful to those who entrusted to him unique evangelistic opportunities. In Fort Augustus, the home of an army garrison since the defeat of the 1715 Jacobite uprising, the military governor ordered the whole garrison to attend church, and at his own initiative ordered a drummer to go through the village with a drum to give notice of the sermon. At least 300 attended, including the governor and other officers.

At the same time, Simeon was not blind to weaknesses among his brethren. He wrote, 'Our time passed both pleasantly and profitably. I could wish however that the custom of drinking toasts was banished from the tables of the serious, because it tends to excess, and invites persons to drink more than they would wish. I gave some hints of this kind: and hope they may not be in vain.'[46] He also felt that some services were too long, especially in services of preparation the day before the celebration of the Lord's Supper, one of which lasted for about four and a quarter hours.

A test of any minister of the gospel is how he lives and behaves when away from his own flock; whether, for instance, he shows concern for people's souls if they are not of his flock, and how much his flock is always on his mind and in his prayers. In both areas Simeon proved faithful. He seized opportunities for personal witness and for conversation for spiritual profit, and, as we have noted, actively distributed gospel tracts. When he stayed in homes with servants and was given the opportunity to lead family prayers, his concern was that the servants should be present, although he was sometimes disappointed that this was not allowed.

But wherever Simeon travelled, the flock at Holy Trinity was never far from his mind and his prayers, especially as some had suggested that while he was absent the work there would be at a standstill. That proved to be far from the case—an evidence, he believed, that the work was of God, not of him.

Notes

1 *Memoirs of Charles Simeon*, p. 67.
2 Ibid.
3 Ibid.
4 Ibid., p. 68.
5 Ibid., p. 69.
6 Ibid., p. 70.
7 Ibid., p. 67.
8 Ibid., p. 69.
9 Ibid.
10 Ibid.
11 Ibid.
12 Ibid., p. 70.
13 Ibid., p. 73.

14 Ibid.

15 *Memoirs of the Late Rev. Alexander Stewart, DD, One of the Ministers of the Canongate, Edinburgh, to Which Are Added a Few of His Sermons* (2nd edn.; Edinburgh, 1822), p. 29.

16 Ibid., pp. 30–33.

17 *Memoirs of Charles Simeon*, p. 78.

18 Ibid., p. 71.

19 Ibid.

20 Ibid.

21 Ibid.

22 Ibid., p. 76.

23 Ibid.

24 Ibid., p. 72.

25 Ibid.

26 *Memoirs of the late Rev. Alexander Stewart*, p. 35.

27 Ibid., p. 138.

28 Ibid.

29 Ibid., pp. 143–144.

30 Ibid.

31 *Memoirs of Charles Simeon*, p. 89.

32 Ibid., p. 74.

33 Ibid., p. 69.

34 Ibid., p. 71.

35 Ibid.

36 Ibid., p. 68.

37 Ibid.

38 *Friendly Advice to All Whom It May Concern* (Chapman & Lang, 1800; Edinburgh: Religious Tract & Book Society of Scotland, 1815), p. 1.

39 Ibid., p. 3.

40 Ibid., p. 4.

41 Ibid.

42 *Memoirs of Charles Simeon*, p. 92.

43 Ibid., p. 300.

44 Ibid., p. 64.

45 Ibid., p. 90.

46 Ibid., p. 70.

Simeon and India

The more we consider Simeon's growing ministry in Cambridge, together with his commitment to taking the gospel elsewhere, the more amazing do we find his energy, enterprise and organizational ability.

Although he never held any office in the church apart from minister of Holy Trinity Church, Cambridge, he could have said with John Wesley, 'I look upon the world as my parish.'[1] His missionary interest was neither casual nor peripheral, but deeply felt and maintained. He did nothing by halves: commitment to his Saviour demanded active involvement in the Great Commission.

The beginnings of missionary work in India

It was not surprising that in God's providence India became a focal point of missionary interest in the second half of the eighteenth century. Protestant work had begun there in the early 1700s when in 1706 German Lutherans arrived at Tranquebar in South India. Sent by Frederick IV of Denmark to his trading post, they were not particularly welcomed by either the Danish authorities or the chaplains to the European community. But it was a significant beginning, and it led to the translation and printing of the Tamil New Testament, the first in any Indian language.

By the end of the eighteenth century Britain had won political power in India, and Christian employees of the East India Company began to feel the burden of the spiritual darkness that existed there, prompting them to share their concern with their home constituencies. Prominent among these were some who identified themselves with the influential Clapham Sect, a small group of reformers who lived in South London and worshipped at Clapham parish church, the congregation where both Henry and John Venn served as minister at different periods.

Among the Clapham Sect's concerns were keeping Sunday special, education and the needs of the poor. Their principal achievement was the abolition of slavery, and William Wilberforce was the best known among them. Although the East India Company had some respect for the missions that came into being, it, like the Danish, saw them as a threat to the exercise of their trade and for a couple of decades forbade missionaries entry.

The East India Company's opposition

The company's prohibition explains why, when William Carey arrived in Calcutta in 1793, he worked as a manager of indigo plantations and set about learning Bengali and Sanskrit. Forbidden to engage in missionary work anywhere within the East India Company's territory, Carey and his colleagues found a home in Serampore, part of Danish India, only sixteen miles from Calcutta. Serampore has been described as the birthplace of the modern missionary movement. There they set up a college in 1819 and by the time Carey died translations of the Bible were complete in Bengali, Oriya, Assamese, Sanskrit, Hindi and Marathi, achieved in the face of many difficulties.

The Anglican advantage

In accord with the principle that 'As iron sharpens iron, so one man sharpens another' (Prov. 27:17), there seems little doubt that Anglican evangelicals found their own missionary concern stimulated and sharpened by the enterprise of Dissenters or Nonconformists like William Carey. But as Anglicans they had a distinct advantage over the Nonconformists. The East India Company employed Anglican chaplains, and by this means evangelicals like Simeon were able to get men with a missionary vision into India, the most famous of whom was Henry Martyn.

Chapter 11

The first mention of India in Simeon's *Memoirs* relates to 1787; the editor describes this as 'a most eventful period in Mr Simeon's history' because from this moment on 'his thoughts and efforts were no longer to be limited to the scene of his immediate duties at Cambridge'.[2] This was five years before the Baptist Missionary Society was founded and twelve years before the Church Missionary Society's beginnings. It was also twenty-two years before the start of the London Jews' Society.

A timely conversion

Another significant providence was the conversion of Charles Grant (1746–1823), a prominent East India Company employee. Brought to personal faith in Christ when convicted of his ungodliness at the time of the deaths of his two daughters from smallpox in 1776, his life was turned around by his new-found relationship with God. It made him ashamed of much of the behaviour of his fellow-countrymen in India and convinced him of the British responsibility to share the gospel with those native to India.

He had first arrived in Bengal in 1768 and in 1787 was made a member of the Board of Trade, with responsibility for the whole of the East India Company's business in Bengal. He eventually became a director of the company. Many within it did not appreciate his Christian convictions, and no doubt he was open to criticism—as we all are—but Wilberforce described him as one of the best men he ever knew. After finishing his work in India in 1790 he became MP for Inverness in 1802. His contact with many prominent people gave him considerable influence as he discovered the good works God had prepared in advance for him to do. His two sons later had considerable influence for good in India.

A strategic proposal

In 1787 Charles Grant and two Christians working in India, David Brown and William Chambers, drew up a document for submission to the British East India Company entitled 'A Proposal for Establishing a Protestant Mission in Bengal and Bahar'. It presented the claims of the people of India upon the British government and the duty of imparting to them the privileges enjoyed by those in Britain, not only in civil matters but also in religious and spiritual. It recommended the translation of the Scriptures into the different languages of the East and the sending of missionaries to instruct them—'fit men, of free minds, disinterested, zealous, and patient of labour, who would accept of an invitation and aspire to the arduous office of a missionary'.[3]

It addressed pertinent questions about missionary enterprise: 'What sort of men are to be chosen? In what manner are they to be supported? And what plan is to be pursued by them?'[4] It was inevitable at this stage that men and not women should be thought of as candidates, since the only vehicle for getting missionaries to India was by means of East India Company chaplains. After giving reasons for wanting young clergymen of the Established Church, the document comments, 'But genuine piety seems to be the grand requisite in a missionary ... men who are ready to endure hardship, and to suffer the loss of all things.'[5] Practical in its proposals, it envisaged that the missionaries should reside in the eight main divisions of the country that existed at that time and that, 'at their respective stations, they should set up schools, employ catechists and establish churches'.[6]

The beginning of Simeon's involvement
Copies of this submission to the East India Company were sent with accompanying letters to a group of influential people: the Archbishop of Canterbury, the Bishop of Llandaff, the Secretary of the Society for Promoting Christian Knowledge, John Newton, the Revd Henry Foster, the Revd Richard Cecil, William Wilberforce, Thomas Raikes, Dr Jackson, Mr M (an unknown correspondent), the Countess of Huntingdon, Robert Robinson of Cambridge and Charles Simeon.

Sadly, it did not achieve all that they hoped but it did bring about Simeon's active involvement and commitment. He knew well two of the men behind the proposal. First, he knew Charles Grant, who upon his conversion had identified himself with the Clapham Sect, the members of which were well known to Simeon. And then, second, David Brown had come to faith under Simeon's preaching in 1782 while a student at Magdalene College and Simeon had encouraged him in 1785 to go to India as an East India Company chaplain. Simeon would also have known of William Chambers through Charles Grant, as Chambers had married Grant's wife's sister, Charity Fraser. Chambers was known too among those concerned for India and the East because of his fluency in Persian and his translation of Matthew's account of the Sermon on the Mount into that language. He was a friend of Christian Friedrich Schwarz (1726–1798), a well-known German evangelical missionary whose work seems to have been exceptionally fruitful.

Representative

The correspondence with Simeon that accompanied the 'Proposal for Establishing a Protestant Mission in Bengal and Bahar' had a more specific purpose than that with the other recipients. Its aim was to invite him to represent the enterprise in Britain.

The invitation read,

From the enclosed papers you will learn the project of a mission to the East Indies. We understand such matters lie very near your heart, and that you have a warm zeal to promote their interest. Upon this ground we take the liberty to invite you to become agent on behalf of the intended mission at home. We humbly hope you will accept our proposal, and immediately commence a correspondence with us, stating to us, from time to time, the progress of our application.7

Simeon's answer has not survived, but David Brown's reply to him on

30 January 1789 reveals his answer. Brown wrote, 'I have before me your two letters of February and May, 1788. You have indeed increased our joy in the Lord, whom we bless for such comforts and encouragements by the way.'[8]

No reaction to the proposal was more significant and eager than Simeon's, although he may well not have realized how demanding the responsibility was to become. David Brown's response was warm and grateful: 'The Lord preserve you, my dear friend, for the spreading of the Redeemer's kingdom in heathen countries. We have great satisfaction in your accepting our invitation to act for the affairs of the mission, and are persuaded of your vigilance and zeal. May we continue equally active and earnest in furthering the same work.'[9]

By 1794, seven years later, the scheme for a mission was in place. Simeon, Wilberforce and Venn were inclining towards it. Grant, with his practical knowledge of India, its people and its requirements, was the man they needed to stimulate and encourage them. The course of his thoughts on this important subject became united with the ideas of Simeon and Wilberforce, and flowed with theirs in one combined current, so that the story of his life becomes completely linked with theirs and at this period cannot be understood without constant reference to them.

Time-consuming

The amount of time that they gave to the project was immense. The first notice of these gatherings occurs in Wilberforce's diary on 22 December 1796: 'House—Went home with Dundas and Pitt, and stayed awhile, discussing Mission business in hand.' The next entry is: 'Breakfasted early with Dundas and Eliot on Mission business; … 26th. Grant, Eliot and Babington at dinner—consultation on East Indian missions and discussing all the evening.'[10] A few weeks later there were further discussions:

14th February ... There is considerable probability of our being permitted to send to the East Indies a certain number of persons—I presume we shall want ten or twelve—for the purpose of instructing the natives in the English language, and in the principles of Christianity. But the plan will need much deliberation. I really dare not plunge into such a depth as is required with previous sounding; lest, instead of pearls and corals, I should come up with my head covered only with sea-weed, and become a fair laughing-stock to the listless and unenterprising. When I return to town, we will hold a cabinet council on the business. Henry Thornton, Grant and myself are the junto.[11]

Simeon's name occurs in Wilberforce's diary on 20 July 1797: 'To town, and back to dine at Henry Thornton's, where Simeon and Grant to talk over the Mission Scheme.' On 22 July 1797: 'Simeon with us—his heart is glowing with love for Christ.' 'How full he is of love, and of desire to promote the spiritual benefit of others.'[12] Again, nearly four months afterwards, success seemed nearer. For 9 November 1797: 'Dined and slept at Battersea Rise for missionary meeting—Simeon—Charles Grant—Venn. Something, but not much, done—Simeon in earnest.'[13]

Schools proposed

The initial approach in India was to set up native schools, and the evangelical chaplains within the East India Company drew up a letter with this suggestion to the governor, Lord Cornwallis. He did not warm to the idea but he did not oppose it. Simeon heard in February 1789 from David Brown that this approach by the chaplains had given Charles Grant the opportunity to share his convictions with the governor, who had asked him to put his thoughts into writing, promising to give attention to his opinion. Brown enclosed a copy for Simeon, hoping that by his giving it to William Wilberforce it might be helpful to him in answering anticipated objections to the scheme. Wilberforce's influence was seen to be strategic.

The proposal was that, to begin with, two young clergymen should be sent to India as missionaries, prepared to spend about three years in language study at Benares, the seat of Hinduism. It was emphasized that zeal and grace alone in the men were not enough; they needed to be well educated—especially in science—so as to be able to converse well with the learned Brahmins.

Practicalities were not ignored. Charles Grant proposed that, until proper funding was available through some public foundation, he himself would provide 300 rupees per month (£300 per annum) for their support. This provision allowed for 'a sufficiency of bread ... but nothing to excite a spirit of adventure, to tempt to worldly views'.[14] While providing subsistence, it gave them nothing from which they could save.

This project of a mission to India set Simeon's mind to work in all kinds of directions, working out how it should proceed and be supported. This led eventually to the foundation of the Church Missionary Society.

Recruiter, adviser and counsellor

Simeon proved conscientious in identifying godly young men to serve as chaplains with the East India Company. All Anglican missionary work had to be done initially by a few of them, who were popularly known as 'the pious chaplains'.

Charles Grant looked to Simeon for recommendations and five stand out: David Brown, Claudius Buchanan, Daniel Corrie, Henry Martyn and Thomas Thomason. The last two appear most frequently in Simeon's correspondence. But there were many others. In March 1816 Simeon wrote to Thomason that within the previous eighteen months he had sent about a dozen, and that two more were soon to follow.

David Brown became the minister of the 'Old Church' in Calcutta, at that time the most important and influential congregation there. Claudius Buchanan became the Vice-Provost of the College of Fort

William, where, among others, William Carey taught. Daniel Corrie served in a variety of chaplaincies, engaging at the same time in missionary work. He was an outstanding Hindi scholar, a governor of the Church Missionary Society and renowned for his generosity. He ended his life as the Bishop of Madras.

Henry Martyn

Henry Martyn is the best-known of the chaplains on account of his brilliant mind, dedication to the service of his Saviour, his significant translations of the New Testament and his early death. His conversion came about like that of many others through his attendance at Holy Trinity Church, Cambridge, and it was from Simeon that he first heard reports of William Carey's work in Bengal.

After his ordination in 1803 he worked for two years as Simeon's curate, with responsibility for a rural congregation. He arrived in Calcutta in early 1806 and served for four years with military cantonments on the Middle Ganges, where he was able to open some schools. There were scarcely any converts in this region during his lifetime, although the first native clergyman of the Church of England in India was a convert from Islam, brought to Christ by the influence of Martyn. In consultation with David Brown and David Corrie Martyn concentrated on learning Arabic, Persian and also Hindustani (Urdu), the principal language of North India, and put his outstanding linguistic skills to use in translating the Bible into these three languages, for distribution in the Arabic script among the Muslims of India and the Middle East. However, suffering from a recurrence of tuberculosis, which made preaching increasingly painful, and despairing of conversions in North India, he decided that Arabia and Persia would provide a more congenial environment, free of colonial restraints, to improve his translations of the Bible into the languages of the Islamic world. Having obtained leave to travel via Calcutta and Bombay, he left

North India in October 1810, but sadly died of tuberculosis at Tokat in Anatolia, on his way to Constantinople, at the age of thirty-one.

Short as his life was, his influence was immense and significant, and continued beyond his death. His translation of the New Testament into Urdu was published in 1814 and that into Persian in 1815. The manuscript of his Arabic New Testament was forwarded to Simeon in Cambridge, who had it published in Calcutta in 1816. Once missionary activity was permitted in 1813—after the East India Company's lifting of its rigid prohibition—the New Testament was available to missionary societies in the languages known to Muslims. Editions of the different translations were repeatedly published. Martyn also had a significant influence upon Simeon. Of the portrait of Martyn that he commissioned and hung in his room, he said, 'There, see that blessed man! What an expression of countenance! No one looks at me as he does; he never takes his eyes off me and seems always to be saying, "Be serious. Be in earnest. Don't trifle. Don't trifle." Then, smiling at the portrait and gently bowing, Simeon would add, "And I won't trifle. I won't trifle."'[15]

Thomas Thomason

Although not so well known as Henry Martyn, Thomas Thomason, six years older than Martyn, was the East India Company's chaplain with whom Simeon had the closest relationship, especially after Martyn's death. A student at Magdalene College, Cambridge, and outstanding in classics, mathematics, Hebrew and Greek, he was one of the many undergraduates who benefited from the time Simeon was willing to give in answering their questions and teaching them how to preach. He was Simeon's curate seven years before Martyn and he named Simeon's friendship as among his greatest blessings.

After a number of years in the ministry in England he sailed for India with his family in June 1808, at the age of thirty-five. His service overlapped that of Henry Martyn for four years, although it appears that they only once had the opportunity of being together. Besides his ministry as a chaplain he founded an orphanage for destitute female orphans of European soldiers and a schoolbook society to provide books for Indian children's elementary education. In 1817 he became the secretary of the Church Missionary Society in India. One of Henry Martyn's manuscripts left incomplete at his death was his translation of the Old Testament into Hindustani, and Thomason gave himself to completing the task, showing marked scholarship.

Simeon's correspondence with Thomason was considerable, although letters sometimes took as long as seven months to arrive. This prompted him in one letter to say that he wished he could send his advice by a carrier pigeon; in another letter, after Thomason had shared a situation with him, he replied, 'Before any observations of mind could reach you your situation would be so changed that they would be quite irrelevant.'[16] He gave advice on Thomason's innovative projects like the Orphan Asylum, the Orphan School and the Book Society, and at the same time spoke to others in England whose support for the projects might help.

The giving of advice

Simeon's spiritual counsel was direct and relevant. Regarding Thomason's relationship with his bishop in India, Simeon wrote, 'I highly approve of your conciliatory conduct towards the bishop. Both duty and policy enjoin that, and I am greatly mistaken, if duty and policy are ever at variance. Honesty is the best policy; so is meekness, forbearance, and rendering good for evil. At all events, they bring peace into the soul, both here and for ever.'[17] He gave similar counsel with regard to Thomason's relationship with his employers, the East India Company.

Another example shows how direct and honest he was in responding when he heard that some of the missionaries had gone beyond what the East India Company allowed in their speaking to the people, and that

Thomason had perhaps not responded as he ought as the company's employee:

In your peculiar situation, a tenfold measure of wisdom is necessary; because as a servant of the Company, you owe obedience to them, at the same time that in your ministerial character you owe obedience to God: and where the two come in competition with each other, your line is, not to violate your duty to the Company, but to renounce your connection with them.[18]

Simeon also made suggestions of a practical nature. In Cambridge, concerned as he was for the poor, he had been involved in the establishment of a Provident Bank, and he wrote to Thomason enclosing a copy of its rules, asking, 'Would not such an institution be of great use amongst you? Might there not be one for the Europeans, and one for the Hindoos? I think you might be a great blessing to that land in promoting such institutions.'[19]

Loco parentis

His involvement with Thomason and the work in India became greater when he undertook the guardianship of James, Thomason's ten-year-old son, when he was sent home to England for his education. He arrived in the summer of 1814 and Simeon wrote to Thomason the next day, expressing 'the happiness of embracing the blessed treasure in my arms, and of bringing him in safety to Cambridge'.[20]

His carefulness in exercising this responsibility revealed a softer and gentler aspect of Simeon's character. He confessed to asking himself, 'What would a father and a mother do?'[21] He showed the same meticulousness in guardianship as in most other things. 'Respecting our dear charge,' he wrote to Thomason, 'we shall steer the medium between excess of care, and want of care. You may be assured we shall have an hundred eyes, whilst we shall seem to have only a dozen. Every attention which he can have he will; but all tempered with wisdom and discretion.'[22]

He sensitively wrote too to Mrs Thomason,

I have weighed him, and measured him; and hope, if I live another year, to tell you how much he has gained in flesh and in height, as well as in knowledge. All his exercises, i.e. one in every month, I shall keep, in order to form a judgment about him, and to enable his father to do the same. Be assured that, if I were indeed his father, I could not feel much more for him than I do.[23]

Simeon related James's many questions and the liveliness of his mind, 'a pledge of the attainments, which, with God's help, I doubt not, he will make in a short time'.[24] His hopes were proved true because James, on the completion of his education, returned to India to pursue a distinguished public career, exercising a Christian influence. At the age of thirty-nine he was appointed Lieutenant-Governor of the North-Western Provinces, and became the father of primary education in North India as he founded a system of village schools. Simeon's guardianship of James proved to be a spiritual investment for the benefit of God's cause in India.

Simeon's giving of advice was not limited to those close to him, like Thomason, a former colleague. To prominent men such as the Bishop of Calcutta, Daniel Wilson, with whom he developed a special friendship, he became something of a confidant and adviser on matters such as the caste system in India.

Provoker of pastors

At home in Britain Simeon provoked his friends and colleagues in the ministry to see the importance of fulfilling our Lord Jesus Christ's final commission. On 8 February 1796 he opened a discussion at the Eclectic Society (see Chapter 13) with the question, 'With what propriety, and in what mode, can a Mission be attempted to the Heathen from the Established Church?'[25] This was not the first time a discussion of this sort had taken place, and he urged that there should be no further delay, although sadly there was. Three years later, on 18 March 1799, at another of the society's meetings, John Venn proposed the question, 'What methods can we use most effectually to promote the knowledge of the Gospel among the heathen?'[26] It is hardly necessary to say that Simeon was there!

John Venn laid down five principles: (1) Follow God's leading; (2) Begin on a small scale; (3) Put money in the second place, not the first; (4) Under God, all will depend on the type of men sent forth; (5) Look for success only from the Spirit of God. The person who recorded the details of the meeting wrote of Simeon's 'characteristic distinctness of purpose and promptitude of zeal'[27] and that he himself proposed three questions: What can we do? When shall we do it? How shall we do it?

We catch a glimpse here of Simeon's typical desire for action and the forcefulness of his contribution. The consequence of this meeting was a proposal that a society should now be established with these missionary ends and placed before the leadership of the Established Church. A fortnight later, on 1 April, the discussion took the matter further and was followed on 12 April by the foundation of the Church Missionary Society, with Simeon as one of the principal founders.

Once the Church Missionary Society was on its feet and missionary work in India no longer dependent on the recruitment and employment of East India Company chaplains, Simeon's interest and involvement were shared by many others. He maintained his commitment for forty-two years and testified to it being 'a principal and an incessant object of my care and labour'.[28]

Notes

1 *John Wesley's Journal*, 11 June 1739.

2 *Memoirs of Charles Simeon*, p. 45.

3 Chas. Simeon, (ed.), *Memorial Sketches of the Rev. David Brown with a Selection of His Sermons Preached at Calcutta* (London: T. Cadell & W. Davies, 1816), p. xiii.

4 Ibid., p. xiii.

5 Ibid., p. xiv.

6 Ibid.

7 *Memoirs of Charles Simeon*, p. 45.

8 Ibid.

9 Ibid., p. 47.

10 *Life of William Wilberforce, by His Son Samuel Wilberforce*, vol. ii (London: John Murray, 1868), p. 165.

11 Ibid., pp. 189–190.

12 Henry Morris, *The Life of Charles Grant* (London: John Murray, 1904), p.191.

13 Ibid., p. 191.

14 *Memoirs of Charles Simeon*, p. 47.

15 Ibid., p. 224.

16 Ibid., p. 247.

17 Ibid., p. 248.

18 Ibid., p. 226.

19 Ibid., p. 256.

20 Ibid., p. 226.

21 Ibid., p. 227.

22 Ibid., p. 228.

23 Ibid., p. 229.

24 Ibid., p. 66.

25 Ibid.

26 John H. Pratt, (ed.), *The Thought of the Evangelicals: Notes of the Discussions of the Eclectic Society, London, During the years 1798–1814* (Edinburgh: Banner of Truth, 1978), p. 96.

27 Ibid., p. 98.

28 *Memoirs of Charles Simeon*, p. 45.

Simeon and the Jews

An aspect of Simeon's life and ministry often overlooked and perhaps ignored is his concern for the salvation of the Jews. This does not seem to have arisen from any special prophetic convictions, as with some of his contemporaries. Only once, for example, in all his sermons does he mention the Millennium. The inclusion and length of this chapter reflects the place the Jews had in his thoughts. If we are inclined to think that the time he gave to the subject was excessive, what he said in another context may be appropriate: 'Who ever rode a favourite hobby without going now and then a little too fast?'[1]

Basically, his concern for the Jews arose from his being a gospel man. He knew that the gospel of Jesus Christ is for all people and every nation, for the 'whoever' of John 3:16. Its roots were in his systematic study of the whole of the Bible, and that included careful study of Romans 9–11. He tried to give equal attention to the whole of God's revelation in Scripture; and integrity demanded, therefore, a concern for the salvation of the Jews and the fulfilment of God's promises to them, as to the Gentiles. A further concern that he voiced was the indifference towards and lack of prayer for them and their inclusion in the missionary endeavours of the church.

Romans 9–11

As he expounded the key passages in Romans relating to the Jewish people Simeon found that he could not escape a developing spiritual burden for them and a compulsion to do something in response. Titles he gave to his sermons on these key chapters reveal the source of his motivation: for example, 'The Privileges of Jews and Gentiles' (Rom.

9:1–4); 'Our Duty Towards the Jews' (Rom. 9:1–5); 'Paul's Love for His Brethren' (Rom. 10:1); 'Salvation by Christ to Be Universally Proclaimed' (Rom. 10:12–15); 'The Restoration of the Jews—A Blessing to the Gentiles' (Rom. 11:11–12); 'Neglect of the Jews Reproved' (Rom. 11:17–21); 'The Dispensations of God towards Jews and Gentiles' (Rom. 11:22–24); 'The Future Salvation of all Israel' (Rom. 11:25–27); 'The Jews Still Beloved of God, for their Fathers' Sake' (Rom. 11:28–29); and 'The Gospel Given to Us as a Deposit for the Jews' (Rom. 11:30–31).

A mystery

He readily admitted that the present state of the Jews is a mystery, but one so great that we should want to understand it. He used the word 'mystery' in the biblical sense of a divine secret that we can never understand apart from God's revelation of it to us. The principal example of this biblical use of the word is in relation to the incarnation of our Lord Jesus, something that was a secret hidden for centuries but has now been revealed to us in his coming and in the New Testament Scriptures. In Paul's letter to the Ephesians the mystery is also equated with the inclusion of the Gentiles with the Jews in the church (Eph. 3:3–6). God's sovereign purposes in the Jews' rejection of their Messiah and their restoration to him are similarly a 'mystery' which we would not be able to understand apart from God revealing and explaining it in his Word.

It is important that we let Simeon here speak for himself. In a sermon on Romans 11:28–29 he summed up this 'mystery' regarding the Jews in this way:

God originally chose the Jews for his peculiar people, and vouchsafed to reveal himself exclusively to them. When, by their abuse of his blessings, they had 'provoked him to become their enemy', he determined to make himself known to the Gentiles, and to transfer to them the blessings which had been so wantonly despised. Therefore he cast off the Jews, and adopted the Gentiles in their place ... This does, I confess, appear a strange and almost incredible statement: and, if it were founded on one particular expression of the Scriptures, we might well doubt the justness of it. But this truth is so often repeated, that we cannot possibly entertain a doubt respecting it. The Apostle tells us, that, 'through their fall, *salvation is come unto the Gentiles*': that their fall was *the riches of the world*; that the diminishing of them was the *riches of the Gentiles*; and that the casting away of them was *the reconciling of the world*.[2]

A growing burden

Simeon's sense of responsibility for the Jewish people increased the more he understood their God-given privileges and promises which they are conspicuously not now enjoying. Empathizing with Paul's great heaviness and continual sorrow that all the time they continued in unbelief they were perishing in their sins, he recognized his duty of sharing his concern for their salvation, as we should for *all* people everywhere who continue in unbelief. 'If we bear in mind what they once were, and what they are yet destined to become, we shall regard them with veneration, for their fathers' sakes, and seek their welfare with earnestness for their own sakes.'[3] If Paul, the apostle to the Gentiles, was willing to suffer anything for the Jews' sakes in order to be instrumental to their salvation, so should all believers.

Basic convictions

Because Simeon recognized the danger of systematization we do not find him putting together all his convictions in one place; we have to gather them from what he said and wrote on a variety of occasions.

First, he was convinced of the future restoration of the Jews. He believed that God's sure purposes for them are built upon the implications of God's everlasting covenant with them and the truth that God's gifts and call are irrevocable (Rom. 11:29). Reflecting upon God's sure promises to Abraham, Simeon believed that it was in no way possible that the Jews should be cast off for ever. 'The Jews were chosen in Abraham their father; and all his posterity were comprehended in the promises made to him: not indeed in their individual capacity ... but nationally, and in their collective capacity; and to them, sooner or later, shall all the promises be fulfilled.'4

Second, Simeon was convinced that what we may feel to be a delay does not mean that God's promises have failed. As God intervened for the Jews during their time in Egypt, so also

will he act yet once more towards that chosen people. They are now dispersed almost beyond the hope of conversion to God. But there is a period when they shall as universally, and perhaps too as suddenly, commit themselves to the government of Christ, as ever they did to the direction of Moses; nor is it improbable that they will yet again inhabit that very land, from which they have been driven for their iniquities.5

But Simeon consistently and steadfastly refused to speculate about the details.

Deep regret

Simeon frequently expressed his sorrow at what he felt was the general attitude of Gentile believers to the Jews. First, we so easily forget or lose sight of our proper response to God's sovereign purposes. 'Perhaps you have never yet thought how much you are indebted to God for the present state of the Jews?' he suggested. 'Surely if salvation comes to us through them, it should return to them through us.'6

Second, we tend to be indifferent to the needs of Jewish people. He was aware that most Christians feel and express little concern for the salvation of the Jews. Speaking of Paul's expressed burden for them, he said, 'It is a shame to the whole Christian world that so little of it is felt amongst us ... we have had no more heaviness or sorrow of heart for them, than if they had been in a state of perfect safety.'[7] When he raised the subject with many Christians they appeared content to be ignorant of God's purposes for the Jews. At the same time they could be quite dogmatic in their views of the prophecies relating to the Jews, as if they had made them a special study. 'Some will tell us, confidently, that the time for the conversion of Israel is not yet come; and that, when it shall be come, it shall be effected by miracle: and that, consequently, it is both unnecessary and presumptuous in us to attempt it.'[8]

Third, a lack of concern for the Jewish people leads to an absence of prayer for them.

Alas! When have we spent one single hour in prayer for them? What sacrifices have we made, or what exertions, for the enlightening of their minds, and the saving of their souls? If we should say, 'My heart's desire and prayer to God for Israel is, that they might be saved,' would not our daily experience give the lie to our profession? Surely we have need to blush and be ashamed, every one of us.[9]

Fourth, sadly, neglect of the Jews and prayerlessness for their well-being are often accompanied by a despising of them. Simeon observed how contemptuously many Christians speak of the Jews 'as if *they* were *by nature* worse than ourselves; and as if they were never again to be restored to the favour of their God'.[10] He placed the blame upon people like himself in spiritual leadership. 'Good men, especially in later ages, have been so fond of spiritualising the Scriptures, that they have, in many instances, totally overlooked their primary meaning.'[11]

Reasons for involvement

He maintained that active involvement in seeking the salvation and spiritual welfare of the Jews is eminently right and reasonable. First, it is God's concern and his honour is involved. 'Put to yourselves this question, "Am I like-minded with God?" Ought I to be like-minded with him? and am I desirous of being a co-worker with him? I will not say for the restoration of the Jews; I will not say for the salvation of the world; but I will say for the honour of the Lord Almighty.'[12] Part of like-mindedness with God is concern for Israel.

Second, since the gospel is given to every believer as a trust (1 Cor. 4:2; 9:17) or deposit (2 Tim. 1:14) to be passed on to all, its proclamation must be *as much* to the Jew as to the Gentile.

I call upon you to pay your arrears … and now, by your personal efforts, or through the instrumentality of others, impart to them the mercy which you yourselves have received. Nor do I suggest this as a matter of advice merely, but as an absolute command from God himself. *It is not a thing left to your option. You have a trust; and you must discharge it.*[13]

Simeon felt that Christian neglect of the Jews is so great that it might be imagined Romans 9, 10 and 11 had never been written.

Words and convictions matched by practice

He practised what he preached. First, he wrestled in his mind to explain what he understood by some of the key phrases in those biblical passages that especially relate to God's purposes for the Jews, without trying to systematize them. He tried to help his hearers by explaining the assertions in the New Testament concerning the Jews by promises in the Old.

He was confident that before their restoration there would always be a believing remnant.

'A remnant' there are, and ever have been, whose eyes have been opened to see the light which shines around them: but 'the rest are and have been blinded', according to that prediction respecting them, 'God hath given them the spirit of slumber, eyes that they should not see, and ears that they should not hear, unto this day' (Rom. 11:8).[14]

The London Jews' Society

With such convictions Simeon enthusiastically supported the London Society for Promoting Christianity amongst the Jews (also known as the London Jews' Society). At the time of its foundation in 1809 it was reckoned that there were not more than fifty Christian Jews in Britain.

This society supported workers, some of whom were ordained, in their house-to-house visitation work in the Jewish quarters of London and elsewhere. They distributed literature in a variety of languages and established schools. Services were held in Hebrew, English and German, and the New Testament was translated into Hebrew. Because the society was predominantly Anglican, the liturgy was also translated into Hebrew. Influential figures in both the government and the Church of England were its patrons.

The first mention of Simeon's involvement with the society is in 1811, when he preached on its behalf. The society went through many difficulties in its early days, some self-inflicted. It made the mistake of making too much fuss of Jewish converts before they had had time to prove the reality of their profession of faith. Simeon's judgement was that they wanted 'to glory in their flesh',[15] and that God, to punish their pride, made use of them to expose the society to shame. But that conviction caused him not to dissociate himself from it but rather to help it to learn hard lessons and to put it on a sound footing.

When its management was in a bad way in 1814, resulting in financial embarrassment, Simeon devoted a whole month to the task of extricating it and placing it on a better foundation—no small commitment for someone with so many other responsibilities. Together with others, he presented four different plans so that they could decide upon the best. After discussing one plan for five hours without success, they went to William Wilberforce's home, where Simeon proposed a fifth plan which was unanimously adopted, accomplishing a better method of management and the paying-off of the whole of its debts of £12,500. Later, at the beginning of 1835, its management was placed completely in the hands of members of the Church of England.

Active and sustained involvement

Simeon played a prominent role in encouraging spiritual concern for Jews not only in Britain but also in Europe. In the early nineteenth century the London Jews' Society was the foremost society with this aim and Simeon gave of his best to its support. A member of its committee, he made frequent early-morning starts to get from Cambridge to London for its meetings. The society grew throughout the nineteenth century and established auxiliaries throughout the British Isles and Canada. By 1861 it had workers in thirty-nine stations in Europe, Asia and Africa; by the end of the century there were fifty-two stations and 199 workers scattered throughout England, Austria, France, Germany, the Netherlands, Italy, Romania, Russia, Constantinople, Jerusalem, Africa and Asia. From its somewhat shaky start it became one of the best-organized and most enterprising of missionary societies.

At least once every year Simeon travelled extensively in England, Ireland and Scotland on the society's behalf. In September and October of 1817, for example, he undertook an extensive tour of about 800 miles in England. His itinerary included Norwich, Nottingham, Sheffield, Leeds, Bradford, Manchester, Shrewsbury and Bristol. The visits were remembered for years afterwards.

On some journeys, as in 1819, meetings were convened in large cities, such as Liverpool and Manchester, for him to address gatherings of Jews, and in these he especially delighted. In those two cities he preached from Micah 5:7: 'The remnant of Jacob will be in the midst of many peoples like dew from the LORD, like showers on the grass, which do not wait for man or linger for mankind.' He 'showed that God had mercy in view both for them, and for the world, in their present dispersion'.[16] In his travels, besides preaching, he recruited workers, distributed literature, gave advice and collected funds. He made at least two excursions into Europe, spending time in Amsterdam and Paris—where in the latter he met, among others, Merle d'Aubigné, the great historian of the Reformation.

In establishing auxiliaries of the London Jews' Society, he did not hesitate to get high-profile people to chair the public meetings. In Bristol, for example, the mayor was in the chair, and in Cambridge the vice-chancellor of the university. Simeon usually preached and then someone else drew up the rules for the new auxiliary. The reception he received often astonished him. Sometimes the numbers of people in such meetings were as many as two or three thousand, as, for instance, in Preston in Lancashire and Frome in Somerset.

Each summer he devoted most of his annual holiday to visiting the auxiliaries to encourage them. It made no difference if the audience was large or small, and he was ready to preach in small villages or large towns and cities, sometimes preaching seven times in ten days. He further supported the work by maintaining an extensive correspondence with the secretaries of the local associations, not hesitating to offer his services where he could help. He saw the value of women's contributions to the cause and he took initiative in establishing women's associations within the society.

His final long tour was in 1825, but right up to the end of his life, when diminishing energy dictated shorter journeys, he continued to advocate the Jewish cause. As late as 1836, the year of his death, knowing that his travelling days on behalf of the society were over, he very reluctantly wrote to a friend about an invitation to preach in Reading: 'The offer of a pulpit there to advocate the Jewish cause made me almost leap half-way to accept it. But with all foreign service I have done. I am now only a poor pensioner-soldier, wearing the king's uniform, and just twice a week attending the parade, and discharging the domestic exercise that has been assigned me.'[17]

The gathering of funds

A major purpose of Simeon's travels was to stir up Christians to support financially work on behalf of the Jews. He could do this with integrity because of his own generosity in the support of the work, more often than not anonymously. We know that in 1813 he gave a donation of 300 guineas towards the erection of an Episcopal chapel for the use of Christian Jews in London, a gift that was followed by many more, some substantial.

He was particularly sensitive to the material needs of individual Jewish Christians who suffered on account of their faith. All his travels for the London Jews' Society were at his own expense, whether in Britain or Europe. As the work expanded to the continent, the demands became greater. He wrote in 1819, 'We must this year not only get for our ordinary expenses, but for our augmented expenses of foreign missions.'[18]

Not every place Simeon visited welcomed him. When visiting Leicestershire, the minister at Lutterworth refused Simeon his pulpit but then was persuaded by others in Leicester to change his mind. He invited all the clergy in the neighbourhood of Lutterworth to dinner and gathered together a good congregation to hear Simeon.

These preaching tours produced further fruit. Simeon prepared sermons in support of the Jewish cause for these tours and some were then printed and distributed. In 1817 he spoke in Norwich and the speech he gave was printed and circulated throughout the United Kingdom. Copies went as far afield as India and America for circulation. After he had preached in the Netherlands, it was felt that his sermon might do further good printed, and it was produced for distribution in English, French and Dutch.

Strategy

Simeon was one of those who saw the importance of the London Jews' Society's translation of the New Testament into Hebrew in 1820 and its vital place in the evangelization of the Jews in the United Kingdom and beyond. He discovered that there were two million Jews in the Russian empire, many of whom were anxious to have the Hebrew New Testament.

He thought deeply about the best strategy to employ. In 1819 he wrote,

The more I think of the state of the Jews throughout the world, and of the importance of putting the Hebrew New Testament into their hands with suitable tracts, the more I am convinced, that to send forth missionaries among them is far more likely to be extensively useful, than to confine our attention to any one city, or any one kingdom in the universe.[19]

This, however, was not to the neglect of strategic cities like Amsterdam. Discovering that 30,000 Jews lived in that city, he and others at their own expense funded taking possession of a chapel there and appointing a chaplain, as an experiment for two years, with a view to doing the same in other big cities like Rotterdam and Hamburg.

The inescapable impression we receive is that Simeon's mind was always working on ways to further the interests of his Saviour's kingdom. Faced with either personal or corporate challenges, he sought answers and ways of taking positive initiative. He made constructive suggestions to all who sought his help. Talking to a Dutch Christian Jew about how he could best benefit his countrymen, he was practical: 'I recommended that he should instruct six youths on his Sabbath, and agree with each of them to instruct six others.'[20]

Recognizing the value of relevant literature to stir interest, he made an anonymous arrangement to give prizes for the best tracts on answering Jewish questions and advertised the competition in the Christian press.

Wise counsel

Perhaps his greatest contribution to the London Jews' Society was his availability to its committee as an unconscious role model and also for his advice. These benefits they were able to draw upon to the end of his life. Instances of his wise counsel stand out.

When the society was faced by those who dismissed out of hand the restoration of the Jews, he urged them to be 'gentle toward all men' and to 'instruct in meekness them that oppose themselves', suggesting that then the society's arguments would appear stronger than if they maintained their position 'in language of severity and triumph'.[21] With regard to showing benevolence to the Jewish people, he urged that it was important for Christians to do so without obtrusiveness or ostentation. In the context of his warning against making too much fuss of Jewish converts, he also suggested that it was a serious mistake to imagine that to ask a bishop to baptize them was at all likely to advance their spiritual well-being. Instead, he suggested, such a practice would 'only destroy the simplicity of their minds, and endanger their stability, in proportion as it fosters their pride'.[22]

His spiritual wisdom was seen in the manner in which he used his episcopal connections for the advantage of the church's work among the Jews. As the years passed and he became well established in Cambridge, he gained esteem in the eyes of several bishops, and his correspondence with them was wise and respectful. He developed a particularly happy relationship with the Bishop of St David's. Simeon wrote candidly to Thomas Thomason, one of his former assistants, 'I go next Monday to meet the Bishops of St David's and Gloucester. I hope God will open the heart of the former to enter fully into my views. He has already shown great kindness and done much; but I am not content with drops: I want, if it may please God, a shower.'[23] Through such relationships, one bishop was able to recommend the work among the Jews to another, as when the Bishop of St David's spoke to the Bishop of London on Simeon's behalf for the work among them, since Simeon had not met him.

Part of the fruit of these relationships was the happy news in May 1818 which Simeon communicated to Thomas Thomason, serving in India:

Wonderful are the tidings I have to communicate. It appears to our governors in the church that missionaries are sent out by every denomination of Christians, except the Church of England. They have therefore applied to Government for a king's letter, to ask subscriptions through all the churches of the kingdom in aid of this good work. I am endeavouring to take care that the Jews shall not be forgotten. It will give you pleasure to hear that I am on the best footing with the Bishop of St David's, and that he will do anything I can wish (in prudence) to promote my views. He is going to establish a missionary class in his college. He has taken under his protection Friedenburgh, a converted Jew of great talent and piety, and a young man from New Holland; both at my request. I hope and trust that God will make him an instrument of great good. God is evidently gone out before us: and considerable work, I hope, will ere long be done.[24]

He did not hesitate to speak to those who were close to him about supporting the work among the Jews. He was, however, aware that some might feel bound to give out of regard for him rather than for love of God and his kingdom—a wise cautiousness.

An important determination and conviction

One thing he was determined not to do was to enter into controversy over the Jews. When requested to attack the work of a minister who denied the restoration of the Jews to their own land, his answer was,

I have neither taste nor talent for controversy; nor do I, on the whole, envy those by whom such taste and such talent are possessed. I know you will forgive me, if I say that the very account you give of yourself in relation to controversy is a dissuasive from embarking in it. Let a man once engage in it, and it is surprising how the love of it will grow upon him; and he will both find a hare in every bush, and follow it with something of a huntsman's feelings.[25]

Simeon's understanding of God's purposes grew over the years, along with a matching concern which he expressed at the 27th Anniversary Meeting of the London Jews' Society in June 1835, just a year before he died. In discussing a resolution to be put before the meeting, Simeon said,

I am fearful I shall not be able to make myself heard by all this vast assemblage, yet I could tell them my heart is in this cause—that I think of it more and more, and I perhaps might astonish them by saying—that, though I have studied the subject of the Jewish question for many years, and written upon it not a little, I have never understood it until within the last few months. I might say, without, as I hope, an attempt at arrogance—for God knows I do not speak it in such a sense—that it is not understood.[26]

In saying this he was afraid that he might offend his friends in such a sweeping assertion and what might seem to border on self-complacency.

But he went on to explain that

the apostles, inspired and instructed as they were to understand and preach the Gospel to the Gentiles, did not, for the space of six years, fully comprehend its meaning; and as you all, no doubt, are aware, the Apostle Peter was openly called to account for misconstruing the directions of our Lord. If, then, the apostles did not understand what had been set forth as plain as any truth could have been, it must not be wondered at if we do not comprehend the preaching to the Jews.[27]

A telling testimony

At Simeon's death—the year after these words—a warm tribute was paid to him in the society's monthly periodical, *The Jewish Intelligence*. It spoke of 'the prominent part which he took in promoting throughout these kingdoms a warm and scriptural concern for the spiritual welfare of the Jewish people'[28] and also of 'his successful advocacy of our Society as an important instrument for preaching the Gospel of Christ to them'.[29]

It drew special attention to the profound influence he had in causing Christians to believe in the future restoration of the Jews.

To him was reserved the peculiar honour of rescuing a large portion of the Word of God from a narrow and prejudiced interpretation, according to which every denomination and curse connected with the name of Israel was carefully applied to the present race of the Jews, whilst every invitation, or promise, or blessing was as scrupulously explained to refer to the Gentile Christian Church, to the utter exclusion of this very same people. Seldom by one man has so marked a change been produced. Thirty years ago comparatively few persons believed in the Scripture doctrine of the future restoration of the Jews. At the present moment we venture to hope that a majority, both of studious divines and of pious Christians in the Church of England, are fully persuaded of this truth, and look forward to it as a glorious triumph of redeeming grace—in short, they believe God's faithfulness in performing his promises to be as exact and as sure as his faithfulness in executing his threatenings. To this end Mr Simeon's labours have been eminently blessed.[30]

The tribute also drew attention to how undergraduates who sat under Simeon's ministry in ever-increasing numbers 'were led by him to examine the Scriptures for themselves'[31] with reference to God's purposes for the Jews.

A significant contribution

It is difficult to overestimate the contribution Simeon made to the church's concern for the Jewish people and their salvation. First, he caused Christians to believe in their future restoration. Second, at a time when the church was recognizing more and more its responsibility for proclaiming the gospel throughout the world—especially in India— Simeon brought the church to see its equal responsibility for the Jews.

The many discouragements he knew in the Jewish work prompted him to say, 'Were it not that I know who reigns, my soul would sink within me.'[32] But these were more than matched by encouragements. The Emperor of Russia requested missionaries from the London Jews' Society and Hebrew Bibles. The Bishop of London consecrated the new chapel the London Jews' Society had built at Bethnal Green, and the Archbishop of Canterbury expressed regret at not giving its work his support earlier. Significant members of the Jewish community in Europe embraced the Christian faith. Influential public figures in the United Kingdom shared his concern, such as the Earl of Darnley, once Lord Mayor of London, the Duke of Kent, and Simeon's special friend, William Wilberforce. While feeling himself out of his proper place with such people, he rejoiced at their commitment.

The greatest encouragement

A particular joy to him in the final years of his life was the growing interest Cambridge undergraduates displayed in the Jewish cause in their attendance at the anniversary meetings of the society in Cambridge. He urged them to examine the Scriptures for themselves. Less than a month before his death he dictated a message to be read to the undergraduates at the next meeting of the society in Cambridge. It was listened to 'with earnest and affectionate attention. It was listened to as to a voice from the grave and many asked for copies afterwards'.[33]

Notes

1 *Memoirs of Charles Simeon*, p. 323.
2 Discourse 1900, *Horae Homileticae*, vol. 15.
3 Discourse 1800, ibid.
4 Ibid.
5 Discourse 1145, ibid., vol. 10.
6 *Jewish Intelligence and Monthly Account of the Proceedings of the London Society for the Promoting of Christianity among the Jews*, June 1835,.
7 Discourse 1833, *Horae Homileticae*, vol. 15.
8 Discourse 1899, ibid.

9 Discourse 1883, ibid.

10 Discourse 1899, ibid.

11 Discourse 946, ibid., vol. 8.

12 *Jewish Intelligence*, June 1835.

13 Discourse 1901, *Horae Homileticae,* vol. 15.

14 Discourse 1898, ibid., vol. 15.

15 *Memoirs of Charles Simeon*, p. 383.

16 Ibid., pp. 301–302.

17 Ibid., p. 453.

18 Ibid., p. 294.

19 Ibid.

20 Ibid., p. 278.

21 Ibid., p. 373.

22 Ibid., p. 384.

23 Ibid., p. 294.

24 Ibid., p. 277.

25 Ibid., p. 372.

26 *Jewish Intelligence*, June 1835.

27 Ibid.

28 *Jewish Intelligence*, December 1836.

29 Ibid.

30 Ibid.

31 Ibid.

32 Ibid.

33 Ibid.

Simeon's concern for the future—the Simeon Trust

J ust as business executives may sometimes be said to think and sleep
profit, Simeon thought gospel. He could have identified with David
Brainerd's declaration:

I cared not where or how I lived, or what hardships I went through, so that I could but
gain souls for Christ. While I was asleep I dreamed of these things, and when I awoke
the first thing I thought of was this great work. All my desire was for the conversion of
the heathen, and all my hope was in God.[1]

If Simeon was not thinking of the work at Holy Trinity in Cambridge, his
thoughts were on India or the salvation of the Jews. But he had a further
concern: it was the purchase of *advowsons*—a word from the French for
the right of presentation to a church living when it became vacant.

The problem of advowsons

Jane Austin, a contemporary of Simeon's, illustrated this unhelpful
practice in *Pride and Prejudice* when she invented the character of the
Revd William Collins and his abject dependence upon the patronage of
the Right Honourable Lady Catherine de Bourgh, through whose
bounty and beneficence he had been presented to the parish within her
gift and the house that went with it. If a parish was not within the gift
of a private individual of property, it was likely to be the prerogative of
a bishop and certainly not that of a congregation to call its own
minister.

Advowsons were bought and sold much as property might have been, and were often used to provide a living and career for a son or relative. In times of spiritual deadness, the whole system accentuated the spiritual need of the nation. Evangelical ministers were not generally popular, especially in the universities, and openings for young men were few and far between. Evangelicals tended to be classed as enthusiasts and to be linked in people's minds with Methodism.

Two expedients were resorted to by evangelicals, especially in London: the first was Propriety Chapels, and the second the establishment of lectureships. The Propriety Chapels were built by public subscription and supported by private individuals, often through pew rents. They had no parish rights and were seldom consecrated by a bishop, although a bishop could grant a licence to a minister to preach in one if the parish minister consented. The well-known Countess of Huntingdon used this expedient.

The lectureships were in effect preaching stations and were supported financially by those who attended or by public bodies or individuals, so that they were independent of the Church of England's funds. At least eighteen such lectureships existed in London in the eighteenth century, and evangelicals were the most prominent holders.

Young men with a calling to the ministry were not in a position to remedy the situation but there were two groups with potential to tackle it. The first was the Eclectic Society, and the second was the Clapham Sect, a title the members themselves would have rejected, for they never had any intention of separating themselves from the Church of England. The Eclectic Society may well have discussed the issue but there seems to be no record of their doing so; but the evangelicals at Clapham did, and the reason is understandable. The Eclectics were predominantly ministers of the gospel who met for fellowship and mutual encouragement, whereas the Clapham evangelicals were much more a group of business and professional people with financial means at their disposal.

Chapter 13

Helpful relationships

Simeon had many links with those who met regularly at Clapham, particularly, as we have seen, with Charles Grant, William Wilberforce and John Venn, the last of whom had become the minister of the church at Clapham where the group regularly met. John Thornton (1720–1790), a merchant and devout Christian, had inherited the Clapham estate and about £100,000. He devoted much of his wealth anonymously to gospel ministry in different parts of the world. In his efforts to obtain livings for evangelical curates he bought a number of advowsons, putting them into a trust. A strategic living he controlled in the City of London was St Mary Woolnoth, to which he presented John Newton in 1779 and where, according to the parish register, Simeon preached for Newton on eleven occasions.

Thornton decided that on his death he would not allow the advowsons to devolve to his sons in case they did not execute their duties with spiritual discernment. Instead he set up a trust for the purpose, and Simeon was one of the three trustees. Immediately upon John Venn's death and the need for the appointment of his successor, Simeon wrote to his fellow-trustees, urging them 'to fix their eyes on God, to whom alone we should look in such an important matter'.[2] He shared with them his conviction that William Dealtry should be appointed. Simeon had known him from his Cambridge student days and he had spent a year as tutor to the sons of Charles Grant. The recommendation was acted upon and approved by the congregation.

This appointment in 1813 was Simeon's first experience of exercising trusteeship and it opened his eyes to its potential and set his feet upon a path from which he did not deviate for the rest of his life. Because John Thornton held a number of livings within his gift, Simeon soon had further experiences of acting as a trustee with others, one of which made him aware of a particular danger. Writing to Thomas Thomason on 27 January 1814 he reported that another

Thornton living was vacant, to which he and his two colleagues would have to present a candidate. Simeon felt that he had to meet with them as soon as possible 'to prevent my colleagues from yielding to any solicitations'.[3]

Such a danger prompted him to lay down rules for trustees. The three initial criteria were: first, to consider who was the fittest person for the sphere in view; second, to discover whose removal to a new sphere would be the least detrimental to any other place; and, third, if two people remained equally suitable choices, to prefer the person whose present circumstances were the most financially difficult.

He did not hesitate to give careful and serious instructions to his fellow-trustees:

I think we must not only prefer a good to an evil, but must prefer a greater good to a lesser—provided there be a great and decided preponderance on either side—and I feel persuaded, that on a deathbed, and in the day that we give up our account to the Great Head of the Church, we shall wish that we had acted on this great and broad principle, 'as we believe the Apostle Paul would have acted'.[4]

He affirmed that he did not care who was appointed, provided that the man was worthy of the sphere to which he was called.

He encouraged his fellow-trustees to ask themselves, 'Who knows how many people a man may influence?' He continued,

But I conjure you to reflect, that in the course of his life there will be probably many thousands of souls interested in our decision, any one of which is of more value than the whole world. Should we then listen to the application of any number of individuals, to place in that large sphere a person unfit, when there are multitudes to be found every way fit and proper? I earnestly wish you to consider, what account we shall give of such a measure in the day of judgment, and to beg of God that we may be enabled to act, as we shall wish then that we had acted.[5]

Chapter 13

A timely and influential legacy

In 1812, just a little while before his introduction to the trusteeship of livings on behalf of the Thornton Trust, Charles's third brother, Edward, died in the prime of life after a distressing illness. An eminent merchant in London, and for many years one of the Directors of the Bank of England, he had built up a large fortune. Charles's care for and spiritual counsel to his brother in his illness was of great help to him and he left Charles a legacy of £15,000.

Simeon devoted either the entire legacy or simply the interest arising from it to the acquisition of advowsons. It was probably the latter, but the money undoubtedly gave him the financial security and capacity to buy livings that became available, even if he then had to look to others to support him in the final purchase. As the years passed, the income he received from his published sermons also went towards similar acquisitions. These livings he committed at once to trustees in perpetuity so that in these churches might be preached the doctrines that had been so productive and transforming in his own life.

The evidence points to his dedication to this goal. Once his essential personal needs were met, his purpose was to use his income to buy other advowsons to further the aims of the trust. He was able to report in 1823 to a friend, 'I have bought several, and for above this month past I have expected a demand of £9,000 for fresh purchases: and I am at this moment in treaty for two more livings. I should not have been able to go on thus far, if I had not been helped.'[6] Feeling the matter to be of such importance he unhesitatingly appealed to his friends for help in supplying the necessary funds.

Some probably thought him foolhardy but, as he put it, 'I do not first ask, and then act; but first act, and then ask; and leave it to the Lord to send friends to my assistance, or not, as it shall please him.'[7] He testified in February 1826 that about four years previously,

When I was in my blessed work of purchasing livings, to secure in perpetuity pious and laborious ministers in them, by the advice of a gentleman I wrote to Dr Kilvington, whom I had never seen, to ask some assistance towards it, thinking he might possibly give me £500; and behold he gave me nearly £8,000! And now that I am again engaged to the amount of above £10,000, a gentleman, whom I never saw but once, and then only for half-an-hour, has died and left me, as my informant says, £9,000.[8]

As his intentions to secure livings became known, many people, trusting his good judgement, gave gifts or left him bequests for this purpose.

The growth of the trust

The trust grew quickly. The original trust was formed of churches in Cheltenham, Newcastle-under-Lyme and Colchester, and seven trustees were appointed. They included John Sargent (the biographer of Henry Martyn) and Daniel Wilson (Vicar of St Mary's, Islington, and later Bishop of Calcutta). St Peter's Church at Ruddington, Nottinghamshire, was the fourth acquisition in 1822, and in 1823 William Wilberforce donated the advowson of Drypool in Yorkshire.

A surprise

An unexpected providence brought even more support for Simeon's enterprise. To a number of people who had sent him contributions, he wrote thank-you letters of a confidential nature about his hopes and prospects. Without consulting him, the recipients sent extracts from them to the editor of the *British Magazine*, who published them as one continuous letter from Simeon, which was circulated far and wide. This came as a surprise to both him and his friends, the latter finding such an action out of character.

Simeon did not think that either the editor or those friends who had allowed their letters to be used in this way had intended him any harm but, as he put it, 'they took the best method imaginable to defeat my plans: and from that time I have been careful to restrain my pen from writing anything more than a plain letter of thanks, except to those whom I knew, and could fully trust'.⁹

But, much as Simeon would have forbidden it if he had known what they planned to do, he acknowledged that God had overruled it for good because very quickly more than £24,000 was subscribed. He wrote,

And through the goodness of God, it has brought me aid to a very great extent. By recent donations I am enabled to make some further efforts ... The object is of incalculable importance. The securing of a faithful ministry in influential places would justify any outlay of money that could be expended on it: and if I were able to effect it by any funds of my own, they would be most gladly supplied for the attainment of so great an end. If our blessed Lord came down from heaven, and died upon the cross, for the salvation of immortal souls—sure I am, that nothing which we can do for the promotion of his glory and of man's salvation can be justly deemed superfluous or inexpedient.¹⁰

One of the chief culprits behind the sending of extracts of Simeon's letter to the *British Magazine* seems to have been Revd J. H. Gurney of Lutterworth, to whom he wrote in March 1836,

My dear Sir, It is a duty which I owe to you and to Almighty God, to inform you that the measure which you have adopted has greatly interested many persons and brought me considerable aid ... *I am glad you did not ask my leave to print my letter, for I could not have consented to it.* Ostentation I utterly abhor: nor could I expect the blessing of God upon me, if I were guilty of it. But your unauthorized *exposé* of my plans has called forth the liberality of so many, and the good will of so many, that I shall have no fear of the religious public suffering me to go to jail in such a cause as this. You have made me as it were a centre of union in this glorious cause: and have shown me that if only I act with simplicity *to God*, and in humble dependence upon him, I may yet in a prudent way and with moderation advance, and extend my efforts in full (not stinted) proportion, as my means of advancement are increased.¹¹

Testimony to God's providence

God's gracious and ample provision for Simeon's purchase of livings for his trust prompted him to reflect on what his father's reaction to the providences with which he was surrounded would have been:

My poor dear honoured and lamented father thought that I should ruin myself by giving my money to the poor; and therefore left my little fortune in the hands of trustees, to keep me from this apprehended mischief. Behold, this is the way in which God leaves me to be ruined! Oh, what a master he is! I wonder who ever lost by serving him! It is sufficient for me to know, that 'what we give for his glory, we lend to him; and he will repay us again'. But he will not even take the loan: for on both these occasions he has just interposed (as indeed he has on several other occasions) to forestall and prevent the payment out of my own pocket; so that I am still as strong as ever to prosecute the same good work. Who needs prove to me the providence of God?[12]

Nothing by halves

As we have noticed before with regard to the gospel enterprises in which Simeon engaged himself, he did nothing half-heartedly but everything zealously. Every church which he made part of what we know as the Simeon Trust brought its own responsibility of care for him. He involved himself with architects where buildings needed to be improved and enlarged, and with all the matters of finance involved. He determined that he should visit both the congregations and their pastors. To the latter it must have left behind memorable times of encouragement and wise counsel. In a letter of June 1836 he shared, 'I am just setting off upon a long, long journey of about 500 miles to visit some of my churches, and am quite oppressed as it were with a variety of matters.'[13]

Evident blessing upon the churches in the trust

Heavy burden as it was, Simeon found rich encouragement, as he described after his visit to Holy Trinity, Cheltenham, the church in which Thomas Thomason had worked.

Here at Cheltenham I have almost had a heaven upon earth. The churches so capacious, and so filled: the schools so large, so numerous, so beneficial: the people so full of love: the ministers such laborious and energetic men: and God himself so graciously with me in my exertions: in truth, I can scarcely conceive any higher happiness on earth than I am now privileged to enjoy ...[14]

Not long afterwards he reported,

Had you seen my meetings anywhere, and my partings at Hereford or Lichfield, you would have known a little what love is, and what a savour Christian communion leaves behind it ... with the sight of such places secured in perpetuity for the Lord, I must be the most brutish of mankind, if I did not feel the most lively gratitude to my heavenly Benefactor.[15]

A few weeks later, in touch with another friend on his return home to Cambridge he wrote,

You desired me to write to you when I should be restored in safety to my beloved home. But how shall I declare all the kindness I experienced in every place, or the comfort I enjoyed in communion with the Lord's people! The prosperity of Zion especially in all the different places far exceeded my most sanguine expectation: and the thought of my having been the rod in the hand of God, by whom all these wonders have been wrought, completed my joy. To all this I may add, the hope I entertained of being yet further accessory to the production of similar good in other places, gave to the whole a richness and sweetness which no words can adequately express.[16]

He went on to mention his awareness of the danger of complacency and at the same time his overwhelming thankfulness that, as he thought of his eight weeks of visiting the churches, 'not even the slightest incident occurred to damp my joy'.[17] What is more, preaching on the Sunday after his return to Holy Trinity, he 'preached to a church as full as it could hold, and partook of the Lord's Supper in concert with a larger number than has ever been convened together, on such an occasion, in any church in Cambridge'.[18] His gratitude knew no bounds.

Undying concern

This consuming concern to see evangelical witness maintained was with Simeon to the end of his life. Three months before his death, he wrote to a colleague at King's College that by the same post that day he had received two letters, one wanting him to open a church in Reading and the other to re-open one at Bradford. He declared that at the age of seventy-seven it made him feel young again, although he acknowledged that he needed to act his age.

The progress of his trust exceeded all his expectations.

The bounty of pious friends encourages me to proceed. And I trust that God, who has already carried me on so far, will finally bring me through. The occasion demands it:— immortal souls demand it:—the Established Church demands it:—and my Lord and Saviour demands it at my hands. And their united calls I will endeavour to obey.[19]

One of the last things he did in the October before his death in November 1836 was to make alterations to his will. Most of his assets and fortune had already been disposed of in promoting spiritual and charitable concerns. His reflections on his most recent visits to the churches in which he had an interest had further convinced him of the strategic importance of these trusteeships, causing him to devote the remainder of his assets, with the exception of a few legacies to relatives, to the support of this work. Once he had completed this, he felt he could prepare himself with joy for his departure.

We cannot fully estimate or quantify how strategic and influential Simeon's commitment to the securing of evangelical livings proved to be, but it was considerable. It was more significant than the Thornton Trust, in that Thornton had in view the immediate provision of livings for men he knew without thinking so much of ensuring an evangelical succession for the future.

Simeon's qualifications for the establishment of his trust

None was more acquainted than Simeon with evangelical men who, sensing God's call to the pastoral ministry, needed to find the most suitable church for its exercise. His preaching classes in particular brought to notice many young men's gifts and calling and made him sensitive to discovering appropriate means of matching men to congregations.

He provided a trusted figurehead and channel for funds. Because he had proved his gospel faithfulness throughout a long ministry in Cambridge and had given generously of his own resources for the purchase of livings, people felt they could entrust to his safekeeping funds for the furtherance of the vision. He was a far-sighted leader rather than a short-term enthusiast. As we have seen, he took care and pains to instruct trustees in their duties and to provide them with rules and principles. He underlined the importance of finding not just a good man for each living, but the best.

For example, when a candidate whose surname began with the letter M was being considered, Simeon urged his fellow-trustees to consider carefully the man's record elsewhere.

Why have I bought those livings? Not to present a good man to each, but to fill them with men who shall prove great and leading characters in the Church of God. Mr —, I doubt not, is a good man. But what great stir was there amongst immortal souls under his ministry whilst he officiated in — ? What lamentations were there when he left it?

What great efforts were made to retain him? Is this then the man to place there? He has shown what he could do: and if I cannot find in Britain one, who may with God's blessing do more, I will appoint him; but I will search the whole kingdom, before I will despair of finding a fitter man. I trust you will understand me aright; I am not displeased in the slightest degree with your letter; but I wish you to know, that I am in a few days to give up my account to God, and to answer for all the souls for whom I have engaged to provide, and I will do that, and that only, which God will approve when I stand before him.[20]

Simeon was no sentimentalist and had no hesitation about resisting approaches to him based on unworthy considerations and lack of good judgement. Of the congregation concerned above, he wrote,

They have sent a petition signed by eighty-eight persons. When I presented to — I had two petitions, one signed by 400, and the other by 700: I complied with neither, but sent them Mr —, and within six months I received a letter of thanks, signed by forty of the heads of both parties, saying that I had provided infinitely better for them than they would have provided for themselves. In another living I had, under far more pressing circumstances, a similar acknowledgment.[21]

A charge to the trustees

He expressed the same care and desire in his solemn charge to his trustees, which read as follows:

In the Name and in the Presence of Almighty God I give the following Charge to all my Trustees and to all who shall succeed them in the Trust to the remotest ages. I implore them for the Lord Jesus Christ's sake, and I charge them also before that adorable Saviour who will call them into Judgement for their execution of this Trust.

First, That they be very careful, whenever they shall be called upon to fill up a vacancy in this Trust, which they must invariably do within three months of a vacancy occurring, that they elect no one who is not a truly pious and devoted man, a man of God in deed and in truth, who, with his piety, combines a solid judgement and a perfectly independent mind. I place this first, because a failure in this one particular would utterly defeat, and that in perpetuity too, all that I have sought to do for God and for immortal souls.

Secondly, That, when they shall be called upon to appoint to a living, they consult nothing but the welfare of the people for whom they are to provide, and whose eternal interests have been confided to them. They must on no account be influenced by any solicitation of the great and powerful, or by any partiality towards a particular individual, or by compassion towards any one on account of the largeness of his family or the smallness of his income. They must be particularly on their guard against petitions from the parishes to be provided for, whether on behalf of a Curate that has laboured among them, or of any other individual. They must examine carefully, and judge before God, how far any person possesses the qualification suited to the particular Parish, and by that consideration alone must they be determined in their appointment of him.[22]

Still today, every time new trustees are appointed, these words are read at the first meeting they attend.

Because Simeon was a tested and proven minister of the gospel he brought to trusteeship invaluable understanding of both ministers and congregations—an understanding he did not hesitate to share. A letter to a trustee on his duty as patron of a benefice illustrates this understanding.

Wherever there is a good minister, there will be, if any, a good curate: consequently the curate will ingratiate himself with the parishioners; and consequently in their view he will be the fittest person to present: and therefore petitions will be made in his favour. From every place I have had petitions upon petitions; and for fit persons too. But where then is my knowledge of persons, my judgment, and my right of patronage, and my conscience, if I too readily and without extreme vigilance, comply with them? I must not only do well, but the best that I can possibly do; and I must spare no pains to effect this. It is on this account, that in my dying charge to my trustees I have particularly guarded them against being influenced by petitions for curates.[23]

Simeon's concern was to place ministers in churches without regard to anything other than their clear fitness for the place where they were to minister. 'This', he wrote, 'is the great reform wanted in our Church; and if generally carried into effect by all who have patronage in the Church, it would supersede all occasions for any further reform.'[24] Again, he wrote, 'I would please all men, but it should be for their good to edification; and how to do that, I must judge for myself.'[25] While he expressed his intentions in a forthright and authoritarian manner, they were the highest.

When he died at least twenty-one advowsons belonged to the trust, but not all with the same trustees, although eventually all were brought into one trust with identical trustees. Over the years the number of advowsons has grown as they have been gifted to the trust, and the trustees are committed to holding them 'in perpetuity'.[26] At the time of writing, the trust has an interest in 174 churches (144 of them are Simeon's and 30 are Hyndman's, another trust Simeon's Trust has looked after since 1990). All of them are in England. Some involve a shared patronage (joint, in turns or as part of a patronage board; the last usually when there is a team ministry). The twelve trustees meet every eight or nine weeks. Once a year the churches are invited to make a donation to the running of the trust, since it receives no endorsements or major funding.

The cumulative effect of all the livings that benefited from someone appointed by Simeon and his fellow-trustees cannot be measured. Everyone so appointed clearly had his call to the ministry confirmed and had the benefit of being cared for spiritually by Simeon in his systematic visitation. For not a few he must have presented a role model that provided further good examples for succeeding generations of ministers. The influence of these churches for spiritual good could probably not have been achieved at the time by any other means. They were certainly among the most spiritually fruitful parishes in Anglicanism. The survival and growth of evangelicalism owes much, under God, to the churches in the Simeon Trust.

Simeon gave a completely different face to patronage. The system remained but the manner in which he and his trustees exercised it was totally different from the previous norm because the motivation was now totally spiritual in its goals and its choices. Its goal was the salvation of souls through the perpetuation of the preaching of Christ crucified in strategic areas of dense population; and the men chosen needed to be not only able but also the most appropriate for the demands of the sphere of influence to which they were appointed. More important than thinking whom a church would best suit was discerning who would best suit the church: the needs of the parish were foremost.

Notes

1 **David Brainerd,** *The Diary and Journal of David Brainerd* (Edinburgh: Banner of Truth, 2007), p. 181.
2 *Memoirs of Charles Simeon*, p. 210.
3 Ibid., p. 217.
4 Ibid., p. 218.
5 Ibid., p. 219.
6 Ibid., p. 345.
7 Ibid., p. 346.
8 Ibid., p. 354.
9 Ibid., p. 454.
10 Ibid., p. 455.
11 Ibid., p. 453.
12 Ibid., pp. 354–355.
13 Ibid., p. 456.

14 Ibid., p. 457.

15 Ibid., p. 459.

16 Ibid.

17 Ibid.

18 Ibid.

19 Ibid., p. 460.

20 Ibid., p. 437.

21 Ibid.

22 Ibid., p. 436.

23 Ibid., p. 437.

24 Ibid., p. 436.

25 Ibid., p. 345.

26 Ibid.

Simeon and his
Horae Homileticae

S imeon—like many pastors and teachers—had to be something of a juggler, managing competing concerns and priorities. First and foremost he was the pastor and teacher of the congregation at Holy Trinity Church. Second, he was actively engaged in the work of missions, especially in India and among Jewish communities in Britain and beyond. But over a period of forty years he was compiling a growing collection of his sermons entitled *Horae Homileticae: Discourses upon Every Book of the Old and New Testament.* The vastness of the task becomes evident when we appreciate that if we were to read one sermon every day it would take us seven years to accomplish. How surprised Simeon would have been if he could have anticipated their current availability on a single DVD!

Theological context and background

1. THE CALVINISM AND ARMINIAN DEBATE

The issues represented by Calvinism and Arminianism were fiercely debated throughout the period of Simeon's ministry. What concerned him most was the debate's divisiveness, especially as he was convinced that the doctrines of grace expounded in Calvinism are not incompatible with the doctrine of man's free will that is at the heart of Arminianism. He stood out among his contemporaries by maintaining that we do not have to choose between the two. He argued against the position of those who said that one necessarily must be right and the other wrong.

He conceded that

Doubtless either of these points may be injudiciously stated, or improperly applied. If the doctrines of Election and Predestination be so stated as to destroy man's free agency, and make him merely passive in the work of salvation, they are not stated as they are in the Articles and Homilies of our Church, or as they are in the Holy Scriptures. On the other hand, if the doctrines of free-will and liableness to final apostasy be so stated as to rob God of his honour, and to deny that he is both 'the Author and the Finisher of our faith', they are equally abhorrent from the sentiments of our Established Church, and from the plainest declarations of Holy Writ.[1]

He tried to show 'that there is a perfect agreement between these different points; and that they are equally salutary or equally pernicious, according as they are properly or improperly applied'.[2] His hope was that in putting together all his sermons it would be clear that a faithful preacher of God's Word can preach the whole counsel of God without focusing all the time upon this great controversy that so clearly preoccupied many, stirring up unnecessary animosity and dividing genuine Christians.

2. THE CHALLENGES TO EVANGELICALISM WITHIN THE CHURCH OF ENGLAND

A further element of the theological background to the *Horae Homileticae* was the opposition within the Church of England to those who adhered to the Thirty-Nine Articles, and not least the Articles' view of Scripture—what we would call evangelicalism. Simeon hoped that the balanced approach he aimed at in expounding the Bible and which he exhibited in his *Horae Homileticae* would in some way 'counteract that spirit of animosity'.[3]

3. THE ABSENCE OF INSTRUCTION FOR MINISTERS IN PREACHING.

Horae Homileticae arose naturally from Simeon's instruction sessions for students on sermon composition. Such instruction found no place in the preparation of young men for the ministry of God's Word and no provision was available after ordination. This had been Simeon's own sad experience. As we saw in Chapter 7, his discovery of Jean Claude's *Essay on the Composition of a Sermon* had immense influence upon him. Claude's rules were so similar to those Simeon had settled upon for himself that they confirmed his confidence that he was proceeding in the right direction.

When Simeon discovered Claude's *Essay* he saw at once how invaluable and vital early instruction in the craft of sermon composition is to a young minister. It stimulated him to put together the skeletons of his own sermons—the beginnings of his *Horae Homileticae*—as a practical extension of the help Claude offered. Doing this sharpened his own ability to preach using simple outlines that could be easily remembered and subsequently preached extemporarily. He concluded that he had never really understood Claude until he set about preparing his own skeletons as a guide for others. When we aim to help and teach others, we are often those who profit the most.

Simeon readily acknowledged his debt to Claude's *Essay* and annexed it to his *Horae Homileticae*, and explained why:

The directions given in Mr Claude's *Essay on the Composition of a Sermon*, which is annexed to these Skeletons, cannot fail of being helpful to every one who will study them with care: but there appears to be something further wanted; something of an intermediate kind, between a didactic *Essay* like Claude's, and a complete Sermon; something which may simplify the theory, and set it in a practical light.[4]

His predominant aim was to 'illustrate one *general* rule; namely, to shew how texts may be treated in a *natural* manner'.[5]

He sought to achieve this by regarding 'three things as indispensably necessary in every discourse; UNITY in the design, PERSPICUITY in the arrangement, and SIMPLICITY in the diction'.[6]

Horae Homileticae's evolution

When he began Simeon had no idea what a huge task he had set himself. The appendix he provided in 1792 for his abridgement of Claude's *Essay* proved to be the seed which grew forty-one years later into twenty-one large volumes of sermon skeletons or outlines in 1833. The completion of *Horae Homileticae* proved to be one of the principal fruits of his multifaceted ministry that even now continues to bear further fruit in the Church of our Lord Jesus Christ.

The beginnings were slow. In 1796, with the publication of a revised edition of Claude's *Essay*, he added an appendix of 100 of his own skeleton sermons, several of which he had preached before the university. In 1801, 500 of his skeletons were published by the Cambridge University Press, and then between 1803 and 1814 a number of other sermons preached before the university were added. Simeon felt that he had begun a race which perhaps he did not possess the stamina to complete. He wrote to a friend,

Shall I set about a volume of about three hundred skeletons? Or, shall I set about one hundred half-hour sermons? Or, shall I write sermons of three-quarters of an hour long, and consequently make them occupy three volumes instead of two? Or, shall I mind my own business, and trouble the publisher no more? What an ease would it be to my mind, if two or three friends would join in telling me to adopt the last of these plans! I assure you I would regard them most faithfully, and most joyfully. A sow does not love the mire so much as I do idleness. May God pity, pardon, and renew, me!7

His friends' approval of his efforts greatly encouraged him to continue to issue more skeletons in further instalments, so that in September 1818 he could report to Thomas Thomason, 'I shall probably now in a few months go to press: having finished the Old Testament, and got to 2 Thessalonians in the New, besides at least one hundred sermons from the following epistles. I bless my God that he has spared me to proceed thus far; but the printing of eleven or twelve volumes will occupy two years.'[8] Only the previous year he had told Thomason, 'I feel that I am running a race against time; and I want to finish my work before "the night cometh, in which no man can work".'[9]

He involved himself meticulously in the printer's production of his material. For instance, he was concerned that in the interests of clarity and emphasis, the leading thoughts in each skeleton sermon should be in larger and bolder characters so that they could be easily recognized and thus convey to the reader more immediately the subject in view. At the same time he was concerned that they should be cheaply and economically produced so that what would ordinarily be sold for fifty guineas would be available for ten.

Essential advice for preachers

A prominent conviction behind the production of *Horae Homileticae* was his concern for the encouragement of young ministers and students for the ministry. His advice was clear and to the point.

- Identify one main subject in each sermon. He used the illustration of a telescope that focuses upon one object.
- Aim at a logical sequence of ideas. Although it is helpful to number the divisions in a sermon, the sequence of thought should be obvious without this. Clear divisions and sequence make it easier for people to remember what they hear.
- Be clear about the precise subject of the text or passage so that in what you say no other text in the Bible will suit the discourse. Every text has its proper subject, which should be brought forth without mutilation or addition of any kind. Just as each of us has an identity that distinguishes us from other people, so should every sermon.
- Be varied in your handling of the text or passage. With what may be a complicated or unusual text or passage, the emphasis may need to be upon straightforward explanation and simple application of its

relevance to the hearer. When the text or passage states something that is immediately clear, the approach may then be to apply the truth or principles to situations that are relevant to the hearers as they try to live to please God. Sometimes the right approach may be to identify the particular truth or truths that are in view in the text or passage and suggest the logical consequences of their application to Christian faith and living. Yet another approach may be continuous explanation and application.

• Aim at conciseness, clarity and simplicity.

Over the forty years of their preparation Simeon's convictions about his aims for *Horae Homileticae* found different expression. One subsidiary aim was that the skeleton outlines might be helpful on a daily basis for individuals and families to read as part of their personal or family devotions.

Simeon confessed that the targets he succeeded in accomplishing—which to the reader might seem the most simple—were those that cost him the most effort. Those who preach with the greatest simplicity and clarity are frequently those who work hardest with these aims in view.

He emphasized that he did not want his readers to become slaves to the methods and pattern he advocated and tried to exemplify. The different talents ministers possess mean that it is impossible to say what the best mode of practice is for everyone. Furthermore, following a model must not mean the abandonment of originality of thought and method. What he did insist upon were unity and clarity in developing the main subject and the straightforward arrangement of what was then preached, together with simplicity in diction. Without these characteristics the majority of hearers gain little from the preaching.

Noteworthy sermons

Simeon drew attention to his inclusion of sermons he preached before the university as being of special significance. He preached four sermons on

Deuteronomy 5:28–29 entitled 'The Excellency of the Liturgy', and another on 2 Corinthians 1:13 under the title 'The Churchman's Confession, or Appeal to the Liturgy'. Others were sermons on 1 Corinthians 2:2, entitled 'Christ Crucified, or Evangelical Religion Described' (see Appendix 2) and Psalm 119:128, with the title 'The true Test of Religion in the Soul'.

As these sermons are examined, it is clear that he used every opportunity to proclaim the simplicity of the gospel, with our Lord Jesus Christ and his atoning death at the centre. His conviction was that these sermons comprehended all the topics he regarded as of primary and fundamental importance. Although there might be a diversity of opinion upon some of the subjects raised in them, he expected these fundamental truths to be accepted by all lovers of God's truth.

Criticisms

Simeon's *Horae Homileticae* inevitably provoked criticism, some of which he anticipated. Typical charges against him are easy to identify.

- He was encouraging men to be lazy and idle in using them.
- He was altogether too logical and purposeful in his presentation of the truth.
- He was too deliberate in his use of Bible language.
- He looked at every Scripture strictly in its context rather than in relation to any human systematization of the Bible's teaching.
- Expressing the whole substance of a sermon in a few pages made the sermon too brief.

His answer, for example, to the first criticism, concerning the encouragement of idleness, was that his skeletons were 'so constructed, that they cannot possibly be used at all, unless a considerable degree of thought be bestowed upon them. Nor does he think that any person, who has ever found the pleasure of addressing his congregation in his own words, will be satisfied with reciting the compositions of another.'[10] He maintained that if the alternative for some men was to preach word for word the sermons of others, at least his skeletons demanded some thought and 'flesh' to be added to them, which were steps towards the men composing their own sermons.

He agreed that brevity could lead to truth not being fully expressed, but his purpose was not to do the preacher's work for him. He was, after all, only providing the raw materials that the preacher must polish. His defence of his approach did not mean that he was not open to either criticism or correction. He admitted his fear of appearing presumptuous to his fellow-ministers and hoped that they would pardon any faults they found in his work as they recognized that it was a humble labour of love intended for the greater usefulness of his readers. He wanted 'to render their entrance on their holy and honourable calling more easy and their prosecution of it more useful'.[11]

Nunc Dimittis

The compilation and publication of *Horae Homileticae* was the final task Simeon longed to complete before his death. It took thirty-two men sixteen months to achieve its printing. He wrote on the volumes' publication,

This day God has vouchsafed to me the two richest blessings (next to the enjoyment of himself) that my soul could desire: 1. I have this day received from the Archbishop of Canterbury his permission to dedicate my work to him; 2. I have this day received the last five volumes, and see the work complete—the ship launched. This last was the only thing for which I wished to live, so to speak, and I now sing my *Nunc dimittis*.[12]

In a diary that he kept for a brief while in 1833 he described their completion as one of three great mercies of which he confessed himself aware: 'What wonderful things have I been spared to behold! 1. Union and harmony and love throughout my whole parish, together with an increased attention to religion. 2. My jubilee completed, and kept with such devout affection. 3. My entire work out, presented, and, as far as I know, approved.'[13]

Presentations

Having received the Archbishop of Canterbury's permission to dedicate his work to him, Simeon made the first presentation of the completed volumes to him and then to the Archbishop of York. He knew that the Archbishop of Canterbury's endorsement would abate prejudice in Britain and aid the volumes' acceptance abroad among the foreign courts to which he would send them.

He then had the honour of presenting them to His Majesty King William IV in a private audience in London. All the foreign ambassadors promised to transmit them to the courts they represented. Prince Tallyrand, the French Ambassador, sent his immediately to Paris. All the Cambridge colleges received copies for their libraries, and in the set given to St John's he wrote,

A Present from the Author, in the humble hope, and with earnest prayer to God, that his efforts to diffuse the knowledge of Christ with all the wonders of Redeeming Love may not be in vain. Now if this change alone were wrought in a college so extensively influential, it were worth all the labour and expense I have bestowed on my plan of presentations.[14]

The sales of earlier versions from as early as 1817 and then of the completed sets gave rise to considerable income and this, together with donations from friends, meant that Simeon was able to add some larger livings to his trust.

Notes

1 *Memoirs of Charles Simeon*, p. 106.

2 Ibid.

3 Ibid., p. 102.

4 Preface, *Horae Homileticae*, vol. 1, p. v.

5 Ibid., p. 84.

6 *Memoirs of Charles Simeon*, p. 84.

7 Ibid., p. 87.

8 Ibid., p. 289.

9 Ibid., p. 259.

10 Preface, *Horae Homileticae*, vol. 1, p. xi.

11 Ibid.

12 *Memoirs of Charles Simeon*, p. 417. *Nunc dimittis* are the first two words in Latin of what is known as Simeon's song in Luke 2:29–32, when he expresses his readiness to die because he has witnessed the coming of the Saviour into the world.

13 Ibid., p. 424.

14 Ibid., p. 420.

Simeon and the principle of balance

W hen preparing this chapter, several possible titles came to mind, such as 'Simeon and Calvinism', 'Simeon and Where Truth Is to be Found' or 'Simeon and the Unity of God's People'. I have opted for 'Simeon and the Principle of Balance' because behind each of these contending titles is this basic conviction that motivated him in relation to each and which has had the greatest impact on my thinking.

Calvinism and Arminianism

The issue that separated many Christians at the end of the eighteenth and the beginning of the nineteenth centuries was the Calvinism versus Arminianism debate. Simeon lived close to that period when two figureheads and spiritual leaders represented these apparently opposing positions. George Whitefield had died in 1770, when Simeon was eleven, and John Wesley in 1791, when Simeon was thirty-two. Whitefield's and Wesley's views and understanding of God's sovereignty separated not only them but also those who were in many ways their disciples.

God's sovereignty

Simeon's clear and certain convictions about God's sovereignty were frequently expressed in his exposition of Scripture. He was no enemy of Calvinism in its essentials. Attacks were made upon him by many in the university because of his Calvinism and evangelicalism. None were in doubt that he preached two evangelical essentials: the total corruption of human nature and justification by faith alone. In 1815 and 1816 he wrote letters about 'two most excellent young men' who had been 'refused orders for inclining towards Calvinism'.[1] Always respectful of episcopal authority, he wrote, 'The bishop has acted a most unjustifiable part towards them; but I believe he meant to do right. What will be the issue of it?'[2] Later he described the bishop's action as a 'most cruel persecution'.[3]

A memorable conversation

Although more of a Calvinist than an Arminian, Simeon was not a fierce enemy of the latter. This was demonstrated in the often quoted conversation with John Wesley, recorded by Wesley himself in his journal on 20 December 1784. Simeon had travelled to Hinxworth, a Hertfordshire village thirty miles from Cambridge, where Wesley was conducting meetings. Wesley wrote,

I had the satisfaction of meeting Mr Simeon, Fellow of King's College in Cambridge. He has spent some time with Mr Fletcher of Madeley; two kindred souls, much resembling each other in fervour of spirit and earnestness of their address. He gave me the pleasing information that there are three parish churches in Cambridge (i.e. Holy Trinity, St Edward's and the Round Church) wherein true Scriptural religion is preached, and several young gentlemen who are happy partakers of it.[4]

In both the Preface to his *Horae Homileticae* and his *Memoirs* Simeon recorded the conversation they had together, although without giving their names. It clearly influenced the way he later approached controversies among believers. (Simeon's and Wesley's names have been added below to aid understanding.)

A young minister, about three or four years after he was ordained, had an opportunity of conversing familiarly with the great and venerable leader of the Arminians in this kingdom; and, wishing to improve the occasion to the uttermost, he addressed him nearly in the following words:

'Sir,' ventured Simeon, 'I understand that you are called an Arminian; and I have been sometimes called a Calvinist; and therefore I suppose we are to draw daggers. But before I consent to begin the combat, with your permission I will ask you a few questions, not from impertinent curiosity, but for real instruction … Pray Sir, do you feel yourself a depraved creature, so depraved that you would never have thought of turning to God if God had not first put it into your heart?'

'Yes, I do indeed,' replied Wesley.

'And do you utterly despair of recommending yourself to God by anything you can do; and look for salvation solely through the blood and righteousness of Christ?'

'Yes, solely through Christ.'

'But, Sir, supposing you were first saved by Christ, are you not somehow or other to save yourself afterwards by your own works?'

'No; I must be saved by Christ from first to last.'

'Allowing then that you were first turned by the grace of God, are you not in some way or other to keep yourself by your own power?'

'No.'

'What then, are you to be upheld every hour and every moment by God, as much as an infant in its mother's arms?'

'Yes, altogether.'

'And is all your hope in the grace and mercy of God to preserve you unto his heavenly kingdom?'

'Yes, I have no hope but in him.'

'Then, Sir, with your leave, I will put up my dagger again; for this is all my Calvinism; this is my election, my justification by faith, my final perseverance; it is, in substance, all that I hold, and as I hold it, and therefore, if you please, instead of searching out terms and phrases to be a ground of contention between us, we will cordially unite in those things wherein we agree.'[5]

God's providence in the Christians we meet and the influence of such meetings on our lives may not be immediately obvious but, nevertheless, profoundly important, and that was certainly the case here.

Distortion of truth through extremes

Extremes that distorted the truth particularly disturbed Simeon. He maintained that Calvinism and Arminianism are 'equally salutary or equally pernicious according as they are properly or improperly applied'.[6] It was this debate that brought about his conviction that in matters that divide Christians or which Christians debate, the truth often exists in both extremes and not necessarily in the middle.

He used the illustration of a watch, especially relevant before the invention of digital watches and batteries. If we look at the inner workings of a grandfather clock or an old pocket watch, we see wheels going in different directions. We do not need to understand the mechanics of how it all works to benefit from the clock telling us the correct time. 'Don't you know, my dear brother,' he said to a friend, 'that the wheels of your watch move in opposite directions? Yet they are all tending to one result?'[7]

He expressed his conviction more fully in his introduction to *Horae Homileticae*:

He [referring to himself] has no doubt but that there is a system in the Holy Scriptures (for truth cannot be inconsistent with itself); but he is persuaded that neither Calvinists nor Arminians are in exclusive possession of that system. He is disposed to think that the Scripture system, be it what it may, is of a broader and more comprehensive character than some very exact and dogmatical theologians are inclined to allow: and that, as wheels in a complicated machine may move in opposite directions and yet subserve one common end, so may truths *apparently opposite* be perfectly reconcilable with each other, and equally subserve the purposes of God in the accomplishment of man's salvation.[8]

Understanding this principle, he maintained, would bring an end to much controversy and 'polemical bitterness', resulting instead in 'harmony of faith and doctrine'.[9]

Applications of the principle

Simeon's sermons and writings provide a number of illustrations of the existence of truth not in the middle but in both extremes. The first, and primary, application, as we have seen, was to the Calvinist and Arminian debate because he was convinced that the distinctive emphases of both Calvinists and Arminians to the neglect of this principle obscures the fact that they are in harmony.

Using again his picture of the wheels of machinery going in opposite directions, he declared,

The one party have taken all those passages which represent God as a Sovereign, dispensing his blessings according to his own will and pleasure, and have made all the rest of the Scriptures bend to them: the other party have done the same with respect to the passages which assert the freedom of the human will, and which speak of men as the sole authors of their own condemnation. It seems never to enter into the minds of either party, that those passages which they set at variance, may, like wheels moving in opposite directions, be in perfect harmony with each other; and that there may be a subserviency, where they see nothing but direct opposition. If they were once brought to consider this, they would be more candid in their interpretation of each other's sentiments, and more cautious of wresting from their plain and obvious meaning the passages which they cannot reconcile with their own exclusive system.[10]

To use Paul's phrase in 2 Timothy 2:15, he longed that all might 'correctly handle the word of truth'. He expressed his thoughts most clearly in the Preface to the *Horae Homileticae*:

It is supposed by many, that the doctrines of grace are incompatible with the doctrine of man's free-will; and that therefore the one or the other must be false. But why so? Can any man doubt one moment whether he be a free agent or not? he may as well doubt his own existence. On the other hand, will any man who has the smallest spark of humility affirm, that he has 'made himself to differ; and that he has something which he has not received' from a superior power? (1 Cor. iv.7) Will anyone refuse to say with the apostle, 'By the grace of God I am what I am'? (1 Cor. xv.10)[11]

Again; as men differ with respect to the first beginnings of a work of grace, so do they also with respect to the manner in which it must be carried on; some affirming, that God has engaged to 'perfect that which concerneth us'; and others, that even St Paul had reason to fear 'lest he himself should become a castaway'. But why should these things be deemed incompatible? Does not every man feel within himself a liableness, yea, a proneness to fall? Does not every man feel that there is corruption enough within him to drive him to the commission of the greatest enormities, and eternally to destroy his soul? He can have but little knowledge of his own heart who will deny this. On the other hand, who that is holding on in the ways of righteousness, does not daily ascribe his steadfastness to the influence of that grace, which he receives from God; and look daily to God for more grace, in order that he may be 'kept by his power through faith unto salvation'? (1 Peter 1:5) No man can in any measure resemble the Scripture saints, unless he be of this disposition. Why then must these things be put in opposition to each other, so that every advocate for one of these points must of necessity controvert and explode the other? Only let any pious person, whether Calvinist or Arminian, examine the language of his prayers after he has been devoutly pouring out his soul before God, and he will find his own words almost in perfect consonance with the foregoing statement. The Calvinist will be confessing the extreme depravity of his nature, together with his liability and proneness to fall; and the Arminian will be glorifying God for all that is good within him, and will commit his soul to God, in order that he who has laid the foundation of his own spiritual temple, may also finish it.[12]

Simeon argued that gospel truths need to be held in balance, a balance the Bible itself so clearly exhibits. Convinced of the perfect correspondence between God's works of providence and grace, he was concerned that they should be so stated as to profit the souls of men and women rather than perplex them. He wrote,

There seems to be a perfect correspondence between God's works of providence and grace: in the former, 'he worketh all things according to the counsel of his own will', yet leaves men perfectly free agents in all that they do; so in the latter, he accomplishes his own eternal purpose both in calling, and in keeping, his elect; but yet he never puts upon them any constraint, which is not perfectly compatible with the freest operations of their own will.[13]

Expressions of balance in Simeon's sermons

The most powerful illustration Simeon gave of the truth being found in both extremes rather than in an endeavour to reconcile them was of the teaching of our Lord Jesus Christ. In John 5:40 Jesus says, 'you refuse to come to me to have life,' and in John 6:44 he says, 'No one can come to me unless the Father who sent me draws him.' In preaching on John 5 Simeon did not hesitate 'to lay the whole blame of men's condemnation on the obstinacy of their own depraved will', and he did not 'think it at all necessary to weaken the subject by nice distinctions, in order to support a system'.[14] 'On the contrary'; when he preached on John 6:44 he did not hesitate to state in the fullest way possible 'that we have no power to do

good works pleasant and acceptable to God, without the grace of God'—
an important truth he did not wish 'to soften, and palliate, and fritter
away'.[15] Rather than setting the two truths in opposition he wanted to
dwell upon both 'with equal pleasure'.[16]

His introduction to a sermon on 1 Timothy 2:3–4 ('God our Saviour …
wants all men to be saved and to come to a knowledge of the truth') sums
up his convictions on this issue:

It is truly lamentable to see how men, in every age, have strained and wrested the Holy
Scriptures, in order to make them speak the language of their own particular creed.
Some, averse to the idea that God should express his good-will to all the sinners of
mankind, limit the word 'all', and make it signify nothing more than some of all
descriptions and characters; whilst others run to a contrary extreme, and deduce from
this expression a persuasion that none shall ever perish. It were well, if, instead of
contending for human systems, and especially those of Calvin and Arminius, we were
content to receive the Scriptures with the simplicity of little children: for, after all that
has been said or written in support of those two most prominent systems, it is
impossible to reduce the Holy Scriptures either to the one or to the other of them: for,
on both hypotheses, there are difficulties which can never be surmounted, and
contrarieties which man can never reconcile. It is by attempting to be wise above what
is written, that we involve ourselves in all these difficulties.

If we would be content to take the Scriptures as they are, and to leave the reconciling of
them unto God, by whose inspiration they were written, we should find them all
admirably calculated to produce the ends for which they were designed. How delightful
is the truth here intimated! and how strange is it, that, instead of enjoying it, and adoring
God for it, men will make it only a ground of acrimonious contention! I thank God, that
all the Scriptures, whatever be their bearing, are alike acceptable to me; and that,
whether they mark the sovereignty or the mercy of God, I am alike ready to prosecute
them, in accordance with their plain and obvious meaning. By attending to the original,
we shall often find our way clear, when, from a diversity of idiom, a translation scarcely

conveys the precise idea. The passage before us, for instance, does not convey in the original anything like a secret determination in God, but only a willingness, that all should be saved: it is precisely parallel with what is spoken by St Peter, when he says, 'God is long-suffering to us-ward; not willing that any should perish, but that all should come to repentance.' And this is assigned as a reason why God would have us pray for all men. Our intercessions for them are pleasing and acceptable to him, because 'he is willing to save all', without exception and without reserve.[17]

Perseverance of the saints

A further application of this principle of balance relates to the perseverance of the saints and the danger of our making shipwreck of the faith. Simeon suggested,

Suppose a person say, 'I need not be careful about my conduct'; for 'God has begun the good work within me, and has engaged to perform it till the day of Christ': if we were to begin extolling the covenant of grace, and setting forth the truth of God in his promises, we should countenance his error, at the very time that he was turning the grace of God into licentiousness. But if we should warn him against the danger of being given over to a reprobate mind, and of perishing under an accumulated load of guilt, we should counteract his sinful disposition, and stimulate him to flee from the wrath to come. On the other hand, if a humble person should be drooping and desponding under a sense of his own corruptions, and we should spread before him all our difficulties and dangers, we should altogether 'break the bruised reed, and quench the smoking flax': but if we should point out to him the fullness and stability of God's covenant; if we should enlarge upon the interest which Christ takes in his people, and his engagements that none shall ever pluck them out of his hand; it is obvious, that we should administer a cordial to his fainting spirit, or (as God requires of us) we should 'strengthen the weak hands, and confirm the feeble knees, and comfort the fearful heart'.[18]

Church government

The principle of balance and the truth being in both extremes applies to church government. Sadly, Christians are denominated more often by their views of church government than by their allegiance to our Lord Jesus Christ. For example, we are labelled as Episcopalians, Presbyterians, Congregationalists and Independents, according to how we consider Christians should govern their corporate life. While the New Testament lays down principles, it does not provide a dogmatic pattern of church government, perhaps because God's purpose is to give flexibility according to times and circumstances. As Simeon put it, 'There is no precise line in scripture drawn with respect to church government: yet the whole Christian church is filled with dissensions and animosities, because all will dogmatize for others, instead of conceding to each other a liberty to judge for themselves, and being content with that apostolic dogma, "let all things be done decently and in order".'[19]

The Sabbath principle

The principle applies equally to our attitude to Sunday and keeping one day special; an issue in Simeon's day and in our own, although in a different context. Some stress a strict observance of the Sabbath principle and others do not give biblical status to the Sunday tradition as binding for the individual or the church, challenging the theology that has been developed to justify it. The torrent of literature is complex and often confusing to the ordinary Christian.

Simeon's balance, expressed in a letter to someone who was concerned over the issue, is one to be emulated:

My views are these: that the spiritual observance of the Sabbath is to be as strict as ever: but that the ritual observance is not. John came neither eating nor drinking: Christ came both eating and drinking; yea, and wrought his first miracle at a marriage-feast: and why? I answer, To show the character of his dispensation, as contrasted with that which it was to supersede. (Of course you will understand me as referring to the liberal spirit of it, in opposition to the servile spirit of the other.) His dining on a Sabbath with a large party on one occasion marked the same.

Now to give you somewhat of a definite view of my judgment on the question. In my own personal habit I am as strict as most: but in my judgment, as before God, I think that many religious characters—ministers as well as others—are in error. I think that many Judaize too much, and that they would have joined the Pharisees in condemning our Lord on many occasions.

N. B. I do not think that they err in acting up to their own principles (there they are right); but that they err in making their own standard a standard for all others. This is a prevailing evil among religious persons. They will in effect argue thus: I do not walk out on a Sabbath-day; therefore an artisan may not walk out into the fields for an hour on that day. They forget that the poor man is confined all the rest of the week, which they are not; and that they themselves will walk in their own garden, when the poor have no garden to walk in. Now in this I do not think that they act towards others, as they, in a change of circumstances, would think it right for others to act towards them: and if your brother will limit his refreshment to such a relaxation as is necessary for health, or materially conducive to it, I shall agree with him, and shall rank this amongst works of necessity or of charity.

Again, I am not prepared to utter either anathemas or lamentations, if ministers of state occasionally, in a time of great pressure of public business, and in a quiet way, avail themselves of an hour or two for conference with each other on that day. I do not commend it; but I do not condemn it. They cannot command their own times. Public affairs may be full as pressing, and may call for immediate conference as much as an ox or an ass for deliverance from a pit into which it may have fallen; and I think that love to one's country may justify a deviation from a ritual observance of the Sabbath, as much as love or pity for a beast. In fact, if the most scrupulous will examine the frame of their own minds, and the real spirituality of their own conversation for two or three hours on some part of the Sabbath, they will find but little right, whatever their disposition be, to cast a stone at a poor man with his family, or at a minister of state with his compeers. Again I say, they may be right: but the others who think and act differently are not therefore wrong. Those who ate, and those who refused to eat, meats offered to idols, were both right, if they acted to the Lord; as were those also who observed, and those who did not observe, certain days, which under the Jewish dispensation were actually prescribed.

I will tell you what I consider the perfect rule: Let all judge for themselves in relation to the ritual observance of such matters; the strong not despising the weak, and the weak forbearing to sit in judgment on the strong. This will be the surest and best discharge of the duty of all parties, whether to God or man: to God, who has said, 'I will have mercy, and not sacrifice'; and to man, who should be left to stand or fall to his own Master.

Whoever neglects the spiritual duties of the day is assuredly wrong; and whoever accounts the ritual observance of it a burden is wrong also. But to Judaize with Pharisaic strictness is not well; and to condemn others for not acting up to that standard is, I think, very undesirable.[20]

If we keep Simeon's balance, we will neither flood it with the mundane nor freeze it with the forbidden. We will rejoice in Sunday as an opportunity to display our love for God and as the market-day of the soul, not as a tedious burden but as a means of grace, making it special without falling into legalism.

Being in the world but not of it

Another area of life for the application of this principle of balance is our being dead to the world, on the one hand, and our not separating ourselves from the world to the point, on the other hand, where we have no impact for good upon the people of the world. Bearing in mind Paul's admonition in Romans 12:2 to no longer conform to the pattern of this world, Simeon asked,

Who shall draw a precise line in everything, and say, 'Thus far you may go, and no farther'? Who shall undertake to say to a poor man, 'You must not visit a poor neighbour': or to a gentleman, 'You must not show courtesy to a neighbouring gentleman': or to a peer, 'You must not pay a customary respect to him whose peer (by creation at least) he is'! In my mind, it is a question of degrees, as far as acts are concerned; and a question of inclination, as far as the habits are concerned.

In the habit of our mind we should be altogether dead to the world; but in our acts we are not so called to separate from all ungodly persons as to have no intercourse with them whatever; for then, as the apostle says, 'we must needs go out of the world'; whereas our blessed Lord prayed 'not that we should be taken out of the world, but be kept from the evil of it'. If we think that by going out of the world we shall get rid of all difficulties, we shall find ourselves mistaken. We may change our difficulties; but we shall not divest ourselves of them altogether; nor is it unqualified good that we shall do by such conduct. We may make our own path easier: but, if we cast a stumbling-block in the way of multitudes, whom by more temperate measures we might have conciliated, we shall have no reason to glory in the choice that we have made. In my opinion, it is not by abandoning our situation in life that we are to honour God, but by being examples in it, and by filling it to his glory. And, if we desire to fill it to his glory, and pray earnestly to God for grace to do so, we may expect him to direct us in all our way, and to uphold us by his power that our footsteps slip not.[21]

To shut ourselves up entirely from the world, and put our light under a bushel, is the more easy: but to be 'blameless and harmless as sons of God, without rebuke, in the midst of a crooked and perverse nation, shining among them as lights in the world, and holding forth among them the word of life' (Phil. ii. 15–16) is in my opinion more worthy of our profession, more honourable to our God, and more beneficial to those whose welfare we are bound to seek.[22]

Simeon had his own battles to fight on this subject, coming as he did from a background where the pleasures of the world were important and where he had sampled most of them. 'I know in a measure what the blessed word of God says in relation to our separation from the world, and I know in a measure the line of conduct that befits my own situation in life.'[23] But he was hesitant about defining the conduct of others. 'My own habits, instead of inspiring me with confidence in relation to others, only make me the more diffident.'[24] Wisdom and love dictated this attitude.

Missions: their members and the committees that govern them

An interesting and perhaps unlikely application of this principle is from another sphere altogether: the relationship of what may sometimes appear as the competing importance of missionary societies' committees and their members on the field. As we have seen, Simeon was heavily involved in a number of missionary enterprises, especially in India and among the Jews. Inevitably, such endeavours needed the active involvement of God's people at home to support those working in these areas and this meant the setting up of committees. But there is always the danger that committees become too important and forget the priority needs of those they represent. Applying this principle of balance, Simeon stressed that both are equally important in their place.

The societies are nothing without their representatives, and the representatives are dependent upon their committees. They should not, therefore, be considered rivals. He expressed it like this:

Societies are like the cabinet of ministers, who send out armies, and sit at home, and get some credit: but it is the armies that strike the blow, and that are God's instruments to us for good. Yet the cabinets are of use in their place, though they may sometimes be wrong in their judgment … And if all committees were more earnest in prayer to God for direction, they would do better. Still, however, there must be committees, as well as cabinets; and where there are men, there will be mistakes, and errors, and infirmities; and if we expect only from men what savours strongly of human infirmity, we shall be less stumbled by their errors … Let us not expect too much from man; but look simply to the Lord, to act by them, or without them, or against them, as he pleases. We will be thankful for all the good that he does, either by individuals or societies: for whether Paul plant, or Apollos water, it is 'God alone who gives the increase'. And whilst in our desires we will be enlarged to the uttermost, we will be moderate in our expectations (the golden mean[25] may here be used); and let neither our joys so prevail as to dispel our sorrows, nor our sorrows so prevail as to overwhelm our joys.[26]

An appropriate and reasonable approach

Simeon was firmly convinced that this principle of balance is especially appropriate when handling the truths of Scripture. Rather than choosing between two apparently opposite views, it is better to 'dwell with equal pleasure on them both' and to state the 'apparently opposite truths in the plain and unsophisticated manner of the Scriptures, than to enter into scholastic subtleties that have been invented for the upholding of human systems'.[27] He was aware

that they who are warm advocates for this or that system of religion, will be ready to condemn him as inconsistent: but, if he speak in exact conformity with the Scriptures, he shall rest the vindication of his conduct simply on the authority and example of the inspired writers. He has no desire to be wise above what is written, nor any conceit that he can teach the apostles to speak with more propriety and correctness than they have spoken.[28]

The application of this principle meant that in some things he appeared strongly Calvinistic and in others strongly Arminian.

As well as this being an appropriate approach, Simeon believed it to be eminently reasonable. He regarded these sentiments as being confirmed in Paul's clear practice of administering God's Word to believers in the light of his understanding of their spiritual state, apportioning to them 'either "milk or strong meat", according to their ability to digest and improve it'. He added,

In reference to this we may say, that the doctrines of human liberty, and human frailty, together with the other first principles of Christianity, are as milk, which those who are yet 'babes in Christ', must have set before them: but that the doctrines of grace, or 'the deep things of God', are rather as strong meat, which none can digest, unless they have grown to some stature in the family of Christ, and have had their spiritual senses long exercised in discerning good and evil: and that, as strong meat, which would nourish an adult, would destroy the life of an infant; and milk that would nourish an infant, would be inadequate to the support of a man oppressed with hard labour; so it is with respect to the points which we have been considering. Or, if we may be permitted a little to vary this illustration, the one sort of truths are as food proper to be administered to all; whereas the other are rather as cordials for the support and comfort of those who need them.[29]

Convinced that much of the controversy and polemical bitterness that separates true believers arises from systematization, he felt it eminently reasonable that our commitment should not be so much to positions on particular doctrines but to the totality of Scripture, and that we should meet on Scripture ground rather than on the basis of a theological position. He wanted to be committed to God's revelation, wherever that might lead him, always coming to the Scriptures like a child wanting to be taught. This explains why he tried as much as possible to dissociate himself from names and parties, and why he was so cautious about attachment and loyalty to any human system that meant that he could not give his assent to every part of God's Word.

Christian unity

Such a mind-set and determination gives a powerful clue to Simeon's contribution to Christian unity. The danger of systems or systematic theologies is that they become exclusive in the minds of their supporters, not allowing anything else as compatible. They may breed a sense of infallibility in our presentation of our views and a false judgement of others. Truths that should build up believers and unite them then become a stumbling block and a cause of division. Because of our commitment to systems of theology rather than to Scripture, we find ourselves too ready to judge others, contrary to God's intention that we should not do so, and not least on secondary matters. Simeon was grieved at the disunity among believers of his time and of the acrimonious way in which we may speak of fellow-Christians.

His concern was to unite rather than to divide believers, and this made him willing to overlook all smaller differences of sentiment in order to unite in vindicating the great doctrines of salvation by grace through faith in Christ. He vigorously maintained that to meet on Scripture ground rather than on any other, not attempting to be wise above what is written, is the way to avoid many of the controversies and contentions that spoil fellowship and dishonour the church's witness to the truth as it is in our Lord Jesus Christ. He grieved that through needless divisions among God's people it might appear that Christ did indeed come to introduce division, not accidentally, but intentionally; not by a separation of his people from the world, but by an alienation of heart from one another. But when views of secondary issues are held moderately, unity is preserved because unnecessary controversy is avoided. Part of his attachment to the Church of England was due to the moderation of its Thirty-Nine Articles and its ability to include both Calvinists and Arminians. If we disagree with him, we must ask ourselves whether it is because of our attachment to a human system of theology— no matter how good—or because of our attachment to the Scriptures and their balance.

Perhaps the final underlying truth behind Simeon's aim for balance was his determination to act in the spirit of the final words of Paul's letter to the Ephesians: 'Grace to all who love our Lord Jesus Christ with an undying love.' Whatever our views, love must characterize our conduct and presentation of the truth. He was acutely aware of the snare of entering into judgement over fellow-Christians rather than loving them, and that a test of loving his Master was recognizing and loving all who belonged to him.

No doubt remembering how zeal had distorted his judgement when he was a young man, he made this interesting comment in a letter in May 1823, when he was sixty-three:

The difference between young and old ministers, in general, consists in this; that the statements of the former are crude and unqualified, whilst those of the latter have such limitations and distinctions, as the Scriptures authorize and the subjects require. The doctrines of salvation by faith alone and of predestination, &c., are often, it is well known, so stated, as to become a stumbling-block to thousands; whilst, when Scripturally stated, they approve themselves to those who have been most prejudiced against them.[30]

In different ways he pointed out that if we allow ourselves to be sidetracked from the fundamentals of the gospel to subjects upon which Christians may legitimately have different views, we may be led away from the centrality of the cross and the practical and heart-searching doctrines the Bible presents to us. If we allow ourselves to be sidetracked from the main truths of the gospel we may be guilty of sleeping while men and women perish. Get the doctrine of the cross central and everything else will fall into its proper place. We must remember that Simeon was a gospel man.

Biblical moderation
At Simeon's death particular attention was drawn to his moderation—or balance—by Daniel Wilson, the Bishop of Calcutta. He declared, 'He

was full of moderation on doubtful and abstruse questions connected with the commanding truths' of 'the Fall and Recovery of Man—of the Atonement of Christ, and the operations of the Spirit—of justification by faith, and regeneration and progressive sanctification by grace—of holy love to God and man, and of all good works as the fruit of faith, and following after justification'.[31]

His was 'the true scriptural moderation arising from a sense of man's profound ignorance, and of the danger of attempting to proceed one step beyond the fair and obvious import of Divine Revelation. In this sense he was moderate.'[32]

Notes

1 *Memoirs of Charles Simeon*, p. 241.
2 Ibid.
3 Ibid., p. 247.
4 Entry in *John Wesley's Journal* for 20 December 1784.
5 Preface, *Horae Homileticae*, vol. 1, pp. xvii–xviii, footnote.
6 *Memoirs of Charles Simeon*, p. 106.
7 Ibid., p. 394.
8 Ibid., p. 310.
9 Ibid., p. 394.
10 Discourse 2229, *Horae Homileticae*, vol. 18.
11 *Memoirs of Charles Simeon*, p. 105.
12 Ibid.
13 Ibid., p. 108.
14 Preface, *Horae Homileticae*, vol. 1, p. xix.
15 *Memoirs of Charles Simeon*, p. 103.
16 Ibid.
17 Discourse 2228, *Horae Homileticae*, vol. 18.
18 *Memoirs of Charles Simeon*, p. 107.
19 Ibid., p. 343.
20 Ibid., p. 404.
21 Ibid., p. 343.

22 Ibid., p. 344.

23 Ibid., pp. 340–341.

24 Ibid., p. 341.

25 The 'golden mean' expresses the helpfulness of remembering that, on issues that often divide Christians, often the truth is to be found not in the middle, and not in one extreme, but in both extremes at the same time.

26 Ibid., p. 353.

27 Ibid., p. 103.

28 Ibid., pp. 103–104.

29 Ibid., p. 107.

30 Ibid., p. 341.

31 Ibid., p. 486.

32 Ibid., p. 488.

Weaknesses and strengths

Since Simeon stands out as such a significant figure who achieved so much we may be inclined to overlook his faults and weaknesses. Neither he nor his friends did. Essentially, he was a man in whom God's good work of sanctification was proceeding. The failings he manifested, especially as a young man, were brought under control as he grew in the knowledge of his Saviour.

Not having himself in mind, he wrote,

It is of great importance that the infirmities of eminent servants of God should ever be faithfully recorded; in order that we may learn what trials and conflicts they had to endure, and how they gained power and strength to have victory against the devil, the world and the flesh. Thus shall we be the more led to magnify God for his grace bestowed upon them, and at the same time derive comfort and hope for ourselves, when endeavouring to subdue our own besetting sins.[1]

Anger

Simeon identified his quick temper as one of his principal failings. His natural disposition was to maintain his rights. He admitted his 'constitutional vehemence and warmth of temper'.[2] Using a word unfamiliar in contemporary language, he wrote, 'I have all my days felt my danger to lie on the side of precipitancy.'[3] An outbreak of his anger at a servant who put the wrong bridle upon his horse caused him to write a letter of apology, signing it, 'CHAS. PROUD AND IRRITABLE'.[4] As he looked back upon his relationship as a young Christian with his father he acknowledged that, rather than getting angry with him, he should have had compassion upon his father in his old age.

He confessed, 'My own natural disposition would have instigated me to maintain my rights by force; and I knew I could never do wrong in resisting my corrupt nature.'[5] He then took an illustration from the game of bowls.

Like a bowl with a strong bias, I could not go far out of the way on the side opposite to that bias; or if I did, I should have always something to bring me back; but if I leaned to the side where that force was in operation, I might be precipitated I knew not whither, and should have nothing to counteract the impulse, or to bring me back. There was no doubt, therefore, in my mind, which was the safer and better path for me to pursue.[6]

Bad temper was linked with irritability, and that in turn was aggravated by the many occasions he suffered from gout. So severe was his gout that he needed to be carried up and down stairs on men's shoulders or put into and taken out of his 'carriage like a log of wood'.[7] Similarly, he had to be helped into his pulpit on a Sunday.

Personal vanity and pride

His temper and irritability were easily provoked through feelings of vanity and self-importance, a subject of conflict and trial to him during the whole of his life. At school these feelings displayed themselves in too great an attention to the way he dressed, and 'in little peculiarities of manner, which quickly attracted the notice and provoked the ridicule of his companions'.[8] As he looked back upon his life before his conversion he felt the deepest shame and sorrow at his vanity. 'To enter into a detail of particulars would answer no good end. If I be found at last a prodigal restored to his Father's house, God will in no ordinary measure be glorified in me; the abundance of my sinfulness will display in most affecting colours the superabundance of his grace.'[9]

Writing to his good friend John Venn on the latter's ordination, he confessed, 'I am so poor, so weak, so ignorant, and yet so vain, that I stand highly in need of your prayers and intercessions for me.

Lukewarmness and vanity are Scylla and Charybdis.[10] Oh, may the Lord Jesus Christ enable us both to steer clear of them!'[11]

We referred in Chapter 4 to Simeon's encouraging weeks at St Edward's Church soon after his ordination, but that in itself brought problems to the control of his vanity, which was 'fed and indulged'[12] by people's appreciation. The danger continued. Writing much later from Scotland he said, 'I desire to give glory to my God for all the love which I meet with, and ardently wish that it may be the means of humbling me in the dust, and not puffing me up with pride, as though I merited such regard.'[13] He also writes of God dealing with his pride when absent from his congregation for four months of ministry in Scotland. He was foolishly tempted to imagine that the congregation would suffer and diminish through his absence.

Over-attention to detail

On occasions Simeon could have been accused of too great a meticulousness. In August 1831 he entered into correspondence with a lawyer about an exorbitant bill. To ensure all possible accuracy in his accounts, as well as to prevent or detect errors, he not only kept his Journal and Ledger in a way of double-entry, but had them regularly balanced by an experienced person at three different periods of the year.

On one of these occasions an error was observed, to the amount of but one penny. This exceedingly annoyed Simeon, and after some days of fruitless search to discover the mistake, he insisted on the accountant taking away with him the books and never remitting his efforts till he had detected the error. 'There! make it out for me, cost what it will; I'll not have my books wrong even by a penny—make it out for me you shall—and I'll give you twenty pounds!'[14] After a lot of time-consuming work the error was discovered. So great was Simeon's delight that he instantly wrote a cheque for the twenty pounds.

Hasty judgement

Linked with quickness of temper often goes a tendency to pass judgement too speedily upon the conduct of others. What prompts this as an observation of Simeon's weaknesses—and I may be mistaken—is his comment on William Carey and his translation colleagues. In March 1812 a fire broke out at Serampore in the printing works while Carey was in Calcutta. Much more important than the premises were the valuable translation manuscripts that were destroyed, meaning that years of work on them were lost.

In August the following year Simeon wrote to Thomas Thomason in India,

I have always thought that the missionaries were too much warped by a desire to appear great benefactors to India; and when I heard of the fire at Serampore, I could not but think that God designed to teach them by it some valuable lessons. What a joy would it be to my soul, to hear from themselves some acknowledgment of their error in this respect! But that is too much to expect from such proud creatures as we are.[15]

Simeon may have been right in his judgement, but it is perhaps an opinion that he would have done better to have kept to himself and certainly not to have put in writing.

Openness to correction

Observations on Simeon's weaknesses need to be balanced by the spiritual strengths they developed and revealed. For instance, he was grateful to those who sought to correct his failings. To a friend who had ventured to correct him he wrote,

You have no occasion to think of apologies: for I have day and night thanked God for you, and prayed for blessings on your head, and watched and prayed against my besetting sin, or rather, against one out of a thousand of my besetting sins. I know and feel that I am extremely blameable on the side you referred to; but in spite of all my wishes and endeavours, if I am not much upon my guard, l fall again and again into the same sins … God alone knoweth how corrupt I am. It is not for nought that I wonder at the mercy of being out of hell. Go on (but without apologies), and cease to be faithful to me, when I kick at you for it, or when, if I rise against reproof at the time, I do not humble myself for it afterwards with shame and sorrow of heart: or rather, never cease, whether I receive it well or ill; but if you be not a savour of life to me, be, however reluctantly, a savour of death.[16]

Taking up again the illustration of the game of bowls, he said that he knew he needed to live recognizing his bias towards evil and to live accordingly to counteract it. Significantly, the more his soul was filled with self-abhorrence, the 'more admiring' were his 'thoughts of the Saviour's love'.[17]

A desire for Christlikeness

Simeon exhibits the truth mentioned in Hebrews 11 of God's people, 'whose weakness was turned to strength' (v. 34). Writing to Thomas Thomason in March 1816 he referred to the example of the Lord Jesus, who, 'as a lamb before its shearers', was dumb and, without either threatening or complaint, 'entrusted himself to him who judges justly' (1 Peter 2:23). He commented, '[This] appears to me most lovely; and I have unspeakable delight in striving … to tread in his steps. God has long taught you this lesson, and I am endeavouring to learn it day by day.'[18]

The great lesson he learned through the difficult experiences of his early years at Holy Trinity was that his enemies actually did him good. Preaching from 2 Corinthians 6:4–10, he said,

As to all the contempt that shall be poured upon us, or the privations we may be called to undergo, they must be as nothing in our eyes, by reason of our enjoyment of the Divine presence that bears us up above them, and our prospect of the Divine glory, that will compensate for all the labour or suffering that ever we could endure, if our lives were protracted for ten thousand years.[19]

Remembering the misbehaviour of students who tried to disrupt services in the early years at Holy Trinity, he wrote, 'I endeavoured always to act with mildness, but yet with firmness; and, through the goodness of God, was enabled to keep in awe every opposer.'[20] In several sermons on anger he stressed that anger should be replaced by a patient spirit.

While once his anger would have made it easy to plunge into controversy, his pursuit of Christlikeness put a restraint upon such desires:

I wish to avoid controversy: not that I desire to shun it on account of any apprehended weakness in my cause; but because I know and feel within myself ... that controversy is hurtful to the spirit: it leads us to find pleasure in detecting and exposing the errors of an adversary; and gratifies, both in the writers and readers, some of the worst passions of the heart. Happy shall I be ... to have no occasion ever to resume it, and happy to embrace every opportunity of approving myself, in deed as well as in word.[21]

This did not mean that he ruled out debate, but it did determine the spirit of it. He described his visit to a parish minister in Scotland: 'We had a warm debate about justification by faith. I was enabled to speak as I would ever wish to speak on that subject: I contended earnestly for the faith, but I hope with love and modesty.'[22]

As explained earlier, no Scripture influenced him more in his pastoral ministry than 2 Timothy 2:24: 'The Lord's servant must not quarrel.' 'Many hundreds of times has that one word tied my hands.'[23] While moderation was not characteristic of him in his early Christian life, it was a marked feature as his spiritual growth increased. The Bishop of Calcutta testified at the time of Simeon's death, 'His moderation on doubtful matters shed a sort of unction over his conversation and ministry, which in spiritual things is the secret of real influence over others.'[24] Despite the suggestion that he may have been wrong about his judgement on Carey and his colleagues, he wrote some years later:

The longer I live, the more I feel the importance of adhering to the rules which I have laid down for myself in relation to such matters.

1st. To hear as little as possible what is to the prejudice of others.

2nd. To believe nothing of the kind till I am absolutely forced to it.

3rd. Never to drink into the spirit of one who circulates an ill report.

4th. Always to moderate, as far as I can, the unkindness which is expressed towards others.

5th. Always to believe, that if the other side were heard, a very different account would be given of the matter.[25]

Pastoral care

Although a Christian minister may be better at preaching than at pastoral care, or vice versa, Simeon never separated the two throughout his ministry. When as a young Christian he attended St Edward's Church without the minister seeming to notice him, he determined that such should never be the case where he ministered.

Students quickly discovered his concern for their spiritual well-being and he became a role model for those who entered the ministry. One wrote, 'Mr Simeon watches over us as a shepherd over his sheep. He takes delight in instructing us, and has us continually at his rooms ... His Christian love and zeal prompt him to notice us.'[26] Writing to his mother, the student spoke especially of how Simeon's 'kindness to us exceeds all bounds, and whose example is such as we shall do well to imitate, when God in his providence shall place us in the Church'.[27]

'What influence can a minister maintain over his people, if he does not foster them as a brood under his wings?'[28] was the question Simeon asked himself. Part of that fostering of his people was making provision for them to meet in smaller groups during the week other than on a Sunday.

To have some opportunities of meeting my people, I considered as indispensable; for how could I know my sheep, if I did not see them in private; and how was it possible for me to visit so many at their own houses, and to find out all their different states and trials? If there were regular seasons for us to meet together, I could from time to time invite them to state to me, either before others or in private, whatever they might wish to say: and I could learn by conversation something respecting the state of their souls before God.[29]

Simeon was innovative for his times in recognizing the need for delegation of pastoral responsibility and yet at the same time ensuring that he did not forfeit his own pastoral care of the flock. He saw that delegation requires careful supervision, and he used the illustration of a coach and horses.

I considered myself as a coachman upon the box, and them as the reins, by which I had immediate access to every individual in my Church: and, from the most mature reflection, I cannot but consider this as of the greatest importance to the welfare of any people. That it is open to abuse is certain; and what is there that may not be abused? Even the Apostolic Churches were more or less distracted by the conceit of some, or the violence of others; and whilst human nature is what it is, we cannot hope to find any society of men on earth free from some kind of evils; but whilst I was able to attend to all the societies myself, there was as little evil arising from this arrangement, as can be expected in any society on earth.[30]

He underlined the importance of keeping in touch with those to whom responsibility was delegated. 'Where people are left to themselves, the most conceited and the most forward will take advantage of it to shew their evil dispositions; and if they can gain an ascendancy (which they too frequently will), they will prove a plague and a grief to the minister that is placed over them.'[31] This was Simeon's own experience when illness meant that he was not available to the leadership he had established.

The practical nature of his pastoral care was touchingly illustrated in the way in which, while on holiday, he responded to the news of the illness of the woman who had worked for him, together with her husband, Charles, for about ten years. He returned to Cambridge immediately, although it had been suggested to him that he could delay his return. He was wise in his decision, as a letter to the friend with whom he had been staying indicates.

I thought my duty to her demanded my presence here, and now that she is gone, my soul is exceedingly rejoiced in having torn myself from you, to wait upon her. I found her sensible, but not by any means comfortable in her soul. Her fears preponderated, and darkened her mind: nor did anything that I said to her seem to inspire peace into her soul. Fearing the physician might not pay all the attention her situation required, I called upon him, and begged him to attend her twice or thrice a day, till the disorder should abate. He went and called a third time that day, but gave me no very great hopes of her recovery. This morning I was with her about half-past seven, and it appeared that she was about to be taken away from us. I conversed and prayed with her; but still all my inquiries, relative to her views of the Saviour and her affiance in him, were attended with a shake of her head, intimating that she was not able to commit herself to him with confidence.

I returned to my room to breakfast, and then went to her again as soon as I had taken my refreshment, but still I could get nothing but a shake of the head. This was exceedingly distressing to my soul; and I endeavoured, with many tears, to set forth again to her the willingness and sufficiency of Christ. Upon this, with a distinct and audible voice, she cried, 'Lord, save me'; and I then again prayed with her to that God, whom I have long known to be 'a God that heareth prayer'. And O! how gracious was God to his poor suppliants! I still continued talking with her, and on asking her again, whether God had answered our prayer; whether she was now able to trust in the Saviour, and to cast all the burdens of her soul on him, she gave me a most significant and expressive nod. I then told her, if she felt peace in her soul, to squeeze my hand; and she squeezed it instantly. This was the signal for our thanksgiving to God; and immediately with the utmost ardour of our souls, we praised and adored our God, who had heard prayer in her behalf, and had caused light to arise in her darkness. In less than an hour afterwards she departed to her eternal rest. Though I watched her continually, as did also Charles her husband, and attendants, we could not tell what time her soul took its flight. I had her hand in mine, and should not have been convinced at last that she was dead, if a medical attendant had not told me she was dead.[32]

Simeon's pastoral care did not stop there, since the husband was left with a young daughter. Simeon arranged for her to complete her education in Reading and to be trained as a housemaid.

Generosity and social concern

In Chapter 5 we noted Simeon's active involvement in the provision of bread for the villages of Cambridge in a time of scarcity. The letter which he sent round to the principal people in each of the twenty-four villages near Cambridge, with the schedule of queries prepared for their answers, was characteristic of his precision and habits of business. As someone observed,

This benevolent and self-denying conduct, and the personal labour and expense he incurred, made a great impression on the University, and was one of the first things to open their eyes to the real character of the man, who had been so much ridiculed and opposed. They could not but acknowledge, in spite of his eccentricities, that some great and noble principle must be at work within him to occasion such conduct. 'He means well at least,' they said; 'this is not like madness.'33

His light shone before men as his Saviour instructed, and his works brought praise to his Father in heaven.

A further evidence of his practical social concern was his involvement in the establishment of a Provident Bank in Cambridge in 1817, some seven years after the Revd Henry Duncan had done something similar in Dumfriesshire, to encourage people to save. A week before its inauguration in Cambridge he preached a sermon from Proverbs 6:6–10, entitled 'The Sluggard Reproved'. He saw it as a gospel opportunity:

It is a ground of thankfulness that those classes of society who have hitherto scarcely known how to secure any little sums which they might save, have now, by the establishment of Provident Banks, encouragement to provide for themselves against the day of adversity. Happy would it be if a similar zeal were now exerted in relation to the concerns of eternity.34

Attractive personality in spite of eccentricities

Simeon had his eccentricities (as we all do). But these were more than compensated for by the attractiveness of his character. Henry Martyn testified to this just before he left Cambridge for India: 'At night was at church, when, almost for the first time, I observed Mr Simeon's manner, and conceived great admiration of him as a preacher; supped with him alone afterwards: he prayed before I went away, and my heart was solemnly affected.'35 What he was in the pulpit, he was out of it.

Weakness turned to strength

Simeon was acutely aware of the danger of pride and all that went with it. Writing to a good friend, he confessed,

I could tell you more of my state of mind, but I am afraid of pride and boasting. I think, however, I may tell you (for I hope it will excite in you a spirit of thankfulness to God for me) that my hopes and expectations are not disappointed. Amidst all that I feel to mourn over, my soul rejoices exceedingly in God my Saviour. I trust that this joy will be made to abound more and more, when you put your live coal to mine, and blow it with the breath of prayer.[36]

The secret of his spiritual strength and influence was his focus upon the Lord Jesus Christ. He did not deny the necessity of looking at himself in a spirit of self-examination, but he knew that the greater priority was to fix his eyes on his Saviour, convinced that it is by the former that we are to be humbled and by the latter that we are 'transformed into [Christ's] likeness' (2 Cor. 3:18). Writing to a fellow-minister he said, 'You must learn to "glory in your infirmities (so to speak), that the power of Christ may rest upon you". You are nothing, and it discourages you; but you must be content to be nothing, that Christ may be "all in all".'[37] He exhibited a growing awareness of his dependence upon the death of Christ. Asked to speak to four to five hundred children while in Scotland, he felt he had not kept their attention as he ought to have done. 'It did not appear to me a profitable season; the fault was my own; I had not studied any subject, nor was my spirit devoutly impressed with my office and employment.' His immediate and thankful response was, 'Thanks be to God who has given one to bear the iniquity of my holy things.'[38]

His daily Bible reading was his guide not only for his own life, but also for his exercise of pastoral responsibility.

I have been used to read the Scriptures to get from them rich discoveries of the power and grace of Christ, to learn how to minister to a loving and obedient people; I am now reading them really and literally to know how to minister to a conceited, contentious and rebellious people. Two qualities I am sure are requisite, meekness and patience: yet in some cases, I shall be constrained to 'rebuke with all authority'. I have been used to sail in the Pacific; I am now learning to navigate the Red Sea that is full of shoals and rocks, with a very intricate passage. I trust the Lord will carry me safely through; but my former trials have been nothing to this.[39]

That same reading of the Scriptures increased his watchfulness not only of God's flock, but also of his own relationship to God.

I have been reading the Scriptures with pleasure and profit, and bless God, who does not refuse me access to him in prayer. I feel truly thankful for that caution, 'Let him that thinketh he standeth, take heed', &c. I long to have a holy fear of offending God, and a jealousy over myself, lest, after all my privileges, I ruin my soul by sin, 1 Cor. ix. 24 to x. 12.[40]

Human weakness was a frequent theme and subject in his preaching, reflecting the emphasis of Scripture as he systematically expounded it. His sermon on James 3:2 was entitled 'The Best of Men but Weak and Frail'.

It should seem indeed that God has determined to stain the pride of human glory, by recording the faults of his most favoured servants. It is remarkable that those who are most noted in Scripture for their piety, not only fell, but manifested their weakness in those very graces for which they were most distinguished. Abraham yielded to unbelief, Job to impatience, Moses to anger, Peter to fear.

There is not a saint, however eminent, but his faults are reported as faithfully as his virtues. And we are constrained to acknowledge, that the best of men, when they come into temptation, are weak and fallible as others, if they be not succoured from above.[41]

Preaching on Joshua's meeting with the Captain of the Lord's Host, he declared,

We must be strong indeed, and of good courage: but we must 'not lean to our own understanding', or 'trust in an arm of flesh'. In fact, we are really strong only in proportion as we feel ourselves weak, and look to Christ to 'perfect his strength in our weakness'. We must therefore be strong, not in ourselves, but 'in the Lord, and in the power of his might'.[42]

The Puritan pastor Abraham Wright wrote, 'I am mended by my sickness, enriched by my poverty, and strengthened by my weakness.'[43] Such was also Charles Simeon's experience and testimony.

Notes

1 *Memoirs of Charles Simeon*, p. 111.
2 Ibid., p. 2.
3 Ibid., p. 265.
4 Ibid., p. 11.
5 Ibid., p. 51.
6 Ibid.
7 Ibid., p. 417.
8 Ibid., p. 2.
9 Ibid., p. 3.
10 Scylla and Charybdis were two legendary sea monsters of Greek mythology, a threat to sailors. Avoiding one meant passing too close to the other.
11 *Memoirs of Charles Simeon*, p. 18.
12 Ibid., p. 33.
13 Ibid., p. 69.
14 Ibid., p. 393, footnote.
15 Ibid., p. 213.
16 Ibid., p. 113.
17 Ibid., p. 73.
18 Ibid., p. 247.
19 Discourse 2026, *Horae Homileticae*, vol. 16.
20 *Memoirs of Charles Simeon*, p. 53.
21 Ibid., p. 165.
22 Ibid., p. 91.

23 Ibid., p. 39.
24 Ibid., p. 488.
25 Ibid., p. 262.
26 Ibid., p. 58.
27 Ibid.
28 Ibid., p. 81.
29 Ibid., p. 80.
30 Ibid., p. 82.
31 Ibid.
32 Ibid., p. 141.
33 Ibid., p. 49.
34 Discourse 767, *Horae Homileticae*, vol. 7.
35 *Memoirs of Charles Simeon*, p. 114.
36 Ibid., p. 133.
37 Ibid., p. 428.
38 Ibid., p. 73.
39 *Memoirs of Charles Simeon*, p. 199.
40 Ibid., p. 124.
41 Discourse 2366, *Horae Homileticae*, vol. 20.
42 Discourse 247, ibid., vol. 2.
43 'Affliction', in **I. D. E. Thomas,** *A Puritan Golden Treasury* (Carlisle, PA: Banner of Truth, 2000), p. 17.

Simeon's 'exodus'

W hen Moses and Elijah appeared to our Lord Jesus Christ at the Transfiguration they spoke of his impending death as his 'exodus'—in other words, not as a threatening disaster but as a moment of glorious triumph. The apostle Peter uses the same word to describe his own imminent death (2 Peter 1:15; translated as 'departure'), as may every Christian believer. Simeon would undoubtedly have done the same.

Once Simeon was in his seventies, he increasingly began to feel his age. It made him cautious about accepting an invitation in 1833 to be one of the select preachers for the university the following year. 'I declined … because I judged it wiser and better in every view to antedate old age, than to run any risk of exposing myself and paining others, by any unconscious display of my augmented senile infirmities.'[1] He wrote two years later,

I am myself *dying daily*: and I find that to be the best and happiest mode of living. Why should we not be taking Pisgah views of the promised land, and tuning our harps that we may be ready at any moment to join the heavenly choir in their songs of praise to 'him, who hath loved us, and washed us from our sins in his own blood', or rather I would say, to him who loveth and washeth us from our sins? The Psalmist has strongly suggested this distinction, in calling on all that is within him to adore and magnify his God for present and existing blessings; '*forgiveth, healeth, redeemeth, crowneth, satisfieth*'.[2]

To another friend he wrote in 1836,

I shall begin to fancy myself young again, when I receive by the same post two letters, one desiring me to open a church at Reading, and the other to re-open one at Bradford in Yorkshire. But I happen to know the difference between 37 and 77; and I am content to discharge, as God shall enable me, the offices pertaining to the latter age.3

He did not minimize the trials that came with old age.

St Paul (what? was *resigned*? no) *took pleasure* (ευδοκω) in trials of every description: he had scarcely the word 'resignation' in his vocabulary; and we also, according to the grace given to us, should almost banish that word, except in very grievous trials indeed, and should substitute for it the apostle's ευδοκω … tribulation itself is the occasion of nothing but joy to the soul. If only we believe that our very hairs are all numbered, and the minutest occurrences are ordered by Infinite Wisdom for our good, we neither have, nor can have, anything but what should be to us a source of joy.4

Like the apostle Peter when he spoke of his 'exodus', Simeon longed that 'when the closing scene shall actually arrive, I may be thus highly favoured again, and have an abundant entrance ministered unto me into the kingdom of our Lord and Saviour Jesus Christ'.5

The period around his seventy-seventh birthday in September 1836 marked something of a turning point in a downward trend in his health. 'What can I expect? I enter my seventy-eighth year to-day. I never expected to live so long: I can scarcely believe I am so old: I have as yet known nothing of the infirmities of age, though I have seen a good old age. I know however it will all be ordered well.'6

The record of Simeon's health

Throughout Simeon's *Memoirs* there are many references to his health—certainly over fifty—especially in his correspondence to his close friends, perhaps on account of his having neither a wife nor children with whom he could share his concerns. Over a long period he had problems with his voice. This first occurred early on in his ministry, between 1796 and 1799:

'It pleased God ... to afflict me ... with almost a total loss of my voice, so that for the space of two years I could do very little in public, and nothing at all in private.'[7] Again in 1807 his strength 'had become so impaired by over-exertion, and his voice was so feeble, that he was compelled to reduce for a season his ministerial duties'.[8] Even to engage in family prayer twice a day was more than he could do. It grieved him that he could not enter fully into conversation with others, or meet with his ministerial friends when they gathered together. 'I greatly regret indeed that I am able to do very little in the way of reading or conversation.'[9] His reaction was positive:

I humbly hope that this dispensation will be in mercy to my soul; and that God is giving me more leisure for reading, meditation and prayer. That I may second the intentions of his providence, I purpose, during this interval of relaxation, to keep a diary that I may the more carefully observe what benefit accrues to me from this affliction.[10]

Occasional attacks of gout afflicted him and he mentions it some thirteen times in his *Memoirs*. He acknowledged that it prompted a certain irritability of temper on his part. Carus, the editor of Simeon's *Memoirs*, comments, 'No one however could be more sensible of the evil than he was himself; and never was anyone more ready to confess and deplore his failings.'[11] When once his gout meant that he could hold his Friday evening meeting with the students instead of attending a Jews' Society meeting in London, he responded by the observation, 'Who knows whether good may not come even of this? Who can tell but what God may have so ordered it, that something I have said this evening may fix in some of your hearts, to bring forth fruit to his glory? For this I would willingly be laid up with ten gouts, yea, suffer death itself.'[12]

Thomas Thomason was the friend with whom he shared most about his periods of ill-health. Having worked together as vicar and curate, their relationship was close and mutually beneficial spiritually; they maintained a regular correspondence when Thomason worked in India. In November 1811 Simeon reported, 'In the autumn I laid by for five weeks, and had my lips hermetically sealed, except for the introduction of beef and pudding: and I improved more in that time than in two years before.'[13] In July 1813 he wrote from Sandgate near Folkestone, where he was staying with Thomason's mother and daughter, 'My view has been to see no human being, and to be silent as death for the space of three months.'[14] He then greatly improved and was able to visit Henry Venn in his dying days and to pray with him. 'The first of these times he said to me, "Do not pray, but render praise and thanks; let it all be praise." The last time he continued praying aloud after I had finished.'[15]

Later that year he wrote,

I hope to get back to Cambridge about the 10th of October. It has been, indeed, a long vacation; and I hope I am essentially stronger than I was; but I never expect to be able to preach twice in a day for a continuance. I fear I must again suspend my family prayer when I come to have my public duties: for the family prayer alone is, even in my present renewed state, quite as much as I can go through with prudence.[16]

In 1815 Simeon seems to have recovered his health, sufficiently to enable him to resume his ministry at Holy Trinity Church and to travel. He wrote to Thomason,

Within these three weeks I have been so strengthened, that I hesitated not to undertake to preach in the evening at Bourn a sermon for the Jews, after having preached a farewell sermon to my people in the morning at Trinity; and I am now waiting for the arrival of the people to meet in the church, at two o'clock, in order to establish an Association for the villages round this place.[17]

In November 1816 he reported, 'My people, who remained steadfast, are in a blessed state: my church better attended than ever: my delight in my work greater: my health is good: my strength is renewed, so that I preach with ease. I do hope that God has yet something for me to do before I die.'[18] He proved it to be so because in May 1817 he wrote,

My own health, through mercy, is as good as at any period of my life; and by means of constant and extraordinary caution, my voice in public is as strong almost as ever. But I am silent all the week besides. I think I once told you, that I compare myself to bottled small beer; being corked up, and opened only twice a week, I make a good report; but if it were opened every day, I should soon be as ditch-water. I think I do right in saving myself thus, because it enables me to throw an energy into my public discourses which makes them far more interesting than they would otherwise be.[19]

At this stage in Simeon's ministry the students had sometimes become almost one half of the congregation.

Reflecting on the past in 1819 he acknowledged,

Had I, when my voice first failed me, fourteen years ago, been able to lay by entirely, and not expend the little strength which was given me from time to time, I should in all probability have been a strong man at this day. But I loved my work, and I loved my fellow-creatures, and when urged to abstain from any particular work and labour of love, I pleaded, 'Is it not a little one?' And thus I never got forward ...[20]

He found guidance in Paul's attitude to physical weaknesses: 'We know that the Apostle Paul took pleasure in his infirmities and distresses for Christ's sake; and it is our privilege to do the same.'[21] He knew that God could accompany illness 'by abundant discoveries of his incomprehensible love'.[22]

Simeon's jubilees

In the latter years of Simeon's life he celebrated two important jubilees. The first, on Thursday, 29 January 1829, marked fifty years since he went up to Cambridge from Eton, significant most of all because of the events that led to his conversion. Around thirty of his friends arranged to celebrate this important milestone by assembling in his rooms for reading the Scriptures and prayer. In the evening they met together for dinner. William Wilberforce was unable to attend because of ill-health, but his letter explaining his absence drew attention to Simeon's improved health and God's marked blessing upon his ministry:

You are blessed with so much bodily health and vigour, that we may humbly indulge the hope, that the Almighty will still grant you a long course of usefulness and comfort. The degree in which, without any sacrifice of principle, you have been enabled to overcome, and if I may so term it, to live down the prejudices of many of our higher ecclesiastical authorities, is certainly a phenomenon I never expected to witness.[23]

Simeon's second jubilee in November 1832 celebrated his fifty years of ministry at Holy Trinity Church. He wrote his own account of this event and the days surrounding it:

On Tuesday, at half-past 10, about thirty-two assembled. I opened the meeting with observations … founded on the fact that the jubilee was always at the close of the day of atonement; the services of which day prepared those who had received deliverance from spiritual judgments, to set others at liberty and restore their inheritances, and those who were now liberated and restored, to appreciate and improve their mercies aright. Thus our jubilee arose out of, and was a continuation of our previous humiliation, which I desired to pervade all our services, and all our enjoyments. I prayed with tears. Mr Sargent followed in a way of humiliation. Mr Bickersteth followed admirably in behalf of missions. We then retired for the luncheon; and met again at 2, till 4; which time was occupied in a similar way by Mr Hankinson and other brethren.

Then twelve of the residents went home to dinner, and I entertained twenty. About six of the others came back to tea; and we spent the evening till past 9 in discussion.

Wednesday was wholly occupied in most profitable discussions and prayer from 11 to 1: and from 2 to 4. Lunch and dinner as before, and evening as before. Mr Jowett's closing prayer will not soon be forgotten. Mr Marsh gave his views of the reign of Christ, greatly moderated and softened. There would be no controversy if the prophetical people were all like him.

Thursday was spent till dinner time as Tuesday had been, in the word and prayer only.

But behold, to my utter surprise my dear (clerical) brethren presented me with an elegant inkstand. This quite overcame me. I could speak only by silence and tears, from a sense of God's unmerited and unbounded love towards me. As there was to be church-service at half past 6, all except a few dined with me. Mr Cunningham preached on the very same text that I myself had taken on Monday. We then separated, after a season such as no one of us had ever seen before. Friday, Mr Sargent stayed the day with me; and I read what he had printed of Mr Thomason's Life. It is beautiful, and very interesting.

On Saturday I redeemed the time that had been alienated from my work for the press, and got up even with my printer.

Monday, Oct. 8. I have been to visit some of the chief of my friends, who have been so active. It is delightful to see in what a spirit they all are. Truly I could never have conceived it probable, if possible, that such love should abound towards me for the Lord's sake.

Oct. 9. I go to town to-morrow. I shall be two hours there to do my work, and hope to return in the evening.

I returned unconscious that I had gone 100 yards, except from recollection; so wonderfully has God been pleased to strengthen me.[24]

He was overwhelmed by the love that surrounded him. At 3 o'clock on

Chapter 17

1 October 1832 a deputation of five men came to present him with a valuable epergne—a large table centrepiece, probably made of silver, to hold sweets, fruit or flowers.

Their address was most kind and flattering. Such a testimony of love from my hearers quite overcame me. I returned them thanks as God enabled me, and with a prayer of thanksgiving I closed the interview.

At one o'clock, I went to the dinner, which I gave to 250 of my poor parishioners, in the National School-room in King's street (Trinity Parish). They were all seated at three tables. There could not have been more order at a dinner in my own room. The room was decorated with boughs and flowers. I implored a blessing on the food and on the company assembled … All the heads of my parish sat at intervals to carve the dinner. All went off well. Before it was over I went round the middle table, expressing love to those on either side.

When dinner was over I returned thanks. Then the heads of the parish brought me a salver … (Both the salver and the epergne are far too elegant for me: but as expressions of respect and love from my hearers they are of incalculable value.) Having presented it to me in somewhat of a set speech, I returned thanks, as the Lord enabled me, with tears of gratitude and love; especially with gratitude to God, who had spared me to this day to behold such harmony and love in my parish, where for thirty years there was little but enmity and opposition. On the whole, it was a sight which has rarely ever been equalled: the room so noble, and so beautifully arranged; the people so happy; the parish so unanimous, the spectators so delighted: and above all, God so present with us.

I am now come home somewhat fatigued, that I may be still and quiet before the evening service.[25]

At the evening service he preached on 2 Peter 1:12–15:

So I will always remind you of these things, even though you know them and are firmly established in the truth you now have. I think it is right to refresh your memory as long as I live in the tent of this body, because I know that I will soon put it aside, as our Lord Jesus Christ has made clear to me. And I will make every effort to see that after my departure you will always be able to remember these things.

Looking back

Simeon reflected upon the wonderful things he had been spared to see and he listed them:

1. Union and harmony and love throughout my whole parish, together with an increased attention to religion.

2. My jubilee completed, and kept with such devout affection.

3. My entire work [i.e. his *Horae Homileticae*] out, presented, and, as far as I know, approved.

4. My church enlarging so as to hold 1,100 persons, and so beautiful as to be the ornament instead of the disgrace of the town.

5. My school-room built for God's service, and now licensed for it. I preached there yesterday, not without many tears, on 1 Cor. ix. 16.

6. St Mary's given to the entire management of Mr C., and at least 1,200 hearers. I preached there on Sunday evening, 20th, to that number, on Rom. xv. 29.

7. Barnwell (Church) open to me. I preached there on Sunday morning, 27th, on Lev. ii. 14–16.

8. St Mary's now statedly open to me in the mornings. Mr C. is to read the prayers early in the morning on Sundays; and at 12 to read the Litany, and (Communion Service, when) I am to preach. It will commence on Nov. 10. I intend to preach on Luke x. 23, 24. This will continue till my church is open, when I hope to preach at Trinity every Sunday morning, and at St Mary's in the evening. Never did I long more to spend and be spent for the Lord than at this moment. Blessed be God!

Nov. 14. This day has Mr H— consented to let me preach at St Botolph's every Thursday. How incredible is all this![26]

Signs of physical weakness

From this time on his age began to show. He travelled and preached away from his own parish less often, although there were times when he displayed sudden physical energy, to his own surprise and that of his friends. The last sermon he preached at Holy Trinity was on the words of Jehu in 2 Kings 10:16: 'Come with me and see my zeal for the LORD.'

The prospect of heaven was real. While preparing for a journey, he remarked,

The Lord knows that I am thinking and longing, to a certain degree, for a far better journey, which, in a few days, I shall take; but I find it difficult to realize the thought that I am so near the eternal world; I cannot imagine what a spirit is, I have no conception of it. But I rejoice in the thought, that my coffin is already cut down, and in the town at this very time; of this I have no doubt:—and my shroud is also ready; and in a few days I shall join the company of the redeemed above.[27]

He was particularly grateful to God that his putting together of all his sermons for publication was behind him. His mind and spirit were as alert as ever and he began to plan a set of sermons on Ephesians 3:18–19: 'I don't expect or desire to preach them; but if my life be spared, WRITE THEM I WILL.'[28]

Seven weeks before his death he visited Ely to pay his respects to the new bishop, Joseph Allen. Allen had been an undergraduate and then a fellow at Trinity College. But the weather—not untypical of Cambridge and Ely in the winter—was damp and chilly. Simeon did not dress adequately and the illness that followed was the result. 'The next morning early he was seized with a violent rheumatic attack, and, during the day, became so seriously indisposed as to be unable to leave his room for the evening lecture.'[29] The next Saturday was his birthday, and 'when his attendant came to him, he was sitting in a favourite spot before the window to enjoy the first beams of the sun'.[30] He said to his attendant, 'I enter my seventy-eighth year to-day. I never expected to live so long: I can scarcely believe I am so old: I have as yet known nothing of the infirmities of age, though I have seen a good old age. I know however it will all be ordered well.'[31]

For a while his health seemed to improve, but then pain and fever returned, and taking to his bed he was 'fully aware that the hand of death was upon him'.[32] With the exception of the legacies intended for his relatives, he made changes to his will which he had been contemplating for some time, particularly for the promotion of Christian and charitable purposes. When this was done 'his mind seemed relieved from every care, and he prepared himself with joy for his departure'.[33]

By early October his growing weakness was apparent. He confessed to a visiting friend, 'I never felt so ill before—I conceive my present state cannot last long—this exhaustion must be a precursor of death; but I lie here waiting for the issue without a fear—without a doubt—and without a wish.'[34] When told by another friend 'Many hearts are engaged in prayer for you', he replied, 'In prayer? aye, and I trust in praise too— praise for countless, endless mercies.'[35]

The news of Simeon's approaching death quickly spread. John Mason Neale, who attended Holy Trinity Church as a student a month or two before Simeon's death and was later the writer of many well-known hymns and carols, such as 'Good Christian Men, Rejoice', although not a sharer of Simeon's evangelical position, wrote in his journal, 'I do think at this moment Mr Simeon must be the happiest man in the world.'[36] Then, when the end had come, he wrote, 'What a meeting he and Henry Martyn must have had.'[37]

On Friday, 21 October, both Simeon and his friends were aware that nothing more could be done for him, but he 'in consequence seemed more than usually calm and happy'.[38] When asked what he was thinking, 'he immediately replied with great animation, "I don't think now—I am enjoying." He then expressed his entire surrender of himself to God's will, and spoke of his extreme joy in having his own will so completely in unison with that of God, adding with remarkable emphasis, "He cannot do anything against my will."'[39] When asked if he found the Lord Jesus to be present with him and giving him peace, he 'instantly replied, looking up to heaven with the most remarkable expression of happiness on his countenance, "Oh! yes; that I do."'[40]

In his final weeks he could only speak in a whisper and slowly, but his confidence in God was evident. Speaking of his condition he declared,

Infinite wisdom has devised the whole with infinite love; and infinite power enables me (pausing) to rest upon that power; and all is infinitely good and gracious ... All is right—and well—and just as it should be; I am in a dear Father's hands—all is secure. When I look to HIM I see nothing but faithfulness—and immutability—and truth; and I have not a doubt or a fear, but the sweetest peace—I cannot have more peace.[41]

He expressed his thanks to his doctor, with 'his earnest wishes for his best interests in time and eternity'.[42]

Remarkably, a fortnight before his death, his mind was preoccupied with preparing sermon outlines for four sermons upon his favourite passage in Ephesians (3:18–19), with no loss of clarity or appropriateness. What had been his lifetime habit 'brought unspeakable delight to him, and was literally his occupation in death'.[43] When unable to sleep at night 'he would employ himself in meditating on such portions of Scripture as particularly displayed the love and immutability and sovereignty of God, or else tended to deepen his sense of sin and promote contrition of heart'.[44]

His concern for the Jewish people showed itself to the end. Meetings on behalf of the London Jews' Society were due to take place at Holy Trinity Church. 'He wished to deliver, he said, his dying testimony to "its immense importance", and he began to compose an address to be read to the undergraduates at their meeting.'[45] He dictated to his attendant what he wanted to be said.

He began to consider the well-being of his people after his death, especially the appointment of his successor in the ministry of Holy Trinity Church. Having been at Holy Trinity for such a long time, and having visited the Bishop of Ely, the patron of the living, he wrote to him, asking 'that the friend whom the parishioners a few years before had chosen for their lecturer, might be appointed as his successor to the living'.[46] The bishop concurred, intimating that his own thoughts on Simeon's successor were the same.

His physical dependence upon his carers increased. On one occasion, when an attendant

had bathed his eyes, and asked him if they were relieved, he said, opening them and looking up to heaven, 'Soon they will behold all the glorified saints and angels around the throne of my God and Saviour, who has loved me unto death, and given himself for me; then I shall see him, whom having not seen I love; in whom, though now I see him not, yet believing I rejoice with joy unspeakable and full of glory.'[47]

He added, 'Of the reality of this I AM AS SURE as if I were there this moment.'[48]

Chapter 17

William Carus, Simeon's chosen successor to him at Holy Trinity Church and the compiler of his *Memoirs*, declares,

There was a remarkable and rapid maturing of all the finer parts of his character from the very commencement of this illness, and a corresponding diminution, and ultimately a disappearance of those symptoms of haste and irritability, which sometimes were visible in his days of health and vigour. He seemed now to breathe entirely an atmosphere of peace and love; and enjoying such a sense of God's pardoning love himself, he longed to manifest an affectionate and forgiving spirit to all around.[49]

On Sunday, 13 November 1836, at about two o'clock in the afternoon, at the exact moment the bell of St Mary's was tolling for the university sermon, which Simeon had been scheduled to preach, he entered his eternal rest. His will gave instructions about where he should be buried. 'If I die out of college, I am not careful where my body shall be buried; but if I die in Cambridge, I should wish to be buried in my college chapel.'[50]

A memorable funeral

His wish had been that as little fuss as possible should be made at his death, and those responsible sought to fulfil his wishes; but they could not control the feelings and respect felt by the people of Cambridge. Simeon died on the Sunday and the funeral was the following Saturday. It was market day, but all the shops in the town centre were closed and lectures were suspended in most colleges.

The funeral procession began at the college hall of King's. It was led by the choristers, the scholars and the fellows, with the provost walking ahead of the coffin borne by the eight senior fellows. College heads and professors, and men of all classes and ages from every college in the university, came to honour him. The procession around the huge quadrangle of King's was three or four abreast and more or less extended to its four sides.

Many of Simeon's colleagues in the ministry requested permission to be present at his interment. The only other people invited were the congregation of Holy Trinity Church. They were admitted privately into the antechapel of King's College Chapel. The antechapel resembles a huge vestibule preceding the main chapel. Today, fairly central on its floor, a tablet bears simply the initials 'C. S.', indicating where he is buried.

One observer was struck most of all 'to see the young men of the university, as they stood during the service between the coffin and the communion rails, all in mourning; and all, in appearance at least, feeling deeply the loss which had brought us together and the solemnity of the service.'[51] Probably no other funeral in Cambridge's history has seen so many people wanting to be involved.

Many funeral sermons

The next day many congregations in Cambridge and elsewhere listened to funeral sermons related to the life and testimony of Charles Simeon. The most meaningful was preached on the Sunday morning at Holy Trinity Church by Dr William Dealtry, then Chancellor of the Diocese of Winchester. His text was 'Those who honour me I will honour' (1 Sam. 2:30). He drew attention to Simeon's influence:

His known piety and most disinterested and generous disposition led others to join with him in good works, which the zeal of an individual could never have accomplished: God gave to him remarkably the hearts of those who had the means of beneficence—and the provision which he was thus enabled to make for the propagation of religion, both in this country and in the farthest regions of the globe, may justly be held out as a signal fulfilment of the declaration, 'Them that honour me I will honour'.[52]

A monument in Holy Trinity Church

The congregation placed a monument in the chancel of Holy Trinity

Chapter 17

Church, opposite to those of the two curates who had been closest to him: Henry Martyn and Thomas Thomason.

Notes

1 *Memoirs of Charles Simeon*, p. 420.
2 Ibid., pp. 437–438.
3 Ibid., p. 460.
4 Ibid., p. 438.
5 Ibid.
6 Ibid., p. 468.
7 Ibid., p. 82.
8 Ibid., p. 121.
9 Ibid., p. 139.
10 Ibid., p. 123.
11 Ibid., p. 112.
12 Ibid., p. 382.
13 Ibid., p. 174.
14 Ibid., p. 210.
15 Ibid.
16 Ibid., p. 214.
17 Ibid., p. 238.
18 Ibid., p. 254.
19 Ibid., p. 258.
20 Ibid., p. 302.
21 Ibid.
22 Ibid., p. 303.
23 Ibid., p. 368.
24 Ibid., p. 413.
25 Ibid., p. 412.
26 Ibid., p. 424.
27 Ibid., p. 467.
28 Ibid., p. 468.
29 Ibid.
30 Ibid.
31 Ibid.

32 Ibid., p. 469.

33 Ibid.

34 Ibid.

35 Ibid.

36 'John Mason Neale 1818–1866', The Hymns and Carols of Christmas, at www.hymnsandcarolsofchristmas.com/Hymns_and_Carols/Biographies/john_mason_neale.htm. Accessed June 2011.

37 Ibid.

38 *Memoirs of Charles Simeon*, p. 469.

39 Ibid., p. 470.

40 Ibid.

41 Ibid., p. 471.

42 Ibid.

43 Ibid., p. 475.

44 Ibid.

45 Ibid.

46 Ibid., p. 477.

47 Ibid., p. 479.

48 Ibid.

49 Ibid., p. 480.

50 Ibid., p. 481.

51 Ibid., p. 482.

52 Ibid., p. 483.

Chapter 18

Simeon's spiritual legacy

S imeon could never have imagined the continuing influence his life and example would have. He knew, of course, that Holy Trinity Church, Cambridge, was in a far healthier state at his death than it was when he had become its minister. From the human point of view his had been the ministry of a man in but one church all his life, a career unmarked by ecclesiastical preferment or denominational status. Up until this point we have looked at factual aspects of his ministry from the point of view of his *Memoirs* and sermons. To turn to his spiritual legacy inevitably means making subjective judgements, where more room for error exists.

Spiritual children

John Calvin, castigated for being without children, replied, 'My sons are to be found all over the world.'[1] Simeon, a bachelor all his life, could have said, 'My sons are to be found all over Britain and in India.' His great-great-great-grandchildren are also to be found all over the world. He is frequently quoted by contemporary preachers, and his example has been something many aspire to emulate, not only in the land of his birth but also further afield.

Foremost from the point of view of the work of the gospel in India were Henry Martyn and Thomas Thomason. Others served in gospel ministry in Britain: men such as Thomas Lloyd, a member and fellow of Simeon's own college, whom he not only regarded as 'his son in the faith' but also always designated 'the first fruits of Achaia',[2] being probably the first member of King's College whom he saw come to faith in our Lord Jesus Christ. Such men had not only his example but also the benefit of his deliberate endeavours to teach them.

A considerable part of my ministerial usefulness has consisted, to instruct young ministers how to read easily, naturally, distinctly, impressively. This is indeed a kind of instruction which no man gives, and no man desires: but it is greatly needed, and of vast importance, as well to the health of the ministers, as to the edification of their flocks. How often are the prayers of our Church spoiled, and good sermons rendered uninteresting, by bad delivery in ministers! I thank God, I could specify many, some that were in a very hopeless state, who have been exceedingly benefited by my poor endeavours.[3]

Even as many contemporary pastors and teachers were unconsciously moulded and influenced by those under whose ministry they were either brought to faith in Christ or built up in their faith while at college or university, so were hundreds during Simeon's ministry at Holy Trinity. They, in turn, influenced the next generation, and so it continues.

A role model

The good example Simeon provided was that of a pastor and teacher, and not of one more than the other. He did this unconsciously and this made it all the more powerful and influential. His example went beyond simply being a spiritual father or physician to his flock as he gave priority to 'the word of God and prayer',[4] but was also seen in his awareness of the need for spiritual delegation. For nearly fifty years he delegated other duties, always under his superintendence, 'as Moses delegated many of his duties to the seventy employed by him'.[5] In Simeon's case he had 'thirty (male and female) in their different districts', and he preached 'an annual sermon in aid of their efforts'.[6] He cared for both young and old. Besides his regular preaching, he instructed his young people 'twice a week in the chancel, and had a public catechizing and instruction on the Sunday afternoons'.[7] On the evening of their confirmation he preached to all who had been confirmed.

He was a role model in finding his pastoral principles from the Scriptures themselves. Recognizing the priority of love for all believers in their human relationships, he knew that it must be exemplified by a pastor, especially when faced by attitudes and actions that made him unhappy. In an intimate letter to the Bishop of Calcutta he wrote,

I think you know my deliberate and habitual plan, which is not to condemn anything strongly, till I can have an opportunity of putting in contrast with it what must of necessity be commended and admired. And then I am not afraid of appearing to indulge a vain, proud, conceited, censorious disposition. Love breaks through the veil, and shows itself to be the dominant principle in every word I say.[8]

He acknowledged that was not the case at the beginning of his ministry but it happily became so as the years passed.

When met by opposition, as inevitably every gospel minister is at times, he drew his confidence from the examples of Scripture. Faced with the rooted determination of some to create divisions in the church fellowship, he concluded,

there never can be union amongst us again, till God shall be pleased either to change their dispositions, or to separate them from us. My opinion is, that God will ere long make their folly manifest unto all men, as he did that of Jannes and Jambres, and of the opponents of the Apostle Paul. My heart's desire and prayer for them, and my incessant labour too, is, that they should desist from their evil ways and return to a becoming spirit; but if they do not, I must remove them from my society; though I will endeavour to proceed with all tenderness and caution, if I should at last be driven by them to this extremity.[9]

Doing the work of an evangelist

Not all pastors and teachers possess the gift of an evangelist, but all of them are called, like Timothy, to 'do the work of an evangelist' (2 Tim. 4:5). Simeon reminded John Venn of the example he had received from those in his family who had gone before him.

I long that with the wisdom of your honoured father you should combine the zeal and love of your grandfather. He knew … nothing but Christ and him crucified. And what is there else for you to know at Hereford? Speak all that the Scripture speaks, and as the Scripture speaks it: and leave all nice distinctions alone. You are a physician, going to thousands dying of the cholera, and have a sovereign remedy for them. Think of nothing else but the remedy. Get into the spirit of the Apostle Paul. Think what he would say and do in your circumstances. Souls are perishing for lack of knowledge. I wish you had known your honoured grandfather. The only end for which he lived was to make all men see the glory of God in the face of Jesus Christ. My dear friend, let that be your one labour with all, and every day and every hour. I shall die a happier man, if I see you rising superior to all minor points, and wholly engrossed with this.[10]

Simeon practised what he preached in this respect. His domestic helps or servants were a special object of his concern from the time of his conversion to the end of his life. He read the Scriptures to them and prayed with them. While he showed respect for all the ministers of the gospel he met on his travels, he did not fail to share with them the essentials of the gospel, as we have seen when he stayed with Alexander Stewart, the minister of Moulin in Scotland. His evangelistic concern expressed itself in his writing and printing of tracts, providing them for others to use and using them himself, especially when he was travelling.

Fellowship in the gospel

Simeon saw the need for fellowship with other ministers of the gospel. Pastors and teachers are sometimes lonely, and those newly called to the ministry may stand especially in need of fellowship and encouragement. They may have burdens that it would be unwise to share with members of their flock lest they appear to be exercising favouritism.

Fellowship with Christian friends who are not members of a pastor's church fellowship may be particularly beneficial and refreshing.

I drank tea at Mr Wilberforce's. He looked better than I have ever seen him. He took an affectionate interest in the state of my health. I did not come away till after their evening prayers. Mr W. read a prayer. We all continued on our knees a considerable time before he began. This had a sweetly solemnizing effect. He read the prayer with singular propriety, in a low and natural tone.[11]

Visiting London, he sought out friends:

About one o'clock I walked to Highbury Place, having had no exercise since I came to town. I found Mr and Mrs Clayton, with two of their sons and daughters, at home, and spent a very pleasant and profitable hour with them. Our hearts were full of love to each other; and I came away thankful for having breathed in so sweet an atmosphere.[12]

Particularly helpful is fellowship with ministers with whom a pastor may share his concerns and challenges, assured of the confidentiality of their conversation. This Simeon found in the Eclectic Society. The first reference to his being present at one of its meetings is on 8 February 1796, when there was an attendance of seventeen, with ten members taking part. Simeon took the opportunity to propose an important question that was going to have huge implications for the spread of the gospel overseas: 'With what propriety, and in what mode, can a mission be attempted to the heathen from the Established Church?'[13] It did not receive an enthusiastic response, but it was a beginning and resulted eventually in the formation of the Church Missionary Society. The benefit of these meetings in London encouraged Simeon to get ministers elsewhere to gather for the same purposes.

Every year he arranged a get-together for his clerical friends. They met first at the home of his assistant, Thomas Thomason, at Little Shelford near Cambridge, and afterwards at the home of Thomason's successor at Aspenden Hall in Hertfordshire, the home of the Lushington family.

Wives were also invited. Simeon had no doubt about their contribution to their husbands' ministerial usefulness and success. He hoped that they would 'enjoy the benefit of the general conversation which took place after dinner, and also be enabled to compare together their several schemes of parochial usefulness, as the helps-meet [a less common expression of help-mates] of their respective partners'.[14]

The numbers were between twenty and thirty, and accommodation was provided for all three nights. The men spent the mornings discussing the Scriptures or a helpful book, under Simeon's presidency. The wives met in another room, where they 'read together, and endeavoured to edify one another'.[15] They then came together for meals and 'after tea there was usually some leading topic of conversation likely to be interesting and profitable to both sexes'.[16] They 'often said in words, and oftener in their hearts, "It is good for us to be here."'[17] On one such occasion in July 1809 Simeon commented, 'For half a day perhaps I have often known times as precious; but never for nearly three days together. The solemnity, the tenderness, the spirituality and the love were equal to anything I have ever seen. God was truly in "the midst of us". Ladies and gentlemen were both highly favoured in their separate discussions.'[18] The practical logistics of getting husbands and wives together for such a period must have been demanding, as they would be today, but they were eminently worthwhile.

One of the perils of Christian people coming together—and not least ministers—is that they may talk about people, and sometimes unhelpfully. Simeon's concern was always for profitable conversation, for ensuring that it was useful and spiritually helpful. Henry Venn wrote to a friend about a visit Simeon made to him early in 1790:

Oh! how refreshing were his prayers! how profitable his conversation! We were all revived; he left a blessing behind him. How shameful is our depravity, and how exceeding great, when we can be content to live without doing good to the souls of men!—call ourselves Christians, and constantly be in the house of our God, and not desire to instruct, to edify, to animate those with whom we converse! They are the truly excellent of the earth—its salt, who, wherever they go, reach the heart and conscience, and excite the devout wish, 'Oh, that I may follow Christ like these true-hearted disciples!'[19]

Simeon was glad he could write on a visit to a Scottish home, 'The conversation had a very useful turn ... Our conversation was altogether spiritual; and the whole family evidently took pleasure in it.'[20]

Single-mindedness

An illustration of Simeon's dedication to Christ and the care of his flock was his observable single-mindedness. While he often travelled in the interests of the work among the Jews and the establishment of what we know now as the Simeon Trust of evangelical churches, he never neglected the needs and concerns of his own flock and responsibilities in Cambridge.

He did not look for a less demanding or easier sphere of service as he grew older but believed that where he served was in God's good providence, both in Holy Trinity Church and in King's College, and the place to stay unless God indicated otherwise. As the Bishop of Calcutta said at Simeon's death, Simeon knew that 'A steady ministry is likely to be a successful one. Changes rarely answer.'[21]

His work schedule shows his dedication. The demands of Holy Trinity Church and his involvement with missionary enterprise left him little time to see friends or enter into correspondence with them. 'Blessed be God, my work is my meat and drink,' he wrote; 'I only want more spirituality in it.'[22] He recognized, as all ought, the need for physical exercise and so he made a point, weather permitting, of riding every day. He prayed, 'May God enable me to devote myself to him more unreservedly than ever!'[23]

The planting of seeds that grew beyond his death

Even as acorns planted in the earth may in turn become oak trees, giving rise to further generations of acorns and oak trees, so what Simeon did gave rise to many benefits for the advance of God's kingdom.

The Simeon Trust—with 174 churches as its responsibility—still exists, encouraging the evangelical character of its churches' ministries. Simeon's trust stimulated the formation of other similar trusts. When he began his ministry evangelicals in the Church of England were few, but by the end of his ministry it is thought that almost a third of Anglican pulpits were evangelical.

The Church Missionary Society, of which Simeon was a founder, continues and from it came other missionary agencies, such as the Bible Churchmen's Missionary Society, now Crosslinks. The British and Foreign Bible Society was another body to which Simeon gave his energies, and it in turn spawned other Bible societies throughout the world. He was influential in pointing it in the direction of being interdenominational.

Societies for the spiritual well-being of the Jews—so much a focus of Simeon's concern—continued well into the twentieth century and up to today, although not with the support to which they were earlier accustomed.

Perhaps the most exciting and fascinating illustration of Simeon's influence is evangelical witness in the world's universities. It began with 'the acorn' of a sermon that he preached in 1827. As a result of hearing and discussing it a group of students began a Sunday school in Jesus Lane, a poorer part of Cambridge. From that arose in 1862 the DPM—a Daily Prayer Meeting. It provoked opposition, but by 1875 more than one in ten students supported it. Including an evangelistic meeting once a term, it developed into the Cambridge Inter-Collegiate Christian Union—the CICCU. In 1885 the Cambridge Seven went from the CICCU as missionaries to China, the best-known being C. T. Studd, someone who, like Simeon, was also educated at Eton. A hundred years later the Christian Union appealed for a Cambridge Seventy to respond to the same call to missionary service.

The Christian Union at Cambridge became a model for other Christian Unions and their influence throughout universities and colleges in Britain. This developed into the Inter-Varsity Fellowship, now called the UCCF: the University and Colleges Christian Fellowship. In 1947 IFES, the International Fellowship of Evangelical Students, was established; this draws together Christian Unions in more than 130 countries. Little could Simeon or his congregation have anticipated how significant that one sermon would prove to be.

Pastoral insights

Although Simeon may never have addressed his fellow-ministers and those who served with him as curates on the subject of pastoral insights, a number stand out as his life and teaching are surveyed, and I have chosen ten.

1. DIFFICULTIES MAY PROVE OUR BEST FRIENDS

Seldom, if ever, will pastors and teachers escape difficulties in their ministries, perhaps through the toughness of the area in which they serve or the perversity of some church members. They may wish to be anywhere other than where God has placed them and then foolishly look for a different sphere of service. Simeon demonstrated that our difficulties may become our friends, since God furthers his good work in our characters and service by them.

Not a few individuals might fairly have been described as Simeon's enemies in his work at Holy Trinity Church. His daily reading of Scripture corrected and controlled his attitude towards them. After reading 1 Corinthians 13 he confessed, 'Feeling that my wicked heart is differently affected towards some, I began to pray for my enemies, particularly the two or three that are most violent and most inveterate.'[24]

As we have seen, his early years at Holy Trinity Church were marked by persecution, but thirty years afterwards, after twenty years of peace, 'some of a peculiarly malignant spirit'[25] came into the parish and drew up a number of accusations against him and sent them to his bishop.

From such experiences he learned that trials tended to divest him of the high thoughts he might have of himself and made him live more by faith in his Saviour.

Certain it is, that the saints whom God has most approved, have been most abundantly exercised in different manners for the trial of their faith: and they who are most earnest in prayer for grace, are often most afflicted, because the graces which they pray for, e.g. faith, hope, patience, humility, &c., are only to be wrought in us by means of those trials which call forth the several graces into act and exercise; and in the very exercise of them they are all strengthened and confirmed.[26]

The best answer to hostility proved to be 'meek and patient conduct'.[27] He wrote on 30 August 1817, 'I have this moment heard of a most malignant attempt to injure my character: and I take up my pen to record, to the praise and glory of my God, that my soul is kept in perfect peace … It is an unspeakable consolation that God knoweth everything, and will judge righteous judgment.'[28] 'If situations are improved by ministers, so are ministers by situations; they have a reciprocal influence upon each other.'[29]

2. THE GOLDEN MEAN IS A PRINCIPLE TO BE READILY TAUGHT AND APPLIED

Earlier, in Chapter 15, we saw that the application of this principle of 'the golden mean'[30] is a clue to the maintenance of the unity of God's people. By the principle of 'the golden mean' we have in view Simeon's conviction that in issues that may divide Christians 'the truth is not in the middle, and not in one extreme; but in both extremes'.[31] In matters such as Calvinism and Arminianism, or matters of church practice, the principle equally applies. The church has to handle in every generation changing perceptions of ministry, the place of music in worship, the ministry of women and the acceptance of new translations of the Bible.

The key to maintaining unity in the local church over such issues is when the leaders themselves ask, 'What does the Bible teach on this subject? What are the extreme positions people take up? Is it clear that the truth is in one extreme or in the middle? Or is it in both extremes at once?' They will need to teach God's people the importance of this principle, not so that they compromise God's truth but so that they guard it with spiritual integrity, relevance and honesty. Simeon's motto reflected this golden mean: '"Rejoice with trembling", and tremble with rejoicing, has always been my motto. I never pass a day without seeing occasion for both, in all around me; but most of all in [myself].'[32]

3. GROWTH REQUIRES DELEGATION

It is difficult to know whether many ministers of the gospel in Simeon's time delegated pastoral responsibility, but it seems unlikely that they did. He knew his goal to be that of presenting each member of his flock 'perfect in Christ' (Col. 1:28). To that end he laboured, 'struggling with all his energy, which so powerfully' worked in him (Col. 1:29). But he could not do it on his own, especially if he was to give himself to the Word of God and prayer. But in delegating, he did not cease to be in control of what he handed over to others or to be personally involved in the needs of God's people.

In the delegation of pastoral care he saw the essential nature of women's pastoral ministry to women. Not all in the Eclectic Society, for example, agreed with him:

The generality seemed to think they did best by keeping at home, and minding their own business. My ideas did not perfectly coincide with theirs. I thought that there were offices, in which they might be profitably employed, provided they were discreet, and did not neglect their own proper callings. On the whole, I do not think we differed much; but our bias was a little different: *I* rather leaned more to the side of visiting the sick, &c., and *they* to the keeping almost entirely at home.[33]

He was convinced that 'females are but too apt to underrate their influence in society',[34] whereas he saw them as 'God's great instruments for carrying on every benevolent and pious work'.[35]

4. TEST YOUR OWN PREACHING

For his own preaching and writing Simeon had but one basic test:

Does it uniformly tend

TO HUMBLE THE SINNER?

TO EXALT THE SAVIOUR?

TO PROMOTE HOLINESS?

If in one single instance it lose sight of any of these points, let it be condemned without mercy.[36]

That test was one he inculcated in the young men he instructed in preaching, and one that his preaching demonstrated in practice.

While he did not look for evidences of God's presence as his Word was preached, he appreciated every indication of it: 'Preached at a small church … there were about 400 people, and God was remarkably present with us: many were in tears.'[37] But he did not confuse a lack of awareness of God's presence with spiritual ineffectiveness: 'In the afternoon at Mr R.'s church … I had much less liberty; I was enabled however to deliver my message faithfully, and I hope not without effect.'[38]

He came to see that he was helped in having enough time to himself before preaching. 'I had not any comfort in the sermon, for I had no opportunity for retirement.'[39] He felt that the more he came to the pulpit with the Scriptures having clearly spoken to his own soul in his preparation, the more likely he was to know God's unction upon what he said.

At the same time he had learned that, while it was important that his doctrine should be right, his style also mattered. 'It is not by coarseness of expression, or severity of manner, that we are to win souls, but by "speaking the truth in love", and if we are offended at such a suggestion being offered to us in a kind and affectionate way, it shows that humility and love have not a due ascendant over us.'[40]

5. GENTLENESS IS A PRIORITY

This reference to style and 'speaking the truth in love' coincides with the priority of gentleness in a minister of the gospel. By nature somewhat impulsive and easily provoked to anger, Simeon found this a hard lesson he had to learn. At the celebration of his fifty years at King's College he was able to write of his labouring to live his life peaceably with all men and to not having 'an atom of unkind feeling'[41] (so far as he knew) towards anyone. He saw gentleness as an essential part of what it means to 'make the teaching about God our Saviour attractive' (Titus 2:10).

In a sermon on Matthew 5:5 and Christian meekness he emphasized that 'the disposition which distinguishes the persons here spoken of, is not that natural mildness and gentleness with which some are favoured even from the womb … but a meekness found "in poverty of spirit", and in "mourning for sin", a fruit of the operation of God upon the soul'.[42]

Using the picture Paul paints of his relationship to the Thessalonians, Simeon knew that the office of a gentle 'nursing-mother' had been committed to him.[43] Writing to a friend who tried to enlist his support in attacking the convictions of a Christian with whom he disagreed, Simeon responded, 'I would say, if you are "gentle toward all men, and instruct in meekness them that oppose themselves", your arguments will appear stronger than they will, if maintained in language of severity and triumph.'[44]

But there, as elsewhere, he saw the need for balance. 'I think that there is a mistake in the minds of religious persons, in relation to this: in that they think nothing should proceed from a religious character but what is soft, and gentle, and persuasive. I think there are times and seasons when he [a minister] must "contend earnestly for the faith", and "reprove with all authority".'45

6. HAVE CONFIDENCE IN GOD'S SOVEREIGNTY AND PROVIDENCE

Never did Simeon express his confidence in God's sovereignty—not least in salvation—more than in the last month of his life. To some of those gathered around his bed he declared, 'I am, I know, the chief of sinners; and I hope for nothing but the mercy of God in Christ Jesus to life eternal; and I shall be, if not the greatest monument of God's mercy in heaven, yet the very next to it; for I know of none greater.'46 Then after a short pause he added,

And if we are to bring the matter to a point, it lies in a nutshell; and it is here—I look, as the chief of sinners, for the mercy of God in Christ Jesus to life eternal; (then very deliberately) and I lie adoring the sovereignty of God in choosing such an one—and the mercy of God in pardoning such an one—and the patience of God in bearing with such an one—and the faithfulness of God in perfecting his work and performing all his promises to such an one.47

This coincides with what he had written earlier: 'All good is from God, dispensed by him in a way of sovereignty according to the counsels of his own will, and to the praise of the glory of his grace.'48 This assurance proved to be his comfort when opposition faced him: 'Our great comfort is, that God reigneth, and that he will ultimately be glorified in men, whether they will or not. He can not only work without them, but against them, or even by them against their own designs.'49

From confidence in God's sovereignty arose the assurance of God's providence—his gracious ordering of our individual lives for his own praise and our good. As he looked back he reflected on the way in which God used his compulsory attendance at Communion as a new undergraduate at King's to open his eyes to his need of salvation.

He saw too God's timing in the vacancy at Holy Trinity Church and the manner in which God used the opposition he met to benefit his character and likeness to Christ; they 'were the very instruments whom God made use of to fix me among them as their stated pastor ... Truly "the judgments of God are unsearchable, and his ways past finding out".'[50] 'How mysterious are the designs of God, and how marvellously does he make the wrath of man to praise him!'[51]

Having survived an accident with his horse, he found that the only proper response was to put himself afresh in God's hands and say 'in the words of David, that "all my bones should praise him". I could not help putting forth first one limb, then another, stretching them forth to him, and receiving them afresh from him, and devoting them afresh to him.'[52]

He saw God's sovereignty too in the affairs of the college to which he belonged, the invitations given him to preach, and in the appointment of those over him in the Church. He wrote to his bishop, 'Under Divine providence your lordship is now become my immediate superior in the Church, to whom I owe all possible deference and respect.'[53] He learned from the Bible's biographies lessons that he applied to himself and passed on to others, especially when they were going through difficulties: 'The histories of Joseph and of Esther are yet passing before our eyes every day: and sweet they are when we can read a chapter in our own experience.'[54] He believed that God ordains our joys as well as our sorrows. 'But one thing I can say without much self-reproach: viz. that we are in the hands of a Father, who is at this moment doing for us precisely the thing which we ourselves should ask at his hands, if we knew, as he does, what is best for us.'[55] Discerning 'so many links in the chain of Providence' for his good, he exclaimed, 'If I do not bless, and magnify my God, the very stones will cry out against me.'[56] 'How sweet it is to be assured that God reigneth! Well may faith be called "precious faith", when it so composes the mind under all circumstances!'[57]

7. GOD'S WORK NEEDS TO BE DONE WITH GOD'S ENERGY

An early lesson Simeon had to learn and to which he had to return was the importance of serving God not in the strength of human energy, but in the strength that God gives to his servants who look to him for it. Nowhere was this more important than in the work of evangelism. Immediately after his conversion he made many attempts to benefit his friends spiritually and sometimes thought he had succeeded, but on reflection he concluded, 'I now see that I expected too much from my own exertions, and from their resolutions. If good be done to any, the work must be God's alone; the help that is done upon earth, he doeth it himself.'[58]

While God is graciously pleased to use human beings as instruments for the spiritual good of others, 'the change wrought in the heart of man depends altogether on the influence of the Holy Spirit: and however incapable we may be of comprehending the Spirit's operations, we must refer to him the entire change which is wrought in us in the conversion of our souls to God'.[59] What underlined this truth most to him was the evidence of what happened at Holy Trinity Church while he was absent from it for several months in 1798.

Pride and vanity and unbelief would have been ready to suggest (but thanks be to God who did not permit me to listen to them) that if I went away for four months, the work would be at a stand at home. Behold! since my return, no less than nineteen persons have applied to me to be received into my societies, of whom I had no knowledge at all (except in one or two cases) when I went away; and what is wonderfully gracious, there is not one of them that owed his first impressions to my ministry; and but one to the ministry of Mr Thomason. All were awakened either gradually and insensibly by God himself, or by conversation with one or other of my people. Tell me, does not this say aloud in our ears, that if we will endeavour to move in God's way and do his work, he will take care of our concerns? So I construe it; and the reflection affords me infinitely more consolation than if I had been instrumental to their conversion. Let us bless our God and labour for him more and more.[60]

8. PASTORS AND TEACHERS SHOULD AIM AT REPRODUCING THEMSELVES

Paul's instruction to Timothy to teach and train others that they might in turn do the same for the succeeding generation (2 Tim. 2:2) was something Simeon strove after. While a minister's immediate sphere and duties to his flock must be his primary focus, he should also be concerned for the future well-being of the church by reproducing himself in some measure in a new generation of preachers and teachers.

Simeon, probably unconsciously, did this by his weekly tea parties and sermon classes over several decades, and also by the example he set Sunday by Sunday in his preaching. One gave testimony to this:

His sermons are very useful and bold. It is astonishing how free he is from all fear of man. In this respect his character is shining. Although his congregation of a Sunday evening is composed partly of persons who come to scoff, yet he never spares them, but declares faithfully the whole counsel of God. What evidences his zeal in the cause of God more perhaps than anything else, is, that after labouring and labouring for his young men, that his lectures may be as profitable as possible, he then kneels down and thanks God, that he makes him in any degree useful to his 'dear—dear young servants'.[61]

'For the space of about twenty years,' Simeon wrote, 'I have persevered in having a few young men to assist in thus preparing for that which is generally esteemed so difficult—the writing of their sermons; and from the many acknowledgments which have been made by ministers from time to time, I have reason to hope that my labours have not been in vain in the Lord.'[62]

His endeavours extended beyond Cambridge. Two societies at

Elland—a small market town in Yorkshire—and Bristol had already been formed to educate men in preparation for the ministry, but Simeon established a third in an Education Society in London and by 1820 had 'already about twenty young men on the funds, all of them very excellent characters'.[63]

9. MAINTAIN A SPIRITUAL WATCHFULNESS

Throughout his *Memoirs* we catch glimpses of Simeon's growing awareness of his own sinfulness and the priority of alertness to temptation and spiritual dangers. Early in 1787 he wrote,

How long are we learning the true nature of Christianity? a quiet, sober, diligent application of one's mind to one's particular calling in life—and a watchfulness over the evils of the heart, seem very poor attainments to a young Christian: we must be everywhere; and everything, or else we are nothing in his esteem. Oh! thanks to our meek and lowly Teacher, how he bears with us.[64]

Daily reading and application of the Scriptures to his life helped him. In 1807 he kept for a while a diary in which he wrote,

I have been reading the Scriptures with pleasure and profit, and bless God, who does not refuse me access to him in prayer. I feel truly thankful for that caution, 'Let him that thinketh he standeth, take heed', &c. I long to have a holy fear of offending God, and a jealousy over myself, lest, after all my privileges, I ruin my soul by sin, 1 Cor. ix. 24. to x. 12.[65]

Probably he shared his convictions to no one more than to his former assistant Thomas Thomason:

I would fondly hope, that my dispositions have not altered for the worse since you knew me: the mercies I have experienced would have been sadly thrown away, if this were the case; but I feel it good to entertain a godly jealousy over myself, even in matters where my conscience least accuses me, because I know how blind we are to our own failings, and how partial a monitor conscience is.[66]

When younger ministers look at older men who are well established and fruitful in their ministries, they may foolishly imagine that they have little need for watchfulness in this area, but such an assumption is false. In 1796 Simeon's visit to Scotland prompted expressions of Christian love and appreciation. 'I desire to give glory to my God for all the love which I meet with, and ardently wish that it may be the means of humbling me in the dust, and not puffing me up with pride, as though I merited such regard.'[67] One of his reasons for not regularly keeping a diary was 'because there is danger of pride in committing to paper the more spiritual exercises of the soul'.[68]

At a time of ill-health he found himself the object of much concern by some who admired and praised him, and this brought its own dangers to his pride; he expressed the thought that God was using his present circumstances

partly in judgment, to counteract and punish an undue measure of complacency, which I may have felt in my growing popularity. I certainly have seen for a long time back the almost invariable kindness and respect, with which I have been treated by all orders and degrees of men in this place; and it is possible, that God may have seen me more gratified with it than I ought to be.[69]

His conviction grew that one of God's principal purposes in his life was the encouragement of humility. In his pocket book for 1787 he wrote in 'large characters, twice over, on separate pages, "Talk not about myself, Speak evil of no man".'[70] One of the most memorable pieces of Simeon's correspondence came in the following year, when he wrote to John Thornton,

A thousand thanks to you dear sir, for many valuable observations in your last letter; especially that which I hope to remember—that ministers when truly useful, and more perfectly instructed in the ways of God, are 'off their speed', and not so full of their success. Alas, alas! how apt are young ministers (I speak feelingly) to be talking of that great letter I. It would be easier to erase that letter from all the books in the kingdom, than to hide it for one hour from the eyes of a vain person. Another observation, in a former letter of yours, has not escaped my remembrance—the three lessons which a minister has to learn, 1. Humility—2. Humility—3. Humility.[71]

10. STAY UTTERLY DEPENDENT UPON CHRIST
AND HIS ATONING WORK ON THE CROSS

The spiritual watchfulness that made Simeon so aware of his personal sinfulness brought the compensation of increasing his awareness of how much he depended upon the Lord Jesus Christ and his saving work on the cross. In 1819 he wrote,

There are but two objects that I have ever desired for these forty years to behold; the one is, my own vileness; and the other is, the glory of God in the face of Jesus Christ: and I have always thought that they should be viewed together; just as Aaron confessed all the sins of all Israel whilst he put them on the head of the scape-goat The disease did not keep him from applying to the remedy, nor did the remedy keep him from feeling the disease. By this I seek to be, not only humble and thankful but humbled in thankfulness, before my God and Saviour continually.[72]

He declared that the doctrine of the cross 'will to all eternity form, as it does already form, the great subject of praise and adoration in heaven'.[73]

Simeon's monument, placed in the chancel of Holy Trinity Church, directly opposite to the tablets of Martyn and Thomason, erected by the congregation, bears this short but expressive inscription, suggested by Simeon himself:

IN MEMORY OF THE REV. CHARLES SIMEON, M.A., SENIOR FELLOW OF KING'S COLLEGE, AND FIFTY-FOUR YEARS VICAR OF THIS PARISH; WHO, WHETHER AS THE GROUND OF HIS OWN HOPES, OR AS THE SUBJECT OF ALL HIS MINISTRATIONS, DETERMINED TO KNOW NOTHING BUT 'JESUS CHRIST, AND HIM CRUCIFIED'. 1 COR. II. 2 BORN SEPT. 24, 1759. DIED NOV. 13, 1836.

Such an inscription should sum up the ministry of every faithful minister of Jesus Christ.

Simeon continues to be remembered and celebrated at King's College. On the anniversary of his death each year a prayer is offered in the college chapel that sums up his ministry:

Almighty and everlasting God, who by thy holy servant, Charles Simeon, didst mould the lives of many that they might go forth and teach others also; mercifully grant that as through evil report and good report he ceased not to preach thy saving Word, so we may never be ashamed of the Gospel of Jesus Christ our Lord, who with thee and the Holy Spirit liveth and reigneth one God world without end. Amen.

The Simeon Trust uses another collect in contemporary language taken from the Anglican book *Common Worship*:

Eternal God, who raised up Charles Simeon to preach the good news of Jesus Christ and inspire your people in service and mission: grant that we with all your Church may worship the Saviour, turn in sorrow from our sins and walk in the way of holiness; through Jesus Christ your Son our Lord, who is alive and reigns with you in the unity of the Holy Spirit, one God, now and for ever. Amen.[74]

He also appears in *The Cloud of Witnesses*, a book published originally for use with the *Alternative Service Book* calendar, still widely used in Anglican churches:

Hear our prayer, O Lord, that we who give thanks this day for the work of grace in the life of your servant Charles Simeon, may ourselves be given his love of souls, and his zeal for the proclamation of your word; through Jesus Christ our Lord.[75]

The book suggests that intercessory prayer should be made 'For evangelicals in our own church, thanking God for the contribution made by the Evangelical Revival'. Simeon would have rejoiced in that suggestion but been greatly surprised—and humbled—that he should be given a day in the Church's year alongside Timothy and Titus, Polycarp, Thomas Cranmer, John and Charles Wesley, William Wilberforce, John Bunyan, William Tyndale and Henry Martyn.

Notes

1 **Jean Cadier,** *The Man God Mastered,* tr. O. R. Johnston (London: Inter-Varsity Fellowship, 1960), p. 101.
2 *Memoirs of Charles Simeon,* p. 42.
3 Ibid., p. 398.
4 Ibid., p. 374.
5 Ibid.
6 Ibid.
7 Ibid., p. 213.
8 Ibid., p. 391.
9 Ibid., p. 197.
10 Ibid., p. 415.
11 Ibid., p. 124.
12 Ibid.
13 Ibid., p. 66.
14 Ibid., p. 153.
15 Ibid.
16 Ibid.
17 Ibid.
18 Ibid., p. 154.
19 Ibid., p. 50.
20 Ibid., p. 71.

21 Ibid., p. 487.

22 Ibid., p. 95.

23 Ibid., p. 74.

24 Ibid., p. 132.

25 Ibid., p. 187.

26 Ibid., p. 43.

27 Ibid., p. 216.

28 Ibid., p. 263.

29 Ibid.

30 Ibid., p. 351.

31 Ibid., p. 352.

32 Ibid., p. 353.

33 Ibid., p. 127.

34 Ibid., p. 232.

35 Ibid., p. 277.

36 Ibid., p. 108.

37 Ibid., p. 89.

38 Ibid.

39 Ibid., p. 90.

40 Ibid., p. 268.

41 Ibid., p. 368.

42 Discourse 51 on Matthew 5:5, *Horae Homileticae*, vol. 11.

43 1 Thes. 2:7; *Memoirs of Charles Simeon*, p. 372.

44 *Memoirs of Charles Simeon*, p. 373.

45 Ibid., p. 216.

46 Ibid., p. 472.

47 Ibid., p. 473.

48 Ibid., p. 331.

49 Ibid., p. 246.

50 Ibid., p. 433.

51 Ibid., p. 39.

52 Ibid., p. 152.

53 Ibid., p. 156.

54 Ibid., p. 173.

55 Ibid., p. 456.

56 Ibid., p. 189.

57 Ibid., p. 200.

58 Ibid., p. 10.

59 Ibid., p. 462.

60 Ibid., p. 96.

61 Ibid., p. 58.

62 Ibid., p. 37.

63 Ibid., p. 314.

64 Ibid., p. 44.

65 Ibid., p. 124.

66 Ibid., p. 200.

67 Ibid., p. 69.

68 Ibid., p. 261.

69 Ibid., p. 268.

70 Ibid., p. 44.

71 Ibid.

72 Ibid., p. 304.

73 Ibid., p. 384.

74 *Common Worship* (London: Church House Publishing, 2004), p. 145.

75 Collect used on the anniversary of Simeon's death, 13 November. *The Cloud of Witnesses: A Companion to the Lesser Festivals and Holydays of the Alternative Service Book 1980.* Compiled by Martin Draper with collects written by G. B. Timms (London: Collin's Liturgical Publications, 1982), pp. 186–187.

Handwritten and unpublished sermon notes

In the archives of King's College, Cambridge, on small scraps of paper, are notes in Simeon's handwriting of a sermon he preached at Newport on Friday, 28 November 1834, a sermon that does not find a place in *Horae Homileticae*.

Based upon Job 31:15–19 and Matthew 25:40, it has no title but its theme is clearly our duty of Christian giving and of caring for one another in practical ways, and especially for those who are our brothers and sisters in Christ.

It would be interesting to know at which Newport he was speaking. The nearest would have been Newport near Saffron Walden, in Essex, or Newport Pagnall, now identified with Milton Keynes in Buckinghamshire. But places further afield with the name of Newport are also possibilities.

Looking at the notes I am prompted to think that Simeon was speaking either at a prayer meeting or at the establishment of one of the many local societies he encouraged to help the poor and needy.

The verses in full from the NIV read:

Job 31:15–19:
Did not he who made me in the womb make them?
Did not the same one form us both within our mothers?
If I have denied the desires of the poor
or let the eyes of the widow grow weary,
if I have kept my bread to myself,
not sharing it with the fatherless—

but from my youth I reared him as would a father,
and from my birth I guided the widow—
if I have seen anyone perishing for lack of clothing,
or a needy man without a garment …

Matthew 25:40:
The King will reply, 'I tell you the truth, whatever you did for one of the least of these brothers of mine, you did for me.'

The underlinings in the notes below are Simeon's.

Brethren—Job 31:15–19; Matt 25:40
   The command all generally Luke 11:41
   all individually 1 Cor. 16:2
   in the most solemn manner 1 Tim. 6:17
   cheerfully Rom. 12:8
   But only according to our ability 2 Cor. 8:12
   Yet to the full extent of it 2 Cor. 8:1, 2
   Our reward proportioned to this 2 Cor. 9:6
   The neglect of this will be visited with execration [i.e. curses or hatred]
from Man Prov. 28:27
   with dereliction from God Prov. 21:13
   with dismission from his presence Matt. 25:42, 43
   The practice of it shall be rewarded with blessings
      temporal Luke 6:35, 38; Prov. 3:9, 10
      spiritual Isa. 58:7, 10, 11
      eternal Luke 16:9. Luke 14:14 1 Tim. 6:9 Matt. 25:34, 35 for God will
regard it as a loan to him Prov. 19:17

Simeon's sermon on
1 Corinthians 2:2

At first sight this sermon may appear long and perhaps heavy-going, but if Simeon followed his usual practice—and there seems little reason to suggest otherwise—he preached it from a simple skeleton rather than from fully written-out notes. He would have done this with his eyes upon his audience and with great vigour, emphasizing his main points. Subsequently, he would have written up the sermon, and for publication probably amplified it.

Christ crucified, or evangelical religion described[1]

1 Cor. 2:2. I determined not to know any thing among you, save Jesus Christ, and him crucified. (KJV)

In different ages of the world it has pleased God to reveal himself to men in different ways; sometimes by visions, sometimes by voices, sometimes by suggestions of his Spirit to their minds: but since the completion of the sacred canon, he has principally made use of his written Word, explained and enforced by men, whom he has called and qualified to preach his Gospel; and though he has not precluded himself from conveying again the knowledge of his will in any of the former ways, it is through the written Word only that we are now authorized to expect his gracious instructions. This, whether read by ourselves or published by his servants, he applies to the heart, and makes effectual for the illumination and salvation of men. It must be confessed, however, that he chiefly uses the ministry of his servants, whom he has sent as ambassadors to a guilty world. It was thus that he conveyed the knowledge of salvation to the

Ethiopian Eunuch, who was reading an interesting portion of Isaiah's prophecies. He might have opened the understanding of this man at once by the agency of his Spirit; but he chose rather to send his servant Philip, to join the chariot, and to explain the Scripture to him. When the Centurion also had sought with much diligence and prayer to know the way of salvation, God did not instruct him by his Word or Spirit, but informed him where to send for instruction; and by a vision removed the scruples of Peter about going to him; that so the established ministry might be honoured, and the Church might look to their authorized instructors, as the instruments whom God would make use of for their edification and salvation. Thus it is at this time: God is not confined to means; but he condescends to employ the stated ministry of his Word for the diffusion of Divine knowledge: 'The priests' lips keep knowledge'; and by their diligent discharge of their ministry is knowledge transmitted and increased.

But this circumstance, so favourable to all classes of the community, imposes on them a duty of the utmost importance. If there be a well from which we are to receive our daily supplies, it becomes us to ascertain that its waters are salubrious: and, in like manner, if we are to receive instruction from men, who are weak and fallible as ourselves, it becomes us to try their doctrines by the touchstone of the written Word; and to receive from them those sentiments only which agree with that unerring standard; or, to use the words of an inspired Apostle, we must 'prove all things, and hold fast that which is good'. To preachers also there arises an awful responsibility; for, as the people are 'to receive the word at their mouth', and their 'word is to be a savour of life or of death to all that hear it', it concerns them to be well assured, that they set before their people 'the sincere unadulterated milk of the word'; that in no respect they 'corrupt the word of God', or 'handle it deceitfully; but by manifestation of *the truth* commend themselves to every man's conscience in the sight of God' (2 Cor. 2:15–17 and 4:2).

Hence it appears that we all are deeply interested in this one question, What is truth? what is that truth, which ministers are bound to preach, and which their people should be anxious to hear? There will however be no difficulty in answering this question, if only we consult the passage before us; wherein St Paul explicitly declares what was the great scope of *his* ministry, and the one subject which *he* laboured to unfold. He regarded not the subtleties which had occupied the attention of philosophers; nor did he affect that species of knowledge which was in high repute among men: on the contrary, he studiously avoided all that gratified the pride of human wisdom, and determined to adhere simply to one subject, *the crucifixion of Christ for the sins of men*: 'I came not unto you', says he, 'with excellency of speech or of wisdom, declaring unto you the testimony of God: for I determined not to know any thing among you, save Jesus Christ and him crucified.'

To explain and vindicate this determination of the Apostle is our intention in this discourse.

I. TO EXPLAIN IT

By preaching Christ crucified, we are not to understand that he dwelt continually on the *fact* or *history* of the crucifixion; for though he speaks of having 'set forth Christ as it were crucified before the eyes' of the Galatians, and may therefore be supposed occasionally to have enlarged upon the sufferings of Christ as the means of exciting gratitude towards him in their hearts, yet we have no reason to think that he contented himself with exhibiting to their view a tragical scene, as though he hoped by *that* to convert their souls: it was the *doctrine* of the crucifixion that he insisted on; and he opened it to them in all its bearings and connexions. This he calls '*the preaching of the cross*': and it consisted of such a representation of 'Christ crucified, as was to the Jews a stumbling-block, and to the Greeks foolishness; but to the true believer, the power of God and the wisdom of God' (1 Cor. 1:23, 24). There were two particular views in which he invariably spoke of the death of Christ; namely, as *the ground of our hopes*, and as *the motive to our obedience*.

In the former of these views, the Apostle not only asserts, that the death of Christ was the appointed means of effecting our reconciliation with God, but that it was the only means by which our reconciliation could be effected. He represents all, both Jews and Gentiles, as under sin, and in a state of guilt and condemnation: he states, that, inasmuch as we are all condemned by the law, we can never be justified by the law, but are shut up unto that way of justification which God has provided for us in the Gospel (Gal. 3:22, 23). He asserts, that 'God hath set forth his Son to be a propitiation through faith in his blood, to declare his righteousness in the remission of sins, that he may be just, and the justifier of them that believe in Jesus' (Rom. 3:25, 26). He requires all, Jews as well as Gentiles, to believe in Jesus, in order to the obtaining of justification by faith in him (Gal. 2:15,16): and so jealous is he of every thing that may interfere with this doctrine, or be supposed to serve as a joint ground of our acceptance with God, that he represents the smallest measure of affiance in any thing else as actually making void the faith of Christ, and rendering his death of no avail (Gal. 5:2–4). Nay, more, if he himself, or even an angel from heaven, should ever be found to propose any other ground of hope to sinful man, he denounces a curse against him; and, lest his denunciation should be overlooked, he repeats it with augmented energy; 'As we said before, so say I now again, If any man preach any other Gospel unto you than that ye have received, let him be accursed' (Gal. 1:8, 9).

To the death of Christ he ascribes every blessing we possess. We are 'reconciled to God by the blood of his cross'; we are 'brought nigh to him', 'have boldness and access with confidence' even to his throne; we 'are cleansed by it from all sin'; yea, 'by his one offering of himself he hath perfected for ever them that are sanctified'. But there is one passage in particular wherein a multitude of spiritual blessings are comprised, and all are referred to him as the true source from whom they flow. The passage we speak of, is in the first chapter to the Ephesians, where, within the space of eleven verses, the same truth is repeated at least eight or nine times. In order to enter fully into the force of that passage, we may conceive of St Paul as maintaining the truth in opposition to all its most determined adversaries, and as labouring to the uttermost to exalt Christ in the eyes of those who trusted in him: we may conceive of him, I say, as contending thus: 'Have we been *chosen* before the foundation of the world? it is *in Christ*. Have we been *predestinated* unto the adoption of children? it is *in* and *by him*. Are we *accepted*? it is *in the Beloved*. Have we *redemption*, even the forgiveness of sins? it is *in him, through his blood*. Are all, both in heaven and earth, *gathered together* under one Head? it is *in Christ*, even *in him*. Have we *obtained an inheritance*? it is *in him*. Are we *sealed with the Holy Spirit* of promise? it is *in him*. Are we *blessed with all spiritual blessings*? it is *in Christ Jesus*. When the Apostle has laboured thus to impress our minds with the idea that our whole salvation is in, and by, the Lord Jesus Christ, is it not surprising that any one should be ignorant of it? Yet we apprehend that many persons, who have even studied the Holy Scriptures, and read over this passage a multitude of times, have yet never seen the force of it, or been led by it to just views of Christ as the Fountain 'in whom all fullness dwells', and 'from whose fullness we must all receive, even grace for grace'.

But we have observed, that there is another view in which the Apostle speaks of the death of Christ, namely, as *a motive to our obedience*. Strongly as he enforced the necessity of relying on Christ, and founding our hopes of salvation solely on his obedience unto death, he was no less earnest in promoting the interests of holiness. Whilst he represented the believers as 'dead to the law' and 'without law', he still insisted that they were 'under the law to Christ', and as much bound to obey every tittle of it as ever (1 Cor. 9:21; Gal. 2:19): and he enforced obedience to it, in all its branches, and to the utmost possible extent. Moreover, when the doctrines which he had inculcated were in danger of being abused to licentious purposes, he expressed his utter abhorrence of such a procedure (Rom. 6:1, 15); and declared, that 'the grace of God, which brought salvation, taught them, that denying ungodliness and worldly lusts, they should live righteously, soberly, and godly in this present world' (Titus 2:11–12). A life of holy obedience is represented by him as the great object which Christ aimed to produce in all his people: indeed the very name, *Jesus*, proclaimed, that the object of his coming was 'To save his people from their sins'. The same was the scope and end of his death, even to 'redeem them from all iniquity, and to purify unto himself a peculiar people zealous of good works'. His resurrection and ascension to heaven had also the same end in view; for 'therefore he both died, and rose, and revived, that he might be the Lord both of the dead and living'. Impressed with a sense of these things himself, St Paul laboured more abundantly than any of the Apostles in his holy vocation: he proceeded with a zeal which nothing could quench, and an ardour which nothing could damp: privations, labours, imprisonments, deaths, were of no account in his eyes; 'none of these things moved him, neither counted he his life dear unto him, so that he might but finish his course with joy, and fulfil the ministry that was committed to him'. But what was the principle by which he was actuated? He himself tells us, that he was impelled by a sense of obligation to Christ, for all that *he* had done and suffered for him: '*the love of Christ* constraineth us,' says he; 'because we thus judge, that if one died for all, then were all dead; and that he died for all, that they which live should not henceforth live unto themselves, but unto him which died for them, and rose again' (2 Cor. 5:14, 15). This is that principle which he desired to be universally embraced, and endeavoured to impress on the minds of all: 'We beseech you, brethren,' says he, 'by the mercies of God, that you present your bodies a living sacrifice, holy, acceptable to God, which is your reasonable service' (Rom. 12:1). What mercies he refers to, we are at no loss to determine; they are the great mercies vouchsafed to us in the work of redemption: for so he says in another place; 'Ye are bought with a price; therefore glorify God in your body and in your spirit, which are his' (1 Cor. 6:19, 20).

Now this is the subject which the Apostle comprehends under the term 'Christ crucified': it consists of two parts; first, of *affiance in Christ for salvation*, and, next, of *obedience to the law for his sake*: had either part of it been taken alone, his views had been imperfect, and his ministry without success. Had he neglected to set forth Christ as the only Saviour of the world, he would have betrayed his trust, and led his hearers to build their hopes on a foundation of sand. On the other hand, if he had neglected to inculcate holiness, and to set forth redeeming love as the great incentive to obedience, he would have been justly chargeable with that which has been often falsely imputed to him—an antinomian spirit; and his doctrines would have merited the odium which has most unjustly been cast upon them. But on neither side did he err: he forgot neither the foundation nor the superstructure: he distinguished properly between them, and kept each in its place: and hence with great propriety adopted the determination in our text.

Having explained his determination, we shall now proceed,

II. TO VINDICATE IT

It was not from an enthusiastic fondness for one particular point, but from the fullest conviction of his mind, that the Apostle adopted this resolution: and so the Word in the original imports; 'I determined, as the result of my deliberate judgment, to know nothing among you save Jesus Christ and him crucified: I have made it, and will ever make it, my theme, my boast, and my song.' The reasons why he insisted on this subject so exclusively, and with such delight, shall now be stated: he did so,

1. Because *it contained all that he was commissioned to declare*
'It pleased God to reveal his Son in the Apostle, that he might preach HIM among the heathen': and accordingly St Paul tells us, that 'this grace was

given to him to preach *the unsearchable riches* of Christ'. This, I say, was *his* office; and this too is the ministry of reconciliation which is committed to *ministers in every age*; 'to wit, that God was in Christ reconciling the world unto himself, not imputing their trespasses unto them' (2 Cor. 5:18, 19). To the Apostles, indeed, the commission was to 'go forth into all the world, and to preach the Gospel to every creature'; whereas to us is assigned, as it were, a more limited *sphere*: but the *subject* of our ministry is the same with theirs: we have the same dispensation committed unto us; and 'woe will be unto us, if we preach not the Gospel'.

But, as though men needed not to be evangelized now, the term *evangelical* is used as a term of reproach. We mean not to justify any persons whatsoever in using unnecessary terms of distinction, more especially if it be with a view to depreciate others, and to aggrandize themselves: but still the distinctions which are made in Scripture must be made by us; else for what end has God himself made them? Now it cannot be denied, that the Apostle characterizes the great subject of his ministry as *the Gospel*; nor can it be denied that he complains of some teachers in the Galatian Church as introducing *another* Gospel, which was not the true Gospel, but a perversion of it (Gal. 1:6, 7). Here then he lays down the distinction between doctrines which are truly evangelical, and others which have no just title to that name. Of course, wherever the same difference exists between the doctrines maintained, the same terms must be proper to distinguish them; and a just view of those distinctions is necessary, in order to our being guarded against error, and established in the truth.

But we beg to be clearly understood in reference to this matter. It is not our design to enter into any dispute about the use of a *term*, or to vindicate any particular *party*; but merely to state, with all the clearness we can, a subject, about which every one ought to have the most accurate and precise ideas.

We have seen what was the great subject of the Apostle's preaching, and which he emphatically and exclusively called *the Gospel*: and if only we attend to what he has spoken in the text, we shall see what really constitutes evangelical preaching. *The subject* of it must be 'Christ crucified'; that is, Christ must be set forth as the only foundation of a sinner's hope: and holiness in all its branches must be enforced; but a sense of Christ's love in dying for us must be inculcated, as the main-spring and motive of all our obedience. *The manner* of setting forth this doctrine must also accord with that of the Apostle in the text: the importance of the doctrine must be so felt, as to make us determine never to know any thing else, either for the salvation of our own souls, or for the subject of our public ministrations. Viewing its transcendent excellency, we must rejoice and glory in it ourselves, and shew forth its fruits in a life of entire devotedness to God: we must call upon our hearers also to rejoice and glory in it, and to display its sanctifying effects in the whole of their life and conversation. Thus to preach, and thus to live, would characterize a person, and his ministry, as evangelical, in the eyes of the Apostle: whereas indifference to this doctrine, or a corruption of it, either by a self-righteous or antinomian mixture, would render both the person and his ministry obnoxious to his censure, according to the degree in which such indifference, or such a mixture, prevailed. We do not mean to say, that there are not different degrees of clearness in the views and ministry of different persons, or that none are accepted of God, or useful in the Church, unless they come up to such a precise standard—nor do we confine the term evangelical to those who lean to this or that particular *system*, as some are apt to imagine: but this we say, that, in proportion as any persons, in their spirit and in their preaching, accord with the example in the text, they are properly denominated *evangelical*; and that, in proportion as they recede from this pattern, their claim to this title is dubious or void.

Now when we ask, What is there in this which every minister ought not to preach, and every Christian to feel? Is there any thing in this enthusiastic? any thing sectarian? any thing uncharitable? any thing worthy of reproach? Is the Apostle's example in the text so absurd, as to make an imitation of him blame-worthy, and a conformity to him contemptible? Or, if a scoffing and ungodly world will make the glorying in the cross of Christ a subject of reproach, ought any who are reproached by them to abandon the Gospel for fear of being called evangelical? Ought they not rather, like the Apostles, 'to rejoice that they are counted worthy to suffer shame, *if shame it be*, for Christ's sake'? The fact is indisputable, that the Apostle's commission was to preach Christ crucified; to preach, I say, *that* chiefly, *that* constantly, *that* exclusively: and therefore he was justified in his determination to 'know nothing else': consequently, to adopt that same resolution is our wisdom also, whether it be in reference to our own salvation, or to the subject of our ministrations in the Church of God.

We now proceed to a *second* reason for the Apostle's determination. He determined to know nothing but Christ and him crucified,

2. Because *it contained all that could conduce to the happiness of man*

There are other things which may amuse; but there is nothing else that can contribute to man's real happiness. Place him in a situation of great distress; let him be bowed down under a sense of sin; let him be oppressed with any great calamity; or let him be brought by sickness to the borders of the grave; there is nothing that will satisfy his mind, but a view of this glorious subject. Tell him of his good works; and he feels a doubt (a doubt which no human being can resolve), what is that precise measure of good works which will ensure eternal happiness: tell him of repentance, and of Christ supplying his deficiencies; and he will still be at a loss to ascertain whether he has attained that measure of penitence or of goodness, which is necessary to answer the demands of God. But speak to him of Christ as dying for the sins of men, as 'casting out none that come unto him', as 'purging us by his blood from all sin', and as clothing us with his own unspotted righteousness; yea, as making his own grace to abound, not only where sin has abounded, but infinitely beyond our most abounding iniquities (Rom. 5:20, 21); set forth to him thus the freeness and sufficiency of the Gospel salvation, and he wants nothing else: he feels that Christ is 'a Rock, a sure Foundation'; and on that he builds without fear, assured that 'whosoever believeth in Christ shall not be confounded'. He hears the Saviour saying, 'This is life eternal, to know thee the only true God, and Jesus Christ whom thou hast sent'; and having attained that knowledge, he trusts that the Word of Christ shall be fulfilled to him: he already exults in the language of the Apostle, 'Who is he that condemneth? it is Christ that died, yea rather, that is risen again, who is even at the right hand of God, who also maketh intercession for us' (Rom. 8:34).

But if a sense of guilt afflict some, a want of victory over their indwelling corruptions distresses others: and to them also the doctrine of Christ crucified administers the only effectual relief. The consideration of eternal rewards and punishments affords indeed a powerful incentive to exertion; but efforts springing from those motives only, will always savour of constraint; they will never be ingenuous, hearty, affectionate, unreserved. But let a sense of redeeming love occupy the soul, and the heart becomes enlarged, and 'the feet are set at liberty to run the way of God's commandments'. We say not that every person who *professes* to have experienced the love of Christ, will always walk consistently with that profession; for there were falls and offences not only in the apostolic age, but even among the Apostles themselves: but this we say, that there is no other principle in the universe so powerful as the love of Christ; that whilst that principle is in action, no commandment will ever be considered as grievous; the yoke of Christ in every thing will be easy, and his burden light; yea, the service of God will be perfect freedom; and the labour of our souls will be to 'stand perfect and complete in all the will of God'. This the Apostle found in his own experience; and this he found to be the effect of his ministry on the hearts of thousands. What then could he wish for in addition to this? Where this principle was inefficacious, nothing was effectual; and where this was effectual, nothing else was wanted: no wonder then that he determined to insist on this subject, and nothing else; since, whether in the removing of guilt from the conscience, or of corruption from the soul, nothing could bear any comparison with this.

Further, he determined to know nothing but this subject,

3. Because *nothing could be added to it without weakening or destroying its efficacy*

The subject of Christ crucified may, as we have before observed, be considered as consisting of two parts—a foundation, and a superstructure. Now St Paul declares, that if any thing whatever be added to that foundation, it will make void the whole Gospel. If any thing could have been found which might safely have been added to it, we might suppose that the rite of circumcision might have claimed that honour, because it was of God's special appointment, and had had so great a stress laid upon it by God himself: but St Paul says in reference to that rite, that if any person should submit to it with a view to confirm his interest in the Gospel, 'Christ should profit him nothing': such a person would have 'fallen from grace', as much as if he had renounced the Gospel altogether. Again, if any person, who had the foundation rightly laid within him, should build upon it any thing but the pure, the simple, the essential duties of religion, 'his work should be burnt up as wood or stubble'; and though he should not entirely lose heaven, he should lose much of his happiness there, and be saved only like one snatched out of the devouring flames. With such a view of the subject, what inducement could the Apostle have to add any thing to it?

But the Apostle speaks yet more strongly respecting this. He tells us, not only that the adulterating of the subject by any base mixture will destroy its efficacy, but that even an artificial statement of the truth will make it of none effect. God is exceedingly jealous of the honour of his Gospel: if it be plainly and simply stated he will work by it, and make it effectual to the salvation of men; but if it be set forth with all the ornaments of human eloquence, and stated in 'the words which man's wisdom teacheth', he will not work by it; because he would have 'our faith to stand, not in the wisdom of men, but in the power of God'. Hence St Paul, though eminently qualified to set it forth with all the charms of oratory, purposely laid aside 'all excellency of speech or of wisdom in declaring the testimony of God', and 'used all plainness of speech', lest by dressing up the truth 'in the enticing words of man's wisdom, he should make the cross of Christ of none effect' (1 Cor. 1:17; 2:1, 4, 5).

Further vindication than this is unnecessary: for, if this subject contained all that he was commissioned to declare; if it contained all that could conduce to the happiness of man; and if nothing could be added to it without weakening or destroying its efficacy; he must have consented to defeat the ends of his ministry altogether, if he had not adopted and maintained the resolution in the text.

If then these things be so, we may venture to found upon them the following ADVICE—

First, *Let us take care that we know Christ crucified*

Many, because they are born and educated in a Christian land, are ready to take for granted that they are instructed in this glorious subject: but there is almost as much ignorance of it prevailing amongst Christians as amongst the heathen themselves. The name of Christ indeed is known, and he is complimented by us with the name of Saviour; but the nature of his office, the extent of his work, and the excellency of his salvation, are known to few. Let not this be considered as a rash assertion: for we will appeal to the consciences of all; Do we find that the Apostle's views of Christ are common? Do we find many so filled with admiring and adoring thoughts of this mystery, as to count all things but loss for the excellency of the knowledge of it; and to say, like him, 'God forbid that I should glory, save in the cross of our Lord Jesus Christ'? On the contrary, do we not find that there is an almost universal jealousy on the subject of the Gospel, that those who most labour to tread in the Apostle's steps, are often most branded with opprobrious names? Do we not find that his views of the Gospel are calumniated now, precisely as they were in the days of the Apostle himself? Verily, we should be glad to be found false witnesses in relation to these things; and would most joyfully retract our assertions, if it could be shewn that they are not founded in truth. We do hope however that there is an increasing love to the Gospel pervading the whole land; and I pray God it may prevail more and more, and be embraced by every one of us, not superficially, partially, theoretically, but clearly, fully, practically.

Secondly, *Let us adopt the Apostle's determination for ourselves*

Doubtless, *as men and members of society*, there are many other things which we are concerned to know. Whatever be our office in life, we ought to be well acquainted with it, in order that we may perform its duties to the advantage of ourselves and others; and we would most particularly be understood to say, that the time that is destined for the acquisition of useful knowledge, ought to be diligently and conscientiously employed. But, *as Christians*, we have one object of pursuit, which deserves all our care and all our labour: yes, we may all with great propriety determine to know nothing but Christ and him crucified. This is the subject which even 'the angels in heaven are ever desiring to look into', and which we may investigate for our whole lives, and yet leave depths and heights unfathomed and unknown. St Paul, after preaching Christ for twenty years, did not conceive himself yet awhile to have attained all that he might, and therefore still desired to know Christ more and more, 'in the power of his resurrection, and in the fellowship of his sufferings'. This therefore *we* may well desire, and count all things but loss in comparison of it.

Lastly, *Let us make manifest the wisdom of our*
determination by the holiness of our lives

The doctrine of Christ crucified ever did, and ever will appear 'foolishness' in the eyes of ungodly men; so that, if it be preached by an Apostle himself, he shall be accounted by them a babbler and deceiver. But there is one way of displaying its excellency open to us, a way in which we may effectually 'put to silence the ignorance of foolish men'; namely, 'by well-doing'; that is, by shewing the sanctifying and transforming efficacy of this doctrine. St Paul tells us, that 'by the cross of Christ the world was crucified unto him, and he unto the world' (Gal. 6:14): and such is the effect that it should produce on us: we should shew that we are men of another world, and men too of 'a more excellent spirit': we should shew the fruits of our faith in every relation of life: and, in so doing, we may hope to 'win by our good conversation' many, who would never have submitted to the preached Word.

But we must never forget where our strength is, or on whose aid we must entirely rely. The Prophet Isaiah reminds us of this; 'Surely shall one say, In the Lord have I righteousness and strength': and our Lord himself plainly tells us, that 'without him we can do nothing'. Since then 'we have no sufficiency in ourselves to help ourselves', and God has 'laid help for us upon One that is mighty', let us 'live by faith on the Son of God', 'receiving daily out of his fullness that grace' that shall be 'sufficient for us'. Let us bear in mind, that this is a very principal part of the knowledge of Christ crucified: for, as 'all our fresh springs are in Christ', so must we look continually to him for 'the supplies of his Spirit', and 'have him for our wisdom, our righteousness, our sanctification, and redemption'.

Note

1 Discourse 1933, *Horae Homileticae*, vol. 16.

Key questions to be asked of any passage by a preacher

J. I. Packer sums up the Puritan method of biblical interpretation as beginning with

asking six questions of each passage or text that we seek to expound:

(1) What do these words actually mean?

(2) What light do other scriptures throw on the text?

(3) What truths does it teach about God, and about man in relation to God?

(4) How are these truths related to the saving work of Christ, and what light does the gospel of Christ throw upon them?

(5) What experiences do these truths delineate, or explain, or seek to create or cure? For what practical purpose do they stand in Scripture?

(6) How do they apply to myself and others in our own actual situation? To what present human condition do these speak, and what are they telling us to believe and do?[1]

Packer makes the interesting comment that

it was the Calvinistic Anglican evangelicals (who devoured Puritan theology almost as their staple diet) who best sustained its spirit' and that 'Charles Simeon restated its basic principles in a more precise and vigorous form in his edition of Claude's *Essay on the Composition of a Sermon* and illustrated them at length in the 2, 536 skeletons which fill his 21-volume *Horae Homileticae*.[2]

I have found tremendous profit over the years using these questions as my first approach to any part of Scripture. The reader may find it helpful to complement these questions by a set of instructions Alexander Somerville, the great friend of Robert Murray McCheyne, encouraged his preachers' class to apply to their study of Scripture in preparation for preaching.

Alexander Somerville's 'Rules for sermon writing'

1. Pray without ceasing for clear views of your subject, for help in composition, in committing to memory, and in delivery.

2. Pray without ceasing for the people you are to address.

3. Remember you are to speak to souls who must either be impressed or hardened by the sermon you deliver.

4. Write *for* Christ and *of* Christ.

5. Remember that the Holy Spirit not merely can alone show *to the heart* the things that are Christ's, but that he must be recognized as doing so by us. Keep the Spirit's peculiar office and work continually in view.

6. Remember that what you write must have *eternal* consequences.

7. Write as one who must give an account to Christ for so doing.

8. Write for a people who must give an account to Christ for the manner in which they hear.

9. *Never* write for the sake of *magnifying* yourself.

10. Remember the flock of Christ must not be fed with ingenuities, but with the bread of life.

11. Write from the heart with *simplicity, plainness* (so that a little child may comprehend), and *godly sincerity.*

12. Pray for other congregations ... for your own *companions* in the work of preaching.

13. Never write without this before you—and read at least three times in the composition of each discourse.3

Notes

1 **J. I. Packer,** *Among God's Giants* (Eastbourne: Kingsway, 1991), p. 138.
2 Ibid., p. 370.
3 **Alexander N. Somerville,** *A Modern Apostle* (2nd edn.; London: John Murray, 1891), [n.p.].

About Day One:

Day One's threefold commitment:

- To be faithful to the Bible, God's inerrant, infallible Word;
- To be relevant to our modern generation;
- To be excellent in our publication standards.

I continue to be thankful for the publications of Day One. They are biblical; they have sound theology; and they are relative to the issues at hand. The material is condensed and manageable while, at the same time, being complete—a challenging balance to find. We are happy in our ministry to make use of these excellent publications.

JOHN MACARTHUR, PASTOR-TEACHER, GRACE COMMUNITY CHURCH, CALIFORNIA

It is a great encouragement to see Day One making such excellent progress. Their publications are always biblical, accessible and attractively produced, with no compromise on quality. Long may their progress continue and increase!

JOHN BLANCHARD, AUTHOR, EVANGELIST AND APOLOGIST

Visit our website for more information and to request a free catalogue of our books.

www.dayone.co.uk

John Rogers—Sealed with blood
The story of the first Protestant
martyr of Mary Tudor's reign

TIM SHENTON

160PP PAPERBACK, 978–1–84625–084–2

Tim Shenton is the head teacher of St Martin's School and an elder at Lansdowne Baptist Church, Bournemouth. He is married with two daughters. He has researched and written extensively on church history, specializing in the eighteenth and nineteenth centuries. Among his works published by Day One are *Forgotten heroes of Revival*, *Our perfect God*, *Opening up 1 Thessalonians* and an expositional commentary on the prophet Habakkuk.

We in the west sorely need to craft a theology of martyrdom—it would put backbone into our proclamation and living, and help us remember brothers and sisters going through fiery trials even today in other parts of the world. Remembering men like John Rogers is a great help in the development of such a theology.
FROM THE FOREWORD BY MICHAEL HAYKIN, PRINCIPAL AND PROFESSOR OF CHURCH HISTORY AND REFORMED SPIRITUALITY, TORONTO BAPTIST SEMINARY, TORONTO, ONTARIO

'Tim Shenton has produced yet another well-documented, gripping biography of a real hero of faith—John Rogers (d. 1555), renowned biblical editor and first Marian martyr. Follow Rogers's fascinating career from Antwerp to Germany, and back again to England, where he was arrested, remained steadfast under intense interrogation, and paid the ultimate price for confessing Christ. This is a great book about an important epigone; hopefully, Rogers will no longer be marginalized! Highly recommended for teenagers and adults.'
—JOEL R BEEKE, PURITAN REFORMED THEOLOGICAL SEMINARY, GRAND RAPIDS, MICHIGAN

'Shenton weaves a brilliant tapestry from original sources and introduces the reader to many compelling and complex personalities. Well-proportioned in its emphasis, this history will be a vital contribution to studies of Protestant martyrs in Queen Mary's reign.'
—RANDALL J. PEDERSON, CO-AUTHOR OF MEET THE PURITANS

COLIN HAMER

144PP PAPERBACK, 978–1–84625–083–5

Anne Boleyn
One short life that changed
the English-speaking world

Colin Hamer

DayOne

Anne Boleyn, twenty years old, stepped onto the shore at Dover in the winter of 1521 after several years abroad. She had been sent to France to assimilate French culture, and had used the time well. She was all set to make a big impression at the Tudor court—and did, capturing the heart of Henry VIII.

But this woman, who was in the grave by the age of thirty-six and on the throne of England for only three years, provokes strong reactions from many. Was she an immoral woman who seduced Henry away from his rightful wife for the advancement of family and personal gain? In this well-researched, fresh look at Anne, Colin Hamer sets her in her context as a young woman who had come to true faith in Christ, and shows the impact for good she made from her position of influence, an impact we still benefit from today.

Colin Hamer is currently chairman of a charity that works with the homeless and other vulnerable groups. Following his graduation from Liverpool University in 1972 with BA (Hons), he spent a short time teaching then pursued a business career for more than twenty-five years. He has been an elder at Grace Baptist Church, Astley, Manchester, for twenty years. He and his wife Lois have two adult children. His first book, *Being a Christian Husband—a biblical perspective,* was published by Evangelical Press in 2005.

'Colin Hamer's Anne Boleyn is as exciting as fiction as it carefully makes its way through the historical and religious complexities of Henry VIII's England.'
—DAVID B. CALHOUN, PROFESSOR OF CHURCH HISTORY AT COVENANT THEOLOGICAL SEMINARY, ST LOUIS, MISSOURI

TIM SHENTON

176PP PAPERBACK, 978–1–84625–130–6

Christmas Evans (1766–1838) was described by
D. M. Lloyd-Jones as 'the greatest preacher that
the Baptists have ever had in Great Britain'. This
remarkable one-eyed Welshman came from
humble beginnings to exercise powerful
preaching ministries throughout Wales,
particularly in Anglesey and the North. In this
thoroughly researched biography, Tim Shenton
paints an honest picture of Christmas Evans, not
excusing or overlooking his faults, but
demonstrating how this gentle and humble man,
who possessed the spirit of prayer to a
remarkable degree, was used by God for the
extension of his kingdom in Wales.

Tim Shenton is the head teacher of St Martin's
School and an elder at Lansdowne Baptist
Church, Bournemouth, England. He is married
with two daughters. He has written twenty
books, and researched extensively on church
history, specializing in the eighteenth and
nineteenth centuries. His published works by
Day One include *Heroes of revival, Our perfect
God, Jesus in Luke's Gospel* and two other
selections of children's daily readings,
expositional commentaries on some of the Minor

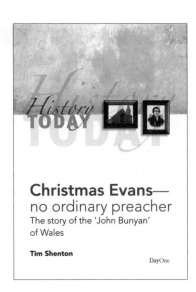

**Christmas Evans—
no ordinary preacher**
The story of the 'John Bunyan'
of Wales

Tim Shenton
DayOne

Prophets, *John Rogers—Sealed with blood,* and
Opening up 1 Thessalonians.

PAUL S. TAYLOR

144PP PAPERBACK, ISBN 978-1-84625-209-9

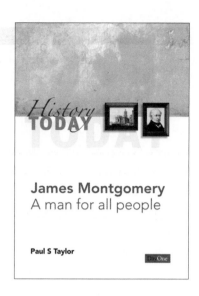

It is quite remarkable that until now no substantial biography has appeared to recount the life of James Montgomery (1771-1854). His memoirs were published in 7 volumes in 1856, several lectures have been given in more recent times and a book of Montgomery's poems was published in 2000. Readers are now able to acquaint themselves with the life, experiences and work of this godly man in a modern biography. .James Montgomery was born in Scotland, educated and nurtured by evangelical Moravians in West Yorkshire and then spent many years of his life in Sheffield serving of the lord, making known the gospel of grace, initiating and supporting many Christian causes. He was a literary figure of some stature, editing a newspaper and writing numerous hymns, many of which are still sung by congregations today.

Paul Taylor is a Yorkshireman. He trained as a Chartered Municipal and Civil Engineer. After working in local government and as a partner in a firm of Civil and Structural Engineers as a partner, he studied at the Nazarene Theological College at Didsbury, and was awarded an MA (Theology) by the University of Manchester in 1997. For many years he was an accredited Methodist local preacher and has served the Lord in a preaching and teaching ministry for 55 years. His written works include *Travelling Man* (with Howard Mellor), the life and work of Rev. Arthur Skevington Wood; *Bold as a Lion* (with Dr Peter Gentry), the life of John Cennick an 18th century Moravian evangelist and hymn-writer; *Sleepers Awake—the Gospel and Post Modernism*; and *Charles Wesle—Evangelist.*

Paul Taylor is a conservative evangelical by conviction and experience with an interest in historical biography and hymnology. He is married to Margaret and they have two children and four grandchildren.

TIM SHENTON

192PP PAPERBACK, ISBN 978–1–90308–770–1

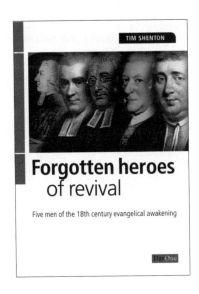

Forgotten heroes of revival

Five men of the 18th century evangelical awakening

The 'forgotten heroes' described here had a deep love for Jesus Christ and for the souls of their listeners which enabled them to stand strong through the storms of persecution and to preach a message that didn't only address the mind with truth, but reached right into the hearts. The Word of Life shook their congregations—it stirred them, and many were saved. Read about the amazing lives of George Thomson, James Rouquet, Captain Jonathan Scott, David Simpson and Thomas Pentycross.

Tim Shenton is the head teacher of St Martin's School and an elder at Lansdowne Baptist Church, Bournemouth, England. He is married with two daughters. He has written twenty books, and researched extensively on church history, specializing in the eighteenth and nineteenth centuries. His published works by Day One include *Heroes of revival, Our perfect God, Jesus in Luke's Gospel* and two other selections of children's daily readings, expositional commentaries on some of the Minor Prophets, *John Rogers—Sealed with blood*, and *Opening up 1 Thessalonians*.

'This fascinating book is recommended to all lovers of historical biographies, but also for all Christians who want to know what preaching the gospel is all about, even today.'
EVANGELICAL TIMES